Three Lives of Gavan Duffy

The Three Lives of
GAVAN DUFFY

CYRIL PEARL

New South Wales University Press

First published in 1979 by
New South Wales University Press Limited
Box 1, P.O. Kensington, N.S.W., Australia 2033

© Cyril Pearl

National Library of Australia
Card Number and ISBN 0 86840 016 5

Library of Congress No. 78 65298

Printed in Australia by
Macarthur Press Pty. Ltd. Parramatta

Contents

Foreword

Charles Gavan Duffy, the Irish rebel who became an Australian patriot, lived three crowded lives. In Dublin, as a young man, he was an ardent nationalist, dedicated to the struggle for Irish independence. In Melbourne, in middle age, he was a perceptive statesman, striving to bring about a federated Australia, and to open up the vast pastoral estates to land-hungry farmers. In Nice, in old age, he was a distinguished man of letters, brilliantly recording the history he had lived through. And the rebel who had been imprisoned on charges of high treason became an honoured Knight Commander of the Most Distinguished Order of St. Michael and St. George.

His story has particular relevance to the troubled Ireland of today. Throughout his long life, he urged his countrymen to free themselves from the poison of sectarianism. He was a devout Catholic, but he declared: 'I hate Catholic Ascendancy and Protestant Ascendancy alike, and while I breathe, I will resist one and the other'. And he never tired of acclaiming Ireland's long line of Protestant patriots; from Wolf Tone to Thomas Davis, from Grattan to Smith O'Brien. His credo was simple: 'We regard all Irishmen who love their country, whatever their creed or pedigree, as equally near and dear to us.'

~Part 1~

One

The Early Years

WHEN Charles Gavan Duffy was a schoolboy he had a fight with one of the boys and was reported to the headmaster for misconduct. The headmaster, a Presbyterian, the Reverend John Bleckley, asked no questions. He summarily stretched Duffy over a desk, according to traditional practice, and flogged him enthusiastically with a leather strap. When he had finished, he said to young Duffy, 'Now, sir, what have you to say for yourself?' 'Say?' Duffy roared. 'I say it is too late to ask for my defence after I have been punished; and that I will never suffer you to lay hands on me again.' With that, he seized his cap and left the school. Recalling the incident in his old age, Duffy wrote: 'Though the result proved a great inconvenience to me I can never regret what happened as a test of character.'

Duffy's character was moulded by Ireland's political condition in his formative years. He was a Catholic brought up in Ulster when Catholics were an oppressed minority, and when, in his own words, 'the Orange drum was heard on every hill from June till August to celebrate the Boyne and Aughrim,' and every office of authority in the province was held by Orangemen or their patrons and proteges. He was barely nine when he heard his father discussing Catholic Emancipation and realised 'dimly and vaguely' that it meant deliverance of his race from subjection to Orange ascendance.

But Duffy's parents were not among what he described as 'the obscure and trampled multitude'. His father, John Duffy, was a wealthy Monaghan shopkeeper who had acquired considerable property and a share in a bleach green. His mother, Anne Gavan, was the daughter of a wealthy gentleman farmer, Patrick Gavan, who cultivated four square miles of land, and was known to his neighbours as 'the King of Aughabog'. Duffy as a child vainly used to pester his mother to show him Grandfather's crown and sceptre. 'The most tedious chapter in a biography is commonly the family pedigree', Duffy says in his autobiography, though in almost the same breath he records that the McMahons, chiefs of Oriel, and the McKennas, chiefs of Truagh, were his near kinsmen and that soldiers, brehons (judges) and scholars, plentifully adorned his family tree.

Duffy seems to have adopted the 'Gavan' early in life. His eldest son was baptised 'John Gavan', but the other sons were just plain Duffies. I

3

have dropped the 'Gavan' in the pages that follow.

DUFFY was born in the town of Monaghan, on Good Friday, 1816, ten months after the Battle of Waterloo. Monaghan is a town with a long history. It was founded by monks in the sixth century, frequently besieged during the Elizabethan wars, and occupied alternately by Irish and English soldiers down to the time of Cromwell. Heber McMahon, chief of the McMahons of Oriel and Bishop of Clogher, then succeeded Owen Roe as commander of the national army. The first men executed during the United Irishmen revolution in 1798 were three 'Croppies' of the Monaghan militia. Many survivors from this heroic, hopeless uprising were still alive in Duffy's boyhood, and one of the Duffy's old servants fed him on the legends and traditions of '98, even promising, if he were a good boy, one day to show him where the Croppies had hidden their arms. Apparently, he was not a good boy, for he never saw the buried treasures.

Duffy was the youngest of six children, four boys and two girls. He was only ten when his father died. As a child he was intensely religious. When he went to bed at night, he took a coarse board with him to kneel upon under the blanket, so that his prayers would not be 'too luxurious', and he brooded on controversial religious books, and 'the abstruse mysteries of religion'. But as he grew older, his first passion was superseded by one that lasted all his life — 'the determination to love, and, if possible, serve Ireland'. His patriotism was kindled, not only by sombre stories of past wrongs but by the glaring injustices he witnessed.

Duffy's first school was a primitive institution, known as a 'poor school'. Ulster Catholics had been deprived of their churches and schools at the beginning of the eighteenth century, and up till 1832, Catholic children were taught in Hedge Schools, held in the open air. The 'poor school', commonly held in a barn or garret, was a considerable improvement on the Hedge School. Though scantily furnished, with bare walls and windows, it had the valuable amenity of a roof. The schoolmaster was a one-handed man, Neil Quin, who, Duffy thought, had probably become a schoolmaster because his deficiency unfitted him for any other employment.

One day Duffy's elder sister met him coming home surrounded by a 'clamorous swarm' of barefooted and ragged fellow-pupils, and peremptorily declared that he would never return to Mr. Quin's school. But no Catholic school was any better. The only alternative was Mr. Bleckley's 'classical academy', which catered for the sons of 'small gentry', professional men, and prosperous townspeople. With the consent of his guardian, the Reverend James Duffy, parish priest of Muckno, Castleblayney, young Duffy became the one Catholic among Mr. Bleckley's fifty pupils. Despite the prevailing anti-Catholic prejudice, Duffy soon made three close friends who were to remain intimates and confidants throughout their lives: a school-fellow, Matt Trumble, and two young men, Henry McManus and Terence Bellew McManus. 'By a happy accident', Duffy wrote, 'these three young men represented three totally distinct elements of Irish society'. Trumble was the son of a

British army officer. Henry McManus, a struggling artist, was the son of a Catholic soldier, brought up as a Protestant by the Government after his father's death with the regiment; Terence McManus, then serving his apprenticeship to a woollen draper, was 'a sprig of the aristocracy', related to the Bellews of Barmeath.

During his first year at Mr. Bleckley's academy, Duffy helped to organise a boys' parliament, a boys' newspaper and a boys' regiment. At first, his connection with them was 'vehemently resisted' in the name of Protestant ascendancy. 'But after a fierce debate', Duffy wrote, 'the majority voted my emancipation, three years before the legislators of larger growth at St. Stephen's made a similar concession to my seniors. I used to boast that I was the first Catholic emancipated in Ireland, but though tolerated I was never allowed to forget that I belonged to the race who were beaten at the Boyne'. (The Catholic Emancipation Bill, which in theory opened public and municipal posts to Catholics, was passed in 1829, when Duffy was thirteen.)

On Sunday afternoons, Duffy and his three friends rambled through the countryside, 'occupied chiefly with speculations and visions of what might be accomplished to reinstate our dethroned people in their rightful position . . . My comrades and I felt our present wrongs deeply, but we knew little of the remote causes from which they sprang. I had never seen a history of Ireland at that time'.

Duffy learned with burning indignation how the Irish had been reduced to serfdom; how it became a crime to teach them to read or write; how their churches were taken away from them, and their priests, under pain of death, forbidden to perform their sacred functions. He heard how little more than a generation ago, a Protestant secret society called the Peep o' Day Boys, had given Catholic farmers in Armagh, Cromwell's choice of 'to Hell or Connaught;' and how the farmers, if they resisted, had their houses burnt over their heads. 'My immature judgment was naturally inflamed with rage at these crimes', Duffy wrote. 'A rage which did not abate when I came to read history and found that the tragic story was substantially true'.

AT the age of eighteen, Duffy was still treated by his guardian as a child, ordained to remain silent in the presence of his elders. But he had begun to express himself in writing ('chiefly about love and patriotism') and one day 'a stately venerable gentleman' walked into his mother's house, and treating him as an adult, invited him to help in the promotion of a projected Belfast newspaper, the *Northern Herald*. The visitor was another United Irishman, Charles Hamilton Teeling, one of the surviving leaders of the rising of 1798. He talked to the enraptured Duffy of the rising, and lent him his *Personal Narrative* of the stirring events. It was the first book Duffy had read dealing frankly with the aspirations of Irish Nationalists, and it thrilled him with 'a new emotion'. He learned how only a generation ago, an Irish army had swept the British forces out of two counties, and, but for accidents, might have swept them out of two-and-thirty.

Duffy reflected that what men had done, men might do again — and do better, and if Heaven were propitious, he might be there to see it done.

'From that time', he wrote, 'my mind was largely occupied with speculations and reveries on Ireland. I read all the books I could buy or borrow on the history and condition of the country, and gradually came to understand the epic of Irish resistance to England, often defeated, often renewed, but never wholly relinquished'.

The policy of the *Northern Herald* was to revive the aims of '98, to unite Catholic and Protestant in the national cause. But these fraternal doctrines were not popular in Ulster in the 1820s. Most Protestants and Presbyterians rejected them, and Catholics thought it futile to talk of fraternity until they were received as equals.

Duffy's three brothers died while he was in his teens. He was haunted by their early death, which seemed to presage his own. 'In all my nonage my health was feeble and uncertain', he wrote, 'and dyspepsia came so early that it must have been hereditary . . . Of the precautions necessary to secure and reclaim health no one had ever spoken to me . . .' Not till he was approaching manhood, did he learn anything about 'the principles of physiology and the structure of the human body . . . so fearfully and wonderfully made'. The enlightenment came from a *Journal of Health* which a young Irishman returned from the United States lent him. From it he adopted a maxim which he never forgot (though we do not know how he put it into practice): 'Keep your head cool, your feet dry, your skin clear, your digestion regular, and a fig for the doctor'.

Duffy made what he described as his 'first formal entry' into public affairs in 1834, when he acted as secretary to a deputation which presented an address of welcome to the Lord Lieutenant, Lord Mulgrave, as he toured Ulster. The occasion was historic. It was the first time since the capitulation of Limerick in 1691 that the King's representative had received Catholics and Protestants on equal terms. The visit evoked a prodigious clamour in Parliament and press. Though boycotted by the gentry, the Monagham welcoming committee included the local doctor, attorney, woollen draper, half-a-dozen priests and a few farmers. Exercising the royal prerogative, Lord Mulgrave reprieved prisoners, among them convicted rebels — an unheard-of procedure — and conducted his undress levees as punctiliously as if he were holding court at Dublin Castle.

The spectacle of priest and rebel honouring the representative of the Sovereign, and being honoured by him, outraged the more intransigent Orangemen. One, the gallant Colonel Blacker, sublimated his wrath in verse:

> Forth starts the spawn of treason, the 'scaped of '98,
> To bask in courtly favour, and away the helm of State.
> He comes the open rebel fierce, he comes the Jesuit sly,
> But put your trust in God, my boys, and keep your powder dry.

The experience, however, had a profound effect on Duffy. 'The era of indolent studies, of perfuming my brain with romances and reviews, was at an end, and the serious business of life had begun', he wrote. Laughingly, he quoted to his mother a line from a folk tale she used to tell him: 'Bake me a bannock, mother, and cut me a collop. I'm going to push my fortune'.

On a visit to Dublin, Duffy met a kinsman, Terence McMahon Hughes, a successful journalist, then special correspondent of the London *Morning Chronicle*. Hughes took Duffy to theatres and public meetings and showed him some of Dublin's best-known citizens: Daniel O'Connell, the 'Uncrowned King' of Ireland, at the Corn Exchange and the lawyers, Plunkett and Bushe at the Four Courts.

Duffy was charmed by the gay independent life Hughes led, and fascinated by his nightly talks on current politics which often appeared next morning transmuted into impressive leading articles. Duffy longed for such a marvellous method of communicating his own ideas to the people and determined to become a journalist. His guardian opened negotiations with Michael Staunton, proprietor of the *Morning Register*, a daily paper founded in 1823 by the Catholic Association, whose proclaimed object was 'to promote concord among all classes of Irishmen'. Staunton had no staff vacancy, but agreed to take on Duffy as an unpaid trainee on trial.

Early in April 1836, when he was just twenty, Duffy moved to Dublin, accompanied by Terence McManus, who had found a job as a shop assistant in one of Dublin's larger stores. Henry McManus had preceded them by a few weeks, and Mat Trumble was an usher in an English school.

Duffy's romantic dreams of journalism as a noble, idealistic profession were soon rudely shattered. He had thought of its practitioners as erudite dedicated men, with a sense of mission, and with settled convictions they were prepared to defend at all costs. He found that his colleagues were 'the gipsies of literature, who lived careless driftless lives, without public spirit or thought of tomorrow'. The staff of the papers which supported O'Connell had little sympathy with O'Connell's policy, or indeed with any policy. For the most part, journalists regarded public life as a stage play, where a man gesticulated and perorated according to the role assigned to him. And, even more surprising, the editors of the three peculiarly Catholic papers were all Protestants, while the co-editors of a pre-eminently Protestant paper were Catholics.

But despite disillusion, Duffy found much to enjoy in his new life. For a time, he shared lodgings with Henry McManus, who guided him to Dublin's art and architectural treasures: the Hogarths in Charlemont House, the historic portraits in Trinity College, the Grinling Gibbons' carved ceilings at Kilmainham, and Gannon's 'noble palaces', the Customs House and the Four Courts, on the Liffey. In the Dublin library he found all the books he had longed for. And he was startled by the revelation that sentiments and experiences which he had long regarded as peculiar to himself were not unique. 'Hazlitt's frank confessions and Montaigne's self-reproaches sometimes read like my personal experience'.

On Sundays, he rambled with McManus and Hughes, visiting sites made famous in history and legend, and in his abundant spare time, he organized a debating society, a class to study French (conducted by a German) and a social club which met over a broiled bone and a jorum of punch. But above all, he steeped himself in Irish history and biography. In imagination, he traversed the panorama of Irish resistance, from St.

Lorcan in the twelfth century to Daniel O'Connell in the nineteenth.

But O'Connell in the flesh proved a great disappointment. He was not the romantic figure, the successor of Owen Roe, Sarsfield and Grattan, whom Duffy had been ready to venerate and obey. Instead, he was a tough, practical man of affairs, with a caustic, humorous and vulgar tongue.

DUFFY worked feverishly and his health, never robust, suffered. But he enjoyed long country walks on Sunday mornings, with a lunch of bread, cheese and porter, and long literary talks on Saturday nights, generally with a new-found friend, the 'delightful and unhappy man of genius', Clarence Mangan. The poet had a prodigious memory for poetry, and would delight Duffy with recitations from Shakespeare, Marlowe and Byron. Another friend whom Duffy made at this time who greatly influenced him was Thomas O'Hagan, then a barrister at the outset of his career, later to become Lord O'Hagan of Tullahogue, and Lord Chancellor of Ireland.

Throughout 1838, Duffy was in constant ill-health. Because his mother had died of consumption he feared he had inherited the disease. He consulted an eminent Dublin physician, Dominick Corrigan, who thirty-four years later, recalled the meeting:

> You asked me, and that was the purpose of your visit, were you going into consumption, that if you were you would work — work while you had life to add something more to the little capital you had laid by for your sister, that if you were not you would make an ambitious move, I think you said to 'The Bar', and you added that on my answer depended your choice of life. It was an anxious moment for me as well as you. I told you you were not on the way to consumption, and thank God my prediction has been true . . .

Duffy's deliverance from what he termed 'the exhausting slavery' of daily journalism took place the following year, when the fifty thousand Catholics of Belfast decided to have a newspaper of their own. Asked to recommend an editor, O'Connell nominated T.M. Hughes. He declined to live in Belfast, and ultimately, Duffy was chosen. On his way to take up his new position, Duffy was entertained at a public dinner by the leaders of the Monaghan Liberal Club. 'In the half century that followed I sat at many feasts', he wrote, 'but the exquisite flavour and intoxicating odour of the first never returned. I was then twenty-three years of age, in impaired health, but devoured with ambition to do something memorable for Ireland and henceforth I was called on to exercise authority instead of obeying it'.

The first number of *The Vindicator*, a bi-weekly, appeared on 1 May 1839. Many friends told Duffy that a Repeal journal could not succeed in such a Protestant stronghold as Belfast. 'At that time', he wrote, 'Ulster was regarded throughout England, and largely regarded in our Southern provinces, as the enemy's country; a territory where Nationality could only appear under some decent disguise'. But *The Vindicator* soon attained a circulation of 1,300; in August, Duffy bought it out.

Duffy soon impressed his own personality on the paper, and proved himself a creative, original editor. He advocated radicalism, home manufactures, the revival of local traditions, and native literature. He enlisted Mangan and T.M. Hughes as poetic contributors, and himself wrote a few ballads, some of which, to his embarrassment, survived in anthologies.

Duffy encouraged the Belfast Catholics who usually supported the Whigs, to speak out for themselves, and to be prepared to abandon the Whigs and choose their own leaders if it became necessary. As a result of his exhortations, meetings were held throughout the northern counties, 'to proclaim the principles of civil and religious liberty'. The Orange papers were furious, but not contemptuous. '*The Vindicator* is to be found in every hamlet', said one. 'It has become the oracle of the peasantry, and the manual of respectable Romanists'. O'Connell was delighted with its success: 'The spirit of the North has been aroused by a free Press', he declared. 'That excellent journal *The Vindicator* has caused a new light to dawn upon the people of Ulster, and still continues to do incalculable service to the cause of freedom'.

Among the few friends Duffy made in Ulster was the Reverend Theobald Mathew, better known as Father Mathew, whose temperance campaign, launched in Cork in 1838, was bringing about a revolution in the social habits of the Irish people. (Subsequently it was so successful that it caused distilleries and breweries to close, some of them owned by members of his own family.) Duffy organised a deputation of Belfast Catholics to meet him, and afterwards attended a banquet to him in Newry, at which Duffy made a speech which he described as the keynote of his whole life.

He insisted that what the Irish people wanted most was education, and that the benefactor who was giving them temperate habits might also give them this kindred blessing. He asked,

> Why should not every teetotal society have its lecture-room where the artisan might be taught the principles of mechanics, the farmer the latest improvements in agriculture, and every one something that would make him a better man and better citizen? I long to see the day when every town will have its temperance hall, and every temperance hall its schoolrooms, its reading rooms, its lecture-rooms, its exhibition rooms, and even its public baths and gymnasium for the operative classes . . . Leisure is the poor man's right, as much as food and clothes; leisure to think, to read, to enjoy . . .

Father Mathew had thirty thousand copies of the speech printed and circulated.

DUFFY was now determined to become a barrister — the one profession, he thought, open to a young Irishman entangled in politics. In Michaelmas Term (2-25 November 1839) he was admitted a law student at King's Inns, Dublin. On a visit to Dublin to keep his first term, he called at the *Morning Register* office, and found that his former editor, Hugh Lynar, had emigrated to the Cape Colony. The paper, traditionally a staid, statistical and stodgy publication, had been left by him in the hands of two young barristers, fresh from Trinity College. Suspected by veteran newspapermen to be slightly crazed, they were playing merry pranks with the paper. One was John Blake Dillon, son of a middle-class Connaught family, who had studied for the priesthood at Maynooth before taking up the law. Duffy described him as tall, strikingly handsome, carelessly dressed, 'with eyes like a thoughtful woman's', and clear olive complexion. He had been brought up among Connaught's impoverished peasantry, and moved by their degradation had made a study of social reform. 'He was neither morose nor cynical', Duffy wrote. 'But he had one instinct in common with Swift — the villainies of mankind made his blood boil'. Dillon, who was occupying Duffy's relinquished chair, introduced him to the other young barrister, Thomas Davis. 'I was less pleased with Davis than with his friend', Duffy recalled. 'He was able and manifestly sincere; but at first sight I thought him dogmatic and self-assured — a strangely unjust estimate as it proved in the end'.

The Davis family was of Welsh origin. Thomas Davis was the son of a Protestant army surgeon, a veteran of the Peninsular War, who had married while serving in Ireland. Thomas was educated at Trinity where his tutor was Thomas Wallis, who called himself 'Professor of Things in General and Patriotism in Particular'. In 1838, at the age of twenty-four, Thomas Davis was called to the bar. Two years later he was elected President of the Historical Society. In a famous speech to the Society, he pleaded for a study of Irish history, and in essays published in a Dublin periodical, he championed, the cause of Irish nationalism.

When he returned to Belfast, Duffy thought much of both young men. He resolved when he saw them next to discuss a project to which he had given much thought — to establish a weekly journal in Dublin on the lines of the London *Examiner* or *Spectator*.

In the session of 1841-2, Duffy entered the class of Logic and Belles Lettres at the Belfast College, which admitted students to lectures without examination. At the same time, he was reading assiduously. From London John O'Hagan sent him a copy of Carlyle's *Miscellanies,* and Carlyle's daring theories moved him 'like electric shocks'. O'Hagan also advised him to read articles by a young man named Macaulay in the *Edinburgh Review*. In his boyhood, the only poets Duffy had known were Moore and Burns. Now he read Scott, Byron, Coleridge and Shelley, 'and pitied somewhat presumptuously those who wasted their time in salons'. He was 'feverish with political designs, and totally indifferent to social success of any sort'.

On Duffy's next visit to Dublin, in the spring of 1842, he strolled through Phoenix Park with Davis and Dillon, discussing Ireland's problems and prospects. When they sat down 'under a noble elm', not far from the Wellington memorial, he expounded his idea of a weekly paper that they should own and edit. Davis and Dillon listened eagerly, for, as Davis put it, they had long wanted to see a paper that would be 'more decided than O'Connell's organs, and less Romanist than *The Freeman's Journal,* both well-established papers. But neither had money to put into it, or was willing to be involved in debt. 'I was able to find capital to a moderate extent', says Duffy, 'and I solved the difficulty by undertaking

10

John Blake Dillon

to become sole proprietor if they aided me in the management, and in this arrangement they gladly concurred'. Thus was conceived *The Nation,* one of the most original and influential newspapers of the century. It owed much of its success to Duffy's energy and skill as an editor, though he later wrote with characteristic modesty: 'Davis was our true leader. Not only had nature endowed him more liberally, but he loved labour better, and his mind had traversed regions of thought, and wrestled with problems still unfamiliar to his confederates'.

The Nation was a young man's paper. At the time of its launching, Davis was 28, Dillon, 27, and Duffy, a veteran journalist of 26.

Duffy returned to Belfast to wind up his affairs. Davis visited him, and they debated the principles on which the new paper should be conducted. Duffy reiterated his 'rooted opinion' that education was the supremely important element of a national struggle. Davis agreed that education was a sure resource, but it was slow. He thought they could win the support of the classes already educated, particularly the Protestant middle class. Dillon, they knew, was impatient for land reform. But as the aims of all three were identical, there would be no difficulty in harmonising their methods.

After restoring the property of *The Vindicator* to the original owners, Duffy returned to Dublin in the autumn of 1842. Before leaving Belfast, he became engaged to Emily McLaughlin, daughter of a well-to-do Belfast merchant, and grand-daughter in the maternal line, of the MacDermott of Coulavin, one of the few Celtic families whose hereditary title had survived into the nineteenth century. Duffy has little to say about Emily, whom he married in Dublin that year.

Among his papers he left a shadowy chronological record of his early romances:

> At eight years, I felt a passionate attachment for a child of my own age. At eleven or twelve my mind was agitated with vague dreams and fantasies of a mistress won by wonderful personal achievements. At fifteen I loved a girl who was my elder and better. I thought her a goddess, she thought me a fool. And faith, she was most in the right. At seventeen first awoke a new sensation turbulent and fierce and meaning I knew not what. At one-and-twenty I was unstained by any breach of the sixth commandment.

What was the new paper to be called? Duffy had suggested the *National,* out of sympathy with the Paris journal of that name. Davis objected on grammatical grounds to the use of an adjective. Among the alternatives were *Tribune, Statesman, Sentinel,* and *Banner.* Ultimately, they decided on *The Nation,* 'a happy and magnificent' choice, Duffy thought, because they desired to make Ireland a nation.

FROM childhood, Duffy had seen how unevenly the scales of justice in Ulster were poised between Catholic and Protestant. In June 1842, his vigorous comments on what he considered a flagrant demonstration of this had led to his arrest on a seditious libel charge.

In Downpatrick, four Orangemen had been tried for the murder of a Catholic named McArdle. The jury, eleven Protestants and one Catholic, found them not guilty, and their friends in court, in the presence of the Judge and Attorney-General, acclaimed the verdict with unrestrained and vociferous enthusiasm.

In Armagh a Catholic, Francis Hughes, had been tried three times for the murder of a Mr. Powell; Hughes was finally found guilty and executed. In each trial, his counsel had unsuccessfully protested that the jury was exclusively Protestant. Under the heading: 'HUGHES' CASE — A LAW FOR THE PROTESTANT AND A LAW FOR THE CATHOLIC', Duffy wrote:

> On his guilt or innocence, it is not our province to pronounce; but we do affirm, without fearing any conscientious man in the Empire will differ from us, that he has not had a fair and impartial trial, such as the law of England intends that every prisoner shall receive. He has not been tried indifferently, as a person under the protection of the law . . . he has been tried as an Irish Catholic, whose guilt ordinarily appears to be assumed, and whose conviction seems to be desired. If we speak strongly and decidedly on this matter, the circumstances demand it; for if we do not *now* and *here* make a stand for justice, no Catholic in the community is safe . . .

On 30 June, Duffy appeared before Chief Justice Pennefather in the Court of Queen's Bench, Dublin, charged with having published 'a false, wicked, malicious, scandalous, and seditious libel' upon the administration of justice. Pennefather instructed the jury that it was immaterial whether what Duffy had written was true or false. 'With the truth or falsehood of those charges', he declared, 'you and I have nothing to do'. Thus guided, the jury took only ten minutes to find Duffy guilty, and he was remanded to come up for sentence at the next sitting of the court.

Many English papers, including the *Morning Chronicle, The Globe* and the *Sun,* denounced the prosecution as characteristic 'Orange Toryism'. The *Morning Chronicle* said the doctrines laid down by Pennefather went 'to the utter extinction of everything bearing the semblance of the Liberty of the Press'. The judge had ruled that all statements not made before the proper tribunals were presumed to be false, even if they were true. 'What would the tribunals be — what would the legislature itself be', asked the *Chronicle,* 'were the doctrine of the Chief Justice to be acted on? What would be the conduct of men in authority were all appeal to the public interdicted'?

There were many protests in the House of Commons, and an unchastened Duffy, in the pages of *The Vindicator,* addressed a long Open Letter to the Rt. Honourable Lord Eliot, Secretary of State for Ireland. In it, he recapitulated the facts about the 'awful and diabolical murder of Hugh McArdle', the 'extraordinary acquittal' of the four men accused of the crime, and the 'indecent exultation' of the Orangemen in court on the announcement of the verdict. He compared this trial with that of Hughes and continued:

> These facts must be in your recollection . . . for they have been repeatedly brought before the government in memorials and petitions . . . as soon as the law permits, I will be sent to a dungeon for stating, in a public journal, what the counsel for Francis Hughes stated in a court of justice — what an English baronet stated in a petition to parliament — and what your Lordship — a

member of the Government which has prosecuted me — stated in the House of Commons.

Much of Duffy's letter was an eloquent plea for the freedom of the press, and a recognition of its dignity and importance. In his summing-up, Justice Pennefather had referred derisively to 'the man with the printing press'. Duffy reminded Lord Eliot that the sneer could be applied to Benjamin Franklin, Cobbett and Leigh Hunt, 'men whose names will be illustrious and world-renowned when their accusers and judges are forgotten'. Moreover the last Lord Chancellor of Ireland, Lord Campbell, had been for many years a reporter on the *Morning Chronicle*, 'the salaried servant of a man with a printing press'.

> It is a mistaken policy to treat the Press with injustice; you cannot extinguish it . . . Be wise, my Lord; and stepping beyond the ignorance and prejudice of your party, declare that, as truth and honesty must triumph in the end, you are not afraid of fair discussion; that you are no friend to a system of sheltering officials behind the barriers of libel laws. . .

In one passage, Duffy referred rhetorically to his ill health:

> It is my misfortune to have a constitution far from robust, and habit has made an intercourse with nature, with the green fields and the blue sky, a necessity of life. A sentence of imprisonment may be equivalent to a sentence of death; but my Lord, if I could evade this evil, great and overwhelming as it is, by the smallest concession of the sacred and inalienable right of the Catholics of Ireland to be tried by their peers, I would not do it. You may send me to a dungeon, if you can reconcile it with equity to do so; you may destroy my property and my prospects, but you cannot deprive me of the consolation of knowing that I have been faithful to my country and my own conscience.

And in another, he continued his defence:

> I do not hold any inflated notions of the power or usefulness of newspapers; but taking them for what they are really worth, observing their immense influence on public opinion, and regarding the honour, ability and fearlessness with which the better part of them is conducted, I am not ashamed to say for myself, that though a few months will see me a member of a profession more sacred in the eye of the Bench, I will not conceive that I have gained anything in honour or usefulness, by ceasing to be a 'man with a printing press' and becoming a man with a wig and gown.

It is hard to reconcile this passage prefiguring his imminent admission to the Bar, with Duffy's two references to the dungeon that awaited him. But he was not to experience the dank rigours of the dungeon. At the next sitting of the Court of Queen's Bench, on 11 November 1842, when he came up for sentence, his counsel, Mr. Robert Holmes, addressing the Court, said he was authorised by Mr. Duffy, who was a Roman Catholic, to state that Mr. Duffy had written the libel 'under the influence of extremely irritated feelings, excited by what appeared to him to be an unequal administration of the same laws, when applied to the Protestants and Roman Catholics, to the prejudice of the latter'. Mr.

Duffy was now satisfied that he did not discuss the matters with 'proper temper and moderation, but was betrayed by the great excitement under which he then acted into the use of strong and unguarded language'. Mr. Duffy thought it was due to himself, as well as to the law officers who had conducted the trials at Downpatrick and Armagh, thus publicly to declare that conviction.

Replying on behalf of the Court, the Attorney-General said that the sole purpose of the prosecution was to rescue the administration of justice from unmerited imputations. The avowal made by the defendant appeared fully to meet this purpose, and he would therefore, with the permission of the Bench, not require Duffy to be brought up for judgment. The Bench graciously agreed.

Two questions must be asked about this incident. Why did Duffy's ruggedly defiant attitude of June ('You may send me to a dungeon . . . You may destroy my property and my prospects', etc.) crumble into a humble breast-beating apologia five months later? And why, when Duffy in 1898 wrote his detailed and well documented memoirs, *My Life in Two Hemispheres*, did he make no mention of this, the first of his many conflicts with the law?

It is easy at least to suggest an answer to the first question. Three weeks before his appearance in Court for sentence, Duffy had launched *The Nation*. A sentence of imprisonment would have been fatal to its prospects. He might have considered its survival more important than his pride. The second question is more difficult to answer. But perhaps, even in his old age, Duffy felt shame for the surrender he had made more than half a century before.

IN the prospectus of *The Nation*, Davis wrote:

> The necessities of the country seem to demand a journal able to aid and organise the new movements going on amongst us; to make their growth deeper and their fruit more 'racy of the soil'; and above all, to direct the popular mind and the sympathies of educated men of all parties to the great end of Nationality . . . a Nationality which may embrace Protestant, Catholic and Dissenter — Milesian and Cromwellian . . . not a Nationality which would prelude civil war, but which would establish internal union and external independence . . . a Nationality which would be recognised by the world, and sanctified by wisdom, virtue and time.

The first number of *The Nation* appeared on 15 October 1842. It was an immediate success. On the day of publication, the day of his twenty-eighth birthday, Davis wrote enthusiastically to his friend, Daniel Owen Maddyn:

> *The Nation* sold its whole impression of No. 1 before twelve o'clock this morning and could have sold twice as many more if they had been printed, as they ought to have been — but the fault is on the right side. The office window was actually broken by the newsmen in their impatience to get more.

And Davis's college tutor, Thomas Wallis, wrote to him: 'One thing you may be sure of: the newsmen are open-mouthed against you . . . They say you might have sold in Dublin *ten times* what you printed for the city circulation. . .'. Twelve thousand copies had been printed, but no reprint was possible, as the type had been distributed. At the end of the day copies were selling for two or three times the published price of sixpence. (In 1842, sixpence represented half the daily wage of an agricultural labourer.)

The sales of the first issue of a paper are no indication of its future prospects. Many readers, prompted by curiosity, buy the first issue only. But within a year, the average weekly circulation of *The Nation*, verified by the penny stamp duty paid on each number, was 10,730. Its nearest rival, *The Weekly Freeman*, had a circulation of just over 7,000. Least popular of Dublin's twelve journals was *The Evening Freeman*, with a circulation of 448! Duffy later estimated that because of its special distribution, *The Nation* had more than a quarter of a million readers.

It consisted of sixteen four-column tightly-packed pages, measuring 17¾ by 12 inches. A good deal of the news content was borrowed from other papers — a practice common to most newspapers at that time. But there was enough original material to justify its motto: 'To create and foster public opinion, and make it racy of the soil'. And in format and typography, as Duffy wrote: 'It departed from the ordinary practice of Irish journals which were immethodical and slovenly . . .'

The front page of the first issue carried advertisements for contributions to 'the O'Connell Tribute' — a tribute to 'Ireland's great moral Regenerator . . . the Patriot Chief of swordless glory . . .', as well as advertisements appealing to less lofty emotions.

Years later, Duffy listed among the virtues of his paper the fact that: 'Quack advertisements universally seen in English or Irish journals were altogether excluded'. Time must have effaced his memory of some of the advertisements that appeared in his first issue, and often subsequently. Thus, while high-minded booksellers offered copies of Augustine's *Confessions*, Butler's *Feasts and Fasts*, and Hay's *Pious Christians* and *Catholic Piety*, more worldly advertisements proclaimed the virtues of 'The Cordial Balm of Syricacum, a gentle stimulant and renovator of the impaired functions of life . . . and debility arising from Syphilis'; and of 'Perry's Purifying Specific Pills, a cure for Gonorrhea, Gleets, Seminal Weakness and Venereal Taint'.

Other pages carried letters from Dieppe and Paris, English parliamentary reports, reports of political trials, 'Musical and Theatrical Chit-Chat'; sporting news; reviews, and a report occupying a page and a half of the weekly meeting of the Royal National Repeal Association in the Corn Exchange, Burgh Quay.

In the main leader, Duffy proclaimed his paper's aims: 'with all the nicknames that serve to delude and divide us', he wrote, 'with all their Orangemen and Ribbonmen, Torymen and Whigmen, Ultras and Moderados, and Heaven knows what rubbish besides — there are, in truth, but two parties in Ireland — those who suffer through her national degradation, and those who profit by it'. The object of *The Nation* was to organise 'the greater and better of these parties' and to restore Ireland's self-respect, without which national feelings could not exist:

> There can be no doubt that all the chief source of the contempt with which we
> are treated by England is our own sycophancy . . . Up to this hour Ireland has

Reading 'The Nation'

Courtesy of the National Gallery of Ireland

no public monuments of any kind except such as commemorate her defeats and degradation. All that she ought to forget is paraded in the face of day; nothing that she ought to be proud of is recorded by a solitary testimonial.

Duffy listed the obelisk on the banks of 'the disastrous Boyne', and the equestrian statue of William of Orange in College Green [it was blown up in 1929], but there was no pillar on the shores of Clontarf where in 1014 Brian Boru defeated the Norsemen, or on 'the memorable banks of the Blackwater'.

The Nation's second leader, written by Davis, condemned the English Army in Afghanistan for 'invading the territory of an independent and unoffending people with no pretext save a lie, and no design save aggrandisement'.

The battle of Waterloo, fought in a foreign country, and for a foreign country, has its testimonial in the Phoenix Park; the battle of the Nile, won by Englishmen and for Englishmen has its memorial in Sackville Street [the Nelson pillar was blown up in 1967]; the holy and peaceful triumphs of '82 and '29 won by Irishmen for Irishmen, are commemorated nowhere. [In 1782 Ireland was given parliamentary independence. In 1829, the Catholic Emancipation Bill was passed.]

John O'Callaghan, who contributed an article on 'Ancient Irish Literature', also had an unfortunate flirtation with the Muses: the first verse of his 'The Exterminator's Song' read:

> *'Tis I am the poor man's scourge,*
> *And where is the scourge like me?*
> *My land from all papists I purge,*
> *Who think that their votes should be free —*
> *Who think that their votes should be free!*
> *For huts only fitted for brutes*
> *My agent the last penny wrings;*
> *And my serfs live on water and roots*
> *While I feast on the best of good things!*
> *For I am the poor man's scourge!*
> *For I am the poor man's scourge!*

Duffy had appealed in *The Vindicator* 'to an old bardic people in passionate popular verse' and resolved to continue the experiment in *The Nation*. In the third number he gave an example of the spirit he hoped to evoke, with a composition of his own, 'Faugh-A-Ballagh, the first national poem' to appear in his paper.

When the poem was reprinted in an anthology, 'The Spirit of the Nation', Duffy explained that it was written in October 1842, 'when the hope and spirits of the people were low'; and published 'as the Charter-song' of *The Nation's* contributors. It was supposed to be sung, as it often was, at their weekly suppers.

'Faugh-A-Ballagh', 'Clear the Road', was the wild yell of the clans of Connaught and Munster which the Royal Irish Fusiliers adopted as their battle-cry in the Peninsular War.

Here is the first of the four verses:

> *Hope no more for fatherland,*
> *All its ranks are thinned or broken':*
> *Long a base and coward band*
> *Recreant words like these have spoken;*
> *But WE preach a land awoken;*
> *And of courage true and tried*
> *As your fears are false and hollow:*
> *Slaves and dastards, stand aside —*
> *Knaves and traitors, Faugh-A-Ballagh.*

Duffy contributed many more poems to *The Nation*. About them, T.W. Rolleston observed:

> None of the Young Irelanders wrote in rhyme and metre with more sinewy force than Duffy. His lines smite home, like the axe of an Irish gallowglass [a Celtic warrior] and though his mind, as his whole career shows, was eminently that of a statesman, he clearly thought and felt as a reckless fighter when he faced the enemies of his cause with the keen blade of verse in his hand.

DESPITE the seriousness of their purpose, the young men whom Duffy gathered around in *The Nation* office, and who had come to be called the Young Irelanders, were a genial, high-spirited community. Once a week, they held an informal conference, meeting in one another's house in succession. Duffy recalls the gaiety and exuberance of these occasions:

> Tea and serious debate occupied the time till 10 o'clock, then a light supper, pleasant talk, fun and song until midnight. It was here the literary and political projects of the party were discussed, and the books and articles to be written, and the places to be visited determined. A cordial friendship warmed and harmonised these pleasant meetings . . . They escaped, I think, the chief danger of such reunions; they were far from being a mutual admiration society. Whoever laid himself fairly open to criticism during the week might confidently expect to be chaffed without mercy on Saturday night . . .

The inner editorial group consisted of Duffy, Davis, Dillon, John O'Hagan and a young law student John Pigot. One night, when the meeting place was Duffy's house at Rathmines, Michael Joseph Barry fell into the Grand Canal at Portobello Bridge, and was hauled out with some difficulty by his fellow poet, Denny Lane. 'It was thought proper to assume he was actually drowned, and his epitaph, his last will and testament, and an account of his premature death were improvised . . . by his comrades'. One ballad had this unflattering verse:

> *Pale, pale, were his bonny cheeks and clammy as the clay:*
> *Pale, pale, were his whiskers twain, the dye was washed away.*

One man who could never be induced to attend these convivial gatherings, and perhaps the only real poet among the Young Irelanders, was the shy unhappy genius, James Clarence Mangan, who summed up his attitude to life in a single haunting sentence: 'I have pleasure in nothing and I admire nothing. I hate scenery and suns'. He had been encouraged by Duffy to write for *The Vindicator* and he contributed to *The Nation* from its first issue until his death, but took no interest in its politics or people.

He lived in a shadowy world of dreams, sustained by opium and alcohol, a ghostly figure in his tattered blue cloth cloak, baggy ill-fitting pantaloons, and fantastic, steeple-shaped hat, under which his blanched golden hair hung in unkempt tangles. His face was like parchment, and his deep blue eyes were sometimes concealed behind large green spectacles. He usually carried a faded voluminous umbrella, and a bottle of what he claimed was tar-water, as a cure for all ills. But his real panacea was whisky. 'He looked like the spectre of some German romance', said Duffy, 'rather than a living creature'. Duffy tried without success to save him from self-destruction. He paid for his contributions in advance, supplemented the payments generously from his own purse, financed the publication of an anthology of his poems, and, with a few friends, guaranteed him an adequate income for six months, if he pledged to give up intoxicating drink for that period. Mangan promised 'in the solemn presence of Almighty God', and 'with His assistance' to do so. But drink was Mangan's only escape from the dark hopelessness of his world. Like his contemporary, Edgar Allan Poe, he could not survive without it. He died of cholera, a burned-out husk, in June 1849 — only a few months before Poe was picked up dying, in a Baltimore street.

Many of Mangan's contributions to *The Nation*, scribbled perhaps with borrowed pen and ink on a bar counter, were mere doggerel. But *The Nation* also published his finest poem, 'Dark Rosaleen', of which another poet, Lionel Johnson, wrote, 'It is among the greatest lyrics of the world'. And James Joyce's first published writing was an article on Mangan in *St. Stephen's*, a Dublin university magazine, in 1902.

Another unhappy man whom Duffy befriended was the novelist William Carleton, who had been rejected by many of his countrymen for abandoning Catholicism, and was struggling to keep a large family on his meagre earnings. 'From my settlement in Dublin I had known him well', wrote Duffy, 'and aimed constantly and not unsuccessfully to restore him to his natural relations to his country and people from which bigots had alienated him'.

One night in April 1843 a twenty-year-old student of Trinity College named John Kells Ingram attended a Nationalist meeting and was greatly stirred by it. When he got home he composed a ballad, 'Memory of the Dead', and dropped it in *The Nation's* letter-box. It was published in the next issue, and with its bold opening line, 'Who fears to speak of '98', was, perhaps, the best-known ballad of the Young Ireland movement. Ingram, the son of a Protestant clergyman, became one of the greatest scholars of his time, and Professor of Oratory and English literature at Trinity College.

Another of *The Nation's* rousing ballads, long remembered, was John O'Hagan's 'The Union':

> *How did they pass the Union?*
> *By perjury and fraud;*
> *By slaves who sold their land for gold*
> *As Judas sold his God;*
> *By all the savage acts that yet*
> *Have followed England's track —*
> *The pitchcap and the bayonet,*
> *The gibbet and the rack.*
> *And thus was passed the Union.*
> *By Pitt and Castlereagh;*
> *Could Satan send for such an end*
> *More worthy tools than they?*

When Duffy received a prose contribution signed 'John Fenshaw Ellis', he was greatly impressed with it, and asked the writer to call at *The Nation* office. The writer replied that this was not possible, and invited Duffy to visit a house in Leeson Street. He was ushered into a drawing room where he discovered that 'Mr. Ellis' was a tall, stately girl with 'flashing brown eyes and features cast in an heroic mould'. Her name was Jane Francesca Elgee, and she was the granddaughter of Archdeacon Elgee, of Wexford.

For years, she contributed verses to *The Nation* under the Pen-name of 'Speranza', but she was to become better known as Lady Wilde and the mother of Oscar Wilde. 'Her little scented notes, sealed with wax of a delicate hue and dainty device, represented a substantial force in Irish politics, and the vehement will of a woman of genius', wrote Duffy. Today she is remembered as a person rather than a poet.

'Educate that you may be free', was a sentence often on Duffy's lips. In 1845, with Davis' enthusiastic co-operation, he launched the *Library of Ireland*, a series of shilling books, originally in paper covers, covering Irish history, literature, and biography. Twenty-two volumes were issued between 1845 and 1847, when the project, for economic and political reasons, had to be terminated. These books, many of which are still in circulation, were the beginning of Ireland's popular national literature. Among the authors were Davis, William Carleton, and D'Arcy McGee. Duffy edited *The Ballad Poetry of Ireland*, a charming anthology, which had an enormous sale. It foreshadowed the Celtic Renaissance of the eighteen-nineties, and was acclaimed even by that unsparing critic, Lord Jeffrey, who described the poems as 'most pathetic and . . . with scarcely an exception, so entirely *national* in character'. He urged his daughter, Mrs. Empson, to get a copy of the book.

Two

The Struggle for Repeal

ON the first anniversary of *The Nation*, which then had a circulation 'far exceeding that of any paper in Ireland', Duffy examined the course it had pursued over the twelve months. 'Nationality was our first great object', he wrote. '*All* social and political movements we valued only if they promoted it...Want of nationality has been the plague of Ireland'. The upper classes were anti-national. Too many of the middle classes aped the vices, the stupidity, and the alienation of the higher.

> The hearts of the poor were always right, but they too often confounded the vices of the landlord with his creed, ignorant that when England and the landlords were good Catholics, the same system existed of delegating to the aristocracy the right by law to rob and hang, in exchange for their labours by keeping Ireland enslaved...We think we can boast that this was the first paper in Ireland, of a political and serious character, which could defy the charge of sectarianism.

The Nation had defended Presbyterians, Protestants and Catholics alike:

> We look upon the Protestant's fear of the Catholic, and on the Catholic's fear of the Protestant, as rank nonsense. Their mutual dislike is something worse. And yet this trash and this crime have ruined the country. We implore the Protestant and Catholic to mix more together, and to judge of each other by observation, not report. The Catholic will find the Protestant an educated gentleman, misled in politics by bigoted training. The Protestant will discover a generous lover of country and of religious equality in the Irish Catholic.

The Nation had also endeavoured to create an independent foreign policy for Ireland, as when it denounced the 'infamy' of England's conduct in Afghanistan and China. And on the question of land tenure, *The Nation's* course had been 'open and decided':

> We seek to secure to the peasant land at a just rent. A just rent would leave him comfort and some leisure. We seek for him the value of all the labour or money he spends in improvements. And we seek *prospective laws*, which shall tend, by a natural and easy change, to reduce the great estates, and create a body of small proprietors in fee throughout every part of Ireland. But we are not ready to jump into a servile war for this purpose.
> On the contrary, we shall do our best to make the landlords recognise that the

postponement of the tenure settlements or the decline of the political agitation, would lead to an anti-rent movement, which might end in a disastrous rebellion, but would begin by reducing them to beggary, and could not be quelled by the defeat of insurgent armies.

'The success of *The Nation*', Duffy concluded, 'has been attributed to the success of the Repeal movement, of which it was *one* of the many moving powers'. At times Duffy's nationalist fervour leads him into absurdity, as when he writes:

> We must deliberately undo all that has been done to assimilate us with Englishmen...There is no people we less desire to resemble. To Anglicise our peasantry would be to teach them the grossest indulgence in the lowest vices. And never is vice so hideous as when engrafted upon the character of an English boor...
> Where an Irish peasant is gay and gallant, an English boor is sullen and sensual. The Saxon plots a vice where the Celt meditates a gallantry; and when he falls into habitual immorality, he wallows like a hog in the stye of his moral filth...
> From such a leprosy as this we have been preserved partly by our poverty, much more by the influence and example of the clergy of the people, but most of all by our national character. The gay, bold, joyous Irishman has no tendency to the darker vices. His animal spirits and his love of fun supply him with abundant materials for enjoyment...

Duffy gives a less flattering picture of 'the gay, bold joyous Irishman' in an article on Father Mathew:

> The drunkenness of the Irish was unlike that of any other people. Many of the happiest, wealthiest, and most moral nations in Europe, drink more than the Irish did, man for man. The Scotch drink more whisky, the Southern nations wine, the English and German porter, and the Swedes and Norwegians potato brandy; but, then, they drink these liquors habitually — every day — as a part of their ordinary sober diet. Far unlike was the Irishman's drunkenness... He drank nothing for some 350 days in the year; but once, or, may be oftener in the month, he got roaring drunk. This occasional debauch was the Lethe-moment of all his sorrows. He then forgot all his wrongs. His cabin was warm, his belly full, his back covered — for an afternoon! But he awoke in the morning penniless, broken-headed, guilty, conscience-sore. During his intoxication he had flung off his chains, and his duties.

But teetotalism had taken from the Irish people 'their only enjoyment'. They were altogether without public sports. They had not 'the out-door amusements of the French peasantry, the fireside enjoyments of the Dutch, the beer and beef of John Bull, or the Militia meetings and anniversaries of Brother Jonathan. He needs some stimulant'. Duffy suggested that education could provide a substitute for alcohol, a proposition that would perhaps be difficult to sustain, even today.

On the last day of 1840, Daniel O'Connell announced his conversion to teetotalism at a crowded meeting held at the Rotunda in Dublin. He declared that he had been a teetotaller for four months and had never felt better in his life. 'As for stuffs and cordials', he urged the audience of men and women 'to avoid all those rascally bowel cordials'.

23

WHILE the young contributors to *The Nation* were cutting their journalistic teeth on its first issues, an experienced London journalist arrived in Dublin. His name was William Makepeace Thackeray, but he was known to readers of *Fraser's Magazine* a leading London monthly, as Michael Angelo Titmarsh. He brought with him the traditional English attitude of patronage and condescension towards the 'primitive' Irish. He had joined the staff of *Punch* in 1842, a year after its birth. Its first editor, Mark Lemon, and his colleagues, were men of social conscience and great compassion, but there was little compassion in Thackeray's treatment of the Young Irelanders, or indeed of the Irish in general.

He toured Ireland for five months in the summer and autumn of 1842, gathering material for his *Irish Sketch Book* a bantering survey of Irish life and manners. 'I wonder who *does* understand the place'? he wrote to his mother on 25 September. 'Not the natives, certainly, for the two parties so hate each other, that neither can view the simplest proceeding of the other without distorting, falsifying or abusing it. And where, in the midst of all the lies that all tell, is a stranger to seek the truth'? Among the liars, O'Connell was 'the greatest liar of all'.

In another letter, which Thackeray wrote to his mother from Dublin on 28 October, Ireland was summed up with some finality: 'The parties never cease quarrelling — the society is under-educated — the priests as illiterate as boors — the clergy reading no profane literature — and shutting their eyes on this world for the next'.

Thackeray rode from Cork to Blackrock on the box of a carriage driven by a talkative driver who had been converted by Father Mathew, and carried a medal in his waistcoat as an amulet against the demon drink. He confessed he had been a 'sad sinner' in the way of drink. 'I used to take from 18 to 20 glasses of whiskey a day', he said. 'I was always at the drink. I often used to be up all night at the public'.

REVIEWING the conditions of Ireland when *The Nation* was established Duffy wrote:

> The whole population was dependent on agriculture...There was no manufacture except linen, and the remnant of a woollen trade, slowly dying out before the pitiless competition of Yorkshire. What the country chiefly produced was food; which was exported to richer countries to pay an inordinate rent...There was no foreign trade; the wines of Spain and Portugal, the silks of France, the drugs and spices of the East, the timber of the north, only reached the island through England...The condition of the two classes who live by agriculture furnished a singular contrast. The great proprietors were two or three hundred; the mass of the country was owned by a couple of thousand others, who lived in splendour; and for these the peasant ploughed, sowed, tended, and reaped a harvest which he never shared. Rent...in Ireland meant the whole produce of the soil except a potato-pit...The food of the peasant was potatoes, with a little milk or salt...butter, beef, mutton or pork was nearly as unknown as an article of diet among the peasantry as among the Hindus...Famines were frequent, and every year destitution killed a crowd of peasants...There were sometimes barbarous agrarian murders — murders of agents and bailiffs chiefly, but occasionally of landlords. It would be shameful

to forget that these savage crimes were often the result of savage provocation...It is charged that the Irish peasant was thriftless and ignorant. He was not free from the faults slavery and misery engender; how could he be indeed?...It is officially recorded that one-half of them lived in mud-wall cabins of one room...The island was now the most ignorant and impoverished of Christian States...On less provocation the sober colonists of North America broke away from the empire, and the grave Belgian *bourgeoisie* broke away from their legislative Union. On less provocation indeed the phlegmatic Hollanders opened their dykes and let in the sea.

Offsetting this 'long catalogue of discouragements' were 'two facts of happy augury'. In 1842, half a million children were being educated in National schools, under a system of religious equality. And Father Mathew's Teetotal movement was at its height, with more than two million enrolled abstainers, and whisky consumption in Ireland diminished one-half.

But the Irish scene was dominated by the giant figure of Daniel O'Connell, whose influence was then at its peak. Burly and boisterous, over six feet tall, with a jolly, ruddy face and bright blue eyes, he strode through life with a splendid swagger, adored by millions of his countrymen. His picture was in every country cottage. His reputation was international. Balzac declared that his aim was to become a fourth member of the band of illustrious men the century had produced. The others were Napoleon, Cuvier, and 'the incarnation of a people', O'Connell. Gladstone thought he was the greatest popular leader the world had ever seen. But to Carlyle, he was 'the chief quack of the then world...a lying scoundrel...the Demosthenes of blarney'.

O'Connell — 'the Liberator' or 'Ireland's Uncrowned King' to his followers, and to his opponents, 'Swaggering Dan' or 'The Big Beggarman' — was born in 1775, the son of a well-to-do Catholic landowner in Kerry. He was educated in France, where he saw the beginning of the French Revolution. He became a law student in London and practised law with great success in Dublin. As a young man, he had witnessed the savage repression of the uprising of '98. This, plus his sense of guilt for killing a man in a duel, convinced him that no struggle justified the spilling of human blood. When he gave up the bar to devote his life to the cause of Irish self-government, his aim was to achieve it by peaceful, constitutional means. He had a lawyer's respect for the British constitution, and he supported the monarchy.

His campaign for the Repeal of the Act of Union, which abolished Ireland's Parliament, was sustained by an organised subsidy, 'the O'Connell tribute', levied on members of the various Repeal bodies, and by a Repeal rent of one penny a head a month, collected from the peasantry. O'Connell drew his salary, made grants, and paid expenses, from the combined fund. At its height, the fund raised £13,000 a year.

He was a superb orator in Gaelic as well as in English, though he believed the old language stood in the way of progress. He had a magnificent voice and presence — wit, ardour and impudence. Dickens tells how, as a Parliamentary reporter, he was so moved by a speech of O'Connell's on the tithe-riot that he was compelled to put down his pencil, unable to continue his work. (O'Connell returned the compliment

Daniel O'Connell

by bursting into tears when he read of the death of Little Nell, and flinging his copy of *The Old Curiosity Shop* out of the window.) But he could be excoriating as well as eloquent. He scattered abuse with glorious abandon. The words 'rogue', 'villain', 'scoundrel', were always on his lips. He labelled the entire House of Commons, 'six hundred and fifty-eight scoundrels'. He declared that the mere mention of the Duke of Leinster's name 'operated like a vomit'. He compared Peel's smile to 'the gleam on the silver plate of a coffin lid'.

During a by-election in 1835, Disraeli had been reported as having denounced O'Connell, as 'an incendiary and a traitor'. The report was inaccurate, but the enraged O'Connell told a Dublin meeting that Disraeli was 'a vile creature', 'a living lie', 'a miscreant' and 'a reptile', and having warmed up, concluded:

> His name shows he is of Jewish origin...He has just the qualities of the impenitent thief on the Cross, and I verily believe, if Mr. Disraeli's family herald were to be examined, and his genealogy traced, the same person would be discovered to be the heir at law of the exalted individual to whom I allude...I leave the gentleman to the enjoyment of his infamous distinction and family honours.

Meetings of Repealers used to be held in the Corn Exchange, Burgh Quay, but it was not big enough. Conciliation Hall, which held three thousand people was opened on the same site in the autumn of 1844.

The success of *The Nation* gave a great stimulus to the Repeal movement. *The Times* warned the Tory Prime Minister, Sir Robert Peel:

> A people labouring under unexampled distress send in their £600 a week to the Repeal Fund...
> The average wage of the Irish farm labourer was about one shilling a day. The rabble of Repealers is joined by respectable and well-intentioned persons, and an insignificant faction has become a powerful party. The people of the United Kingdom were firmly persuaded that it was better to conciliate by repealing bad laws than to pour troops into Ireland for the purpose of enforcing them...

But Sir Robert reassured the Irish gentry, and the world at large, that England would resist Repeal even at the painful cost of civil war; O'Connell replied that Ireland would begin no rebellion, but he warned Peel to beware of causing a contest to take place.

IN 1843, proclaimed by O'Connell 'the great Repeal Year', membership of the Repeal Association grew enormously. Members were issued with cards bearing the names of four battlefields where the Irish had defeated the Danes or the English, and O'Connell began a weekly series of 'monster meetings', demanding repeal. The first, at Trim, in March, was said to have been attended by 30,000. Estimates of attendances at subsequent meetings soared astronomically, sometimes incredibly. When O'Connell rode into Kenagh in May, after a triumphal march, he was said to have been escorted by 100,000 men and to have addressed an audience of 350,000. At a meeting on the historic Hill of Tara, in Meath, the site of Ireland's Royal capital, the number was supposed to have reached between 500,000 and 750,000.

The meetings, held weekly or twice a week, followed a fairly standard pattern. O'Connell would begin by asking if there were a band within hearing? 'If there be', he would say, 'let them play up "God Save The Queen"'. There was always at least one band to respond, and when the anthem had been loyally honoured, he would launch into an impassioned account of the woes Ireland had suffered under 'Saxon' rule, including a moving reference to the three hundred Irish women, 'the loveliness and beauty of Wexford' foully murdered by Cromwell.

Duffy described the significance of the Tara meeting: 'To address such a meeting and be heard was a physical impossibility; but in truth it was not a meeting in the ordinary sense, but what in Southern Europe is called a "pronunciamento" — a muster of men already devoted to a public cause, and no longer needed to be schooled in its principles'. 'The peaceful demonstration of the assembled multitudes is one of the most alarming symptoms', reported the Lord Chancellor of Ireland, Sir Edward Sugden.

O'Connell's speeches grew in vehemence, and though he was careful always to make no explicit appeal to force, he did not rule out the possibility of conflict. 'I am called Washington', he said, 'He was driven into the field and obliged to take up arms; but I know a trick worth two of that. But if the Russians, or the Scotch, aye, or the English, were to assail us against the Constitution and the law, they know little of me who think that I would be amongst the last who would stand up for Ireland'.

In Connaught, he declared that the end of the struggle was near at hand, and at a banquet which followed a monster meeting in Mallow, County Cork, he made a spirited declaration which became known as the Mallow Defiance. 'The time is coming when we must be doing', he said. 'Gentlemen, you may learn the alternative to live as slaves or die as freeman. But, gentlemen, as long as they leave us a rag of the Constitution we will stand on it. We will violate no law and assail no enemy; but you are much mistaken if you think others will not assail you'. When someone in the crowd cried: 'We are ready to meet them'! O'Connell replied: 'To be sure you are. Do you think I suppose you to be cowards or fools'? and later, he added: 'Are we to be trampled under foot? Oh! They shall never trample me, at least. (Cries of "No! No!") I say they may trample me, but it will be my dead body they will trample on, not the living man'. To many people in England, Ireland and America, this seemed to portend revolution.

Even more defiant of Peel's threats were the writers of *The Nation*. A leader published in May 1843 declared that if the Irish were 'not prepared to face delay and persecution...and if they will hereafter hesitate to face suffering, danger and death itself for liberty, let them at once abandon a contest for which nature has never fitted them'. A few weeks later Davis wrote of 'The Morality of War', and from time to time, leading articles extolled the use of arms, and urged readers to learn to handle them. *The Nation* concluded that the use of force was justifiable when all other means had failed. It was on this issue that the Young Irelanders gradually broke with O'Connell.

A six-day meeting was held in New York to declare support for the cause of Repeal. Among the senators, clergymen and wealthy merchants who attended were Governor Seward, later to become Secretary of State under Lincoln, and Horace Greeley, editor of the *New York Tribune* and a future Presidential candidate. The President of the United States, John Tyler, whose father had fought in the War of Independence, excused himself from attending, but declared: 'I am a decided friend of the Repeal of the Legislative Union between Great Britain and Ireland. I ardently and anxiously hope that it may take place, and I have the utmost confidence that Ireland will have her own Parliament in her own capital in a very short time. On this great question I am no halfway man'. The President's eldest son, Robert Tyler, took a keen interest in the proceedings.

The meeting declared unequivocally, if perhaps a little unrealistically, that if England invaded Ireland, she should do so 'with the assured loss of Canada by American arms'. An Irish-born merchant offered 'a princely donation' to fit out a fleet of fast Baltimore clippers to embarrass English commerce, and as an earnest of immediate support, five thousand dollars were transmitted to the Repeal Association. Similar meetings were held in Boston, Philadelphia, and Baltimore. Philadelphia, in one week, raised two thousand dollars for the Association.

The British Government panicked, and the Duke of Wellington was once more called upon. He was an irascible and contentious veteran of 75; no longer the brilliant strategist of the Napoleonic Wars. But he tackled the job of defending Ireland with gusto. As Duffy relates:

> Thirty-five thousand troops of all arms were distributed throughout the island...The barracks were pierced with loop-holes and became fortresses against insurrection. Forts and Martello Towers were put in a state of defence, garrisons were strengthened, the supply of arms and materials of war largely increased, and war steamers stationed on the sea coast and navigable rivers. To provide against the risk of seduction or surprise...the soldiers who attended Catholic churches on Sunday went in marching order, with guns, bayonets and knapsacks ready for immediate use.

Barracks were provisioned against siege, and justices of the peace who were Repealers were dismissed. In this supercharged atmosphere, O'Connell in the autumn of 1843 announced that another 'monster meeting' to be the greatest of all, would be held at Clontarf, on the shores of Dublin Bay, the historic site on which, in 1014, Brian Boru, High King of Ireland, had defeated the Danish invaders. The meeting was planned for Sunday 5 October. On the preceeding Friday the *Evening Mail* announced that the meeting would be suppressed, and that the Privy Council would next day publish a proclamation prohibiting it. On Saturday, in an agony of uncertainty, the organisers of the meeting awaited the proclamation. But throughout the morning, and into the afternoon, the Government gave no sign, other than the arrival of five additional regiments from England and Scotland. Not till half past three in the afternoon was the proclamation issued. It forbade the meeting, cautioned people from attending it, and instructed officers of the law to prevent or disperse it. To reinforce the ukase, the cannon of the Pigeon House fort commanding Dublin Bay were trained on the approaches to the site, which was occupied by horse, foot and artillery.

O'Connell had repeatedly declared that if the right of public meeting were to be assailed by force, he would maintain it by force. 'The Clontarf meeting differed in no respect from the long list of its predecessors', wrote Duffy, 'and if it could be forbidden and dispersed on the authority of an order in the *Dublin Gazette,* that fundamental right was at end. The occasion for making a stand in its defence had clearly come, or it never would come'. Duffy wrote this thirty-seven years after the event. But to O'Connell, faced with the appalling prospect of a bloody encounter, perhaps a massacre, the issue was not so simple. He was not a military leader. He had made no preparations for an armed struggle. He had no staff, no arms, no supplies. As Duffy concedes: 'Looking back...it scarcely admits of doubt that he never deliberately contemplated resistance to the British troops, under any circumstances whatever...But in such circumstances it was a fearful mistake, alike in morals and strategy, to threaten resistance'.

Inevitably, O'Connell had to announce to the Repeal Committee that he would submit to the proclamation. The time for resistance had not come, he said. Swift measures were taken to prevent the expected thousands from assembling. An address issued by O'Connell, exhorting them to obey the proclamation, was posted during the night in centres of population within twenty miles of Dublin, and agents of the Repeal Association, aided by the Catholic clergy, were abroad at dawn to explain and enforce it. These efforts were successful. The troops were left in sole occupation of the Clontarf site. But the damage done to the Repeal cause was irremediable. O'Connell's decision, Duffy wrote later, 'deprived the movement in a moment of half its dignity and all its terror'. At the time, Thomas Reynolds, a colleague of O'Connell's, said 'Ireland was won at Clontarf and she is going to be lost at Clontarf'.

What was Duffy's attitude at the time towards O'Connell's surrender? There is no doubt that the Young Irelanders supported the policy of keeping the peace. 'The man who dares to adopt any policy not sanctioned by O'Connell will deserve the great execration', *The Nation* declared in the issue following the Clontarf debacle. 'We entreat — we implore — we demand of the People to let nobody tempt them to any outrage'. This is very different language from that of Duffy the historian writing in the luxury of retirement:

> They might have failed; but had they fought and failed could the result have been more disastrous? Those who in later times have seen hecatombs slain by famine greater than fell in three French revolutions, and multitudes exiled by political despair...may well doubt whether to fight and fail could have entailed calamities so great as befell them because they incurred the hate of England by threatening resistance and the contempt of England by failing to perform what they threatened.

Summing up events in Ireland during the year 1843, *The Annual Register* said:

> A newspaper called *The Nation,* in particular distinguished itself by the most vehement and stirring advocacy of the Repeal cause, and co-operated powerfully with the leaders of the movement in exciting the popular mind of Ireland towards the prosecution of their object...As if prose, with all the fire and vehemence which the spirit of Irish rhetoric were not a sufficiently powerful engine to work up men's feelings to the required pitch, poetry was called to aid and the columns of the paper filled with songs and odes, many of them turning on the events of 1798, and the efforts and sufferings of the insurgents of that time.

Lord Plunkett, who presided in the Court of Chancery, was reading *The Nation* in the robing-room when a friend asked him: 'What is the tone of *The Nation* today'? 'Wolfe Tone', was the answer.

THE Government pressed on swiftly to consolidate its bloodless victory at Clontarf. A week later, O'Connell, his son John, Thomas Steele ('one of their most active coadjutors'), Thomas Ray (Secretary of the Repeal Association) two little-known priests, Father Peter Tyrell and Father Thomas Tierney, and the editors of the three leading National journals, Dr. (later Sir John) Gray, of *The Freeman's Journal,* Richard Barrett, of *The Pilot,* and Duffy, of *The Nation,* were arrested and charged with conspiring to excite ill-will among Her Majesty's subjects, to weaken their confidence in the administration of justice, and to obtain by unlawful means a change in the constitution and government of the country. They were also charged with exciting dissatisfaction among Her Majesty's troops. Father Tyrell died a few weeks after his arrest.

The Grand Jury, early in November after five days' deliberation found a true bill. On 15 January 1844, the defendants (or 'Traversers', as they were called after they had traversed the indictment) including the most eminent Catholic in the British Empire, appeared in Dublin's Green Street court, to be tried by four judges and twelve jurors. Among them there was not a single Catholic.

The indictment presented to the court was nearly one hundred yards long. Bound into a book, it covered 57 folio pages the size of *The Times.* In it, 43 overt acts of the defendants, were set out, sixteen of which consisted of their attendance at monster meetings. The three journalists were charged with conspiracy because they had reported speeches at these meetings. Six other overt acts related to material published in *The Nation,* including a letter proposing that modern place names in Ireland should be replaced by the old Celtic names. Both sides deployed a huge and costly battery of counsel. An incongruous figure on the Crown side was Robert Holmes, brother-in-law of the patriot Robert Emmet, who had himself been imprisoned as a sympathiser with Emmet's insurrection of 1803. Holmes, despite his sympathy with O'Connell and the other defendants, had felt obliged to accept the retainer sent to him.

The Attorney-General, Mr. T.B.C. Smith, in stating the case against the eight defendants, quoted Ingram's poem beginning 'Who fears to speak of '98'? which he described as 'a single specimen of a whole volume of inflammatory matter'. And he referred to the Tara meeting attended by numbers 'variously estimated at 100,000 to 1,000,000':

> The spot was selected as the scene of the defeat of those engaged in the rebellion of 1798. Actually hundreds — I might I believe say thousands — of people were seen upon their knees, plucking the wild plant [a wild geranium with a red leaf] growing on the graves of those who fell in the rebellion, and who were buried there, under the impression these poor people had that the colour of the leaf arose from the slaughter of those who fell there.

It was hard to see what the sentimental beliefs of poor peasants had to do with the charges of conspiracy, but Mr Smith had cast his net widely. He mentioned a Repeal dinner at which Mr John O'Connell, toasting the Queen, had indiscreetly said:

> Her Ministers may fix her throne amidst bloody fields, and blazing cities, and slaughtered corpses. Let them take care that the ruddiest stream flowing might not be their own blood. Let America be told the whole truth of our position, and she will do her best...
> The French people long to serve us. England is in distress. Her finances are in difficulty. Her colonial empire — India, the Cape, China, Canada, etc, make such a demand on her, that out of one hundred and three battalions, which constitute her infantry of the line, eighty are abroad, and only twenty-three in the three kingdoms...

If this passage could be read as incitement to violence, it was tempered by what followed. Duffy urged the people of Ireland to conciliate such Protestants as had not yet joined them, to organise carefully for repeal agitation, to observe the law strictly, and above all to avoid any collision with the troops or police.

O'Connell, who had laid aside his barrister's costume, and addressed the Court in ordinary dress, said he thought there was no possibility of restoring prosperity to Ireland, or of avoiding ultimate separation from England, save by the restoration of Parliament. He concluded by rejecting 'with contempt' the appellation of conspirator:

> I have acted boldly in the open day, in the presence of the magistracy — there has been nothing secret, or concealed. I have struggled for the restoration of the Parliament of my native country. Others have succeeded before me; but succeed or fail, it is a struggle to make the fairest land in the world possess those benefits which nature intended she should enjoy.

For twenty-five days, to soporific eruptions of fustian oratory, the trial dragged on. The Attorney-General's statement of the case occupied two days. 'He had promised to disclose a foul and wicked conspiracy', Duffy wrote. 'But there was not a single fact relied on which was not long familiar to his audience'. Alone among the Traversers, Daniel O'Connell defended himself: 'I am a hired servant of the people', he declared. 'It may derogate from the chivalry of my position, but I avow it, and am ready to earn my salary'. When the case for the defence closed, the Solicitor-

General replied in an address which lasted three days.

All the Traversers were convicted, a result which surpised no one. Awaiting sentence which, according to practice, was deferred till the opening of the following law term, Daniel O'Connell issued a resounding appeal to his countrymen, urging them to be calm. 'Obey my advice. No riot. No tumult. No blow. No violence. Keep the peace for six months, or at the utmost, twelve months longer and you shall have the Parliament in College Green again'.

On 30 May 1844, the Traversers were brought up for judgment. When O'Connell entered the court, he was greeted with loud applause, and many members of the bar stood up deferentially. The Traversers' counsel asked the Court to suspend judgement till an appeal to the House of Lords for a writ of error was heard. Judge Burton (whose somnolence in court had been apparent) refused the application, and in pronouncing sentence, said that the object of the Traversers was to obtain a Repeal of the Union by means which he should not say were not violent, for excitement, intimidation, and terror were violent means, but without bloodshed. He believed the principal Traverser had that design rooted in his mind, and that it was by his great influence the country had been preserved from civil war. But he had told the people that if he had found it impossible to succeed, he should leave them to themselves; and in case of aggression, they should know how to act. The Court, however they might lament it, was bound to consider that exhortations to keep the peace did not take away the character of conspiracy from the proceedings.

Daniel O'Connell was sentenced to twelve months imprisonment, fined £2,000 and ordered to give security of £5,000, and his personal security in a like amount, to be of good behaviour for seven years. Duffy and the other Traversers were each sentenced to nine months imprisonment, fined £50, and ordered to give security for £1,000 and their personal security in a like amount, to be of good behaviour for seven years.

Calmly and with great dignity Daniel O'Connell rose and spoke a few words: 'I will not do anything so irregular as to reply to the Court', he said, 'but I am entitled to remind Mr. Justice Burton that we each of us have sworn, and that I in particular have sworn positively, that I was not engaged in any conspiracy whatsoever. I am sorry to say that I feel it my imperative duty to add that justice has not been done to me'. In fact, as O'Connell pointed out, the judge's opinion seemed to be that his only conspiracy was a conspiracy to prevent an insurrection.

The prisoners were taken by a circuitous route to Richmond Bridewell, described by Duffy as 'the healthiest of the city prisons' and the imprisonment 'turned out an agreeable surprise'. The metropolitan prisons were under the control of the Corporation of Dublin, and a sympathetic Board of Superintendence, in the best traditions of Irish hospitality, treated the State prisoners as distinguished guests. The Governor and Deputy-Governor of the prison were authorised to sublet their houses and gardens to the prisoners, and, says Duffy,

> members of Mr O'Connell's family, and of the families of the other prisoners, came to reside with them; they employed their own servants; from the first

day presents of venison, game, fish, fruit, and the like began to arrive; and after a little they found themselves established in a pleasant country house, situated in the midst of extensive grounds, bright with fair women and the gambols of children, and furnished with abundant means either for study or amusement. They breakfasted and dined in common, but generally spent the evening apart with their personal friends, each prisoner having a separate sitting-room at his disposal. A gynmasium was set up for exercise, a spacious canvas pavilion erected in one of the gardens for dining in the open air, and each man settled down to some specific work which would occupy the forenoon...It was whispered that the two youngest prisoners were taking lessons from Moore Stack, a noted teacher of elocution, had foils and masks for fencing, and even horses in one of the great yards for daily exercise. After a little time, a weekly journal called the *Richmond Gazette,* the circulation of which was strictly limited to one copy in MS, was read aloud after dinner every Friday, and John O'Connell, who was indefatigable as a Master of Revels, projected private theatricals, and got *Julius Caesar* into rehearsal. No Cassius being forthcoming among the convicted conspirators, he brought from the outer world beyond the walls, his cousin Maurice Leyne, to undertake the part...

The only interruption to these genial and diverse activities came from the constant stream of visitors, to whom the prisoners were compelled to give audience. The prisoners had access to two gardens. In one, was a mound, which they christened. 'Tara Hill', and a summerhouse, christened 'Conciliation Hall'. On 'Tara Hill' the Liberator formally received deputations. One day a party of American admirers arrived. They deferentially doffed their hats and remained at the foot of the hill until summoned to the presence. 'You are probably more visited here', said one, 'than if you were at large'. 'Yes,' replied O'Connell, 'and here I cannot use the excuse of "not at home".' It became necessary to control the flow of visitors, and O'Connell and his colleagues inserted a notice in the Dublin papers announcing that no person would be admitted any day before twelve or after four o'clock, or admitted at all on Mondays or Wednesdays. Immediate political associates, of course, were not affected. Twice a week a conference was held to discuss the affairs of the Association. The dinner table was never set for less than thirty and an artist's studio and a daguerrotypist's camera were set up to multiply likenesses of the prisoners and their guests. One patriotic Dublin shopkeeper sent them seven music boxes and another, two monster cakes. Davis wrote to Pigot in London that he was concerned for Duffy's health, but believed that the enforced rest had done him good.

The week Duffy went to gaol, *The Nation* was printed in green ink; the articles which had been declared seditious were published in a little book titled *The Voice of the Nation* and the prosecuted verse in a new and costly edition of *The Spirit of the Nation*. 'You have imprisoned three newspaper proprietors', Richard Lalor Shiel said in Parliament, 'and the Irish press is as bold and as exciting as it was before. Eleven thousand copies of *The Nation* newspaper circulate every week through the country, and administer the strongest provocation to the most enthusiastic spirit of nationality which the highest eloquence in writing can supply.'

IN July 1844, the Young Irelanders formed the '82 Club. It was named after the historic events of 1782, when Protestant patriots of the landlord class raised eighty thousand armed and uniformed volunteers, ostensibly to defend Ireland against American privateers. The formidable force was able to persuade the English Government to give Ireland a 'Free Constitution' and its own Government, concessions which led Henry Grattan, a colonel in the Volunteers, to exclaim exultingly but prematurely 'Ireland is now a nation'!

Members of the '82 Club wore a resplendent uniform designed by Davis, which cost twelve guineas — nearly as much as the year's earnings of an Irish labourer. Davis wrote to Denny Lane about the importance of wearing the uniform. In the letter, he added: 'Poor Duffy has lost his eldest child, and his wife is dying'. The child was a girl named Anna Eva.

'Though the convicted conspirators took their imprisonment gaily', remarked Duffy 'it moved the gravest indignation of the country and of other countries'. In Ireland Catholic bishops distributed a special prayer beseeching God to grant O'Connell grace to bear his trials with resignation. Catholic colleagues in France and Germany reminded O'Connell how blessed were they who suffered persecution for righteousness' sake. Belgian and Rhenish papers reported that prayers for O'Connell's deliverance were being offered in churches from Ostend to Dusseldorf.

Walter Savage Landor, that leonine champion of liberty, addressed a petition to Queen Victoria, asking a free pardon for the prisoners, on the grounds that the Act of Union was brought about by improper practices; and that Ireland was at present treated with less liberality in regard to religion than Greece had been under Turkish dominion, a dominion which England had helped to overthrow. He pointed out that two millions of British subjects in America, with incomparably less cause for complaint than the people of Ireland, were driven to secure their independence without the aid of any free state, whereas Ireland had seven millions of malcontents, and the nearest and most powerful nations omitted no opportunity of exhibiting sympathy for her cause. It was his opinion that in such a condition of affairs, only the influence of Daniel O'Connell had restrained the passions of his countrymen; and for these reasons his imprisonment ought to end.

Her Majesty does not seem to have made any direct acknowledgment of Landor's plea, but, when Parliament met on 1 February 1844, before sentences were pronounced, she said in her prepared Speech from the Throne: 'I forbear from observations on events in Ireland in respect to which proceedings are pending before the legal tribunals'. The Opposition, not to be silenced, assailed the Government with a barrage of questions about the conduct of the trial, and Lord John Russell, the leader of the Liberal party, moving a vote of censure against the Irish administration, said that in England, the Government was a government of opinion, in Ireland it was 'notoriously a government of force'.

The Traversers, Lord Russell continued, had been indicted for exciting ill-will among the people of Ireland against the people of England. Did the Government know of no man in England who had done the same thing, just transposing the words Ireland and England? Was there not an eminent person who had endeavoured to excite that feeling among the English people by calling the people of Ireland aliens. (The eminent person was the Lord Chancellor, Lord Lyndhurst, who had spoken of the Irish as 'aliens in blood, language and religion'. Lyndhurst spoke with authority. He was the grandson of an Irish emigrant to Boston, Massachusetts!) But Lyndhurst had not been prosecuted. Could anything be more monstrous than this injustice? Lord Russell asked. And was there to be no excuse for Irish Catholics whose priests had been called 'surpliced ruffians', and who had themselves been described as 'barbarians and New Zealanders' by partisans of the present Government?

In the same debate, the brilliant, reckless, profligate and ill-fated George Smythe (later Lord Strangford), leader and idol of the 'Young England' group, who fought the last duel on English soil, said he would rather see Ireland governed in the spirit of Tyrconnell than in the spirit of Cromwell. Disraeli, Smythe's friend and mentor, in one of his most celebrated speeches, asked what was the Irish question:

> One says it is a physical question, another, a spiritual. Now it is absence of aristocracy, then the absence of railways. It is the Pope one day, potatoes the next. Consider Ireland as you would any other country similarly situated. You will see a teeming population which, with reference to the cultivated soil, is denser to the square mile than that of China; created solely by agriculture, with none of the resources of wealth which develop with civilisation; and sustained, consequently, upon the lowest conceivable diet, so that in the case of failure they have no other means of subsistence upon which they can fall back. That dense population in extreme distress inhabits an island where there is an established Church which is not their Church and a territorial aristocracy the richest of whom live in distant capitals. Thus you have a starving population, an absentee aristocracy, and an alien Church, and in addition, the weakest executive in the world. This is the Irish question.

The duty of a wise English Minister, Disraeli continued, was to effect by policy all the changes which a revolution would effect by force. Unfortunately, when Disraeli was in a position to effect these changes, he had temporarily forgotten his noble sentiments. And it is instructive to recall what he had written about the Irish in 1836: 'This wild, reckless, indolent, uncertain and superstitious race had no sympathy with the English character. Their fair ideal of human felicity is an alternation of clannish brawls and coarse idolatry. Their history describes an unbroken circle of bigotry and blood...'

The bluff sea-dog, Admiral Sir Charles Napier, the hero of Acre, asked Parliament to consider what would have happened had Napoleon conquered England, as he might have done,

> and brought over French bishops and French priests, and forced on the English a religion they did not like, would not the English be anxious to drive every man Jack of them out of the country, religion and all? And if the Irish were treated as a conquered people it was no wonder if they would do the same sort of thing.

NIGHT-SCENE IN A DUBLIN-STREET.

Illustrated London News, 14 September 1844

Sir Thomas Wilde, who had been the official head of the English Bar, denounced the indictment and the trial as a disgrace to the law, and affirmed 'the cardinal proposition', that O'Connell had not had a fair trial. And Thomas Babington Macaulay asked the House: 'How was Ireland governed? Not by love but by fear...Not by the confidence of the people in the laws...but by armed men and entrenched camps.'

In spite of the eloquence of those who supported the motion, it was defeated by ninety-seven votes. A similar motion in the House of Lords was also defeated.

ON 4 September 1844, when Duffy and his colleagues had been more than three months in prison, the five judicial members of the House of Lords assembled in Westminster Hall to decide whether or not they had been legally convicted. For the Traversers it was argued that the offence for which they had been tried was not legally charged in the indictment; that the jury had been chosen from a spurious list and was not a lawful jury of the country; that the verdict had been based on a serious misdirection by the Chief Justice and was not a legal verdict, and that the judgment of the Court was bad in law. After much learned argument, the Appeal Court, by a majority of three to two, quashed the convictions. The Chancellor, Lord Lyndhurst, and Lord Brougham upheld the judgment of the Irish court. Their noble Whig brothers in ermine, Lord Denham, a former Lord Chancellor, Lord Cottenham and Lord Campbell, rejected it. One of them spoke of the administration of justice becoming 'a mockery, a delusion, and a snare' (Lyndhurst, a notorious lecher, had no reason to favour O'Connell who a few years before in a letter to a London press had threatened to describe 'with hideous details' his private life.)

As they assembled for dinner on the evening of 13 September, the prisoners were told they were free. Duffy describes the event: 'Pale and panting', their aged attorney William Ford, 'who had posted day and night from London with the Lords' judgement in his pocket, stumbled into the room' with the good news. When the train stopped at Chester on his race back to Dublin, Ford, unable to contain his excitement, had announced to the assembled passengers and porters at the top of his voice 'O'Connell is going to get out'! 'Indeed', said a courteous English porter. 'Did you say 'twas at this station the gentleman would get out'?

The Governor of the gaol was so overcome with emotion that he almost fainted, and water was thrown on him to revive him. The Deputy-Governor rushed from the room, weeping.

A deliriously joyful reception greeted the released prisoners. In a massive three-tier triumphal car, profusely decorated with purple velvet, gold fringe, gold nails and gaudy paintings, the Liberator, his son John, and his two grandsons, were driven to his house in Merrion Square. Daniel O'Connell stood on the topmost stage, about twelve feet from the ground, bowing incessantly to the cheering multitude, while a harpist played Irish tunes. 'His head, thrown proudly back, was covered with the green and gold velvet Repeal cap', reported the *Annual Register*. They were preceded by the marshalled trades of Dublin, banners flying and bands playing, and the Lord Mayor in full costume and members of the Corporation in their handsome equipages; and followed by O'Connell's seven prison colleagues in carriages, hundreds of other vehicles, and men on horseback. Finally, came the defence lawyers in a coach, carrying the 'monster indictment'. The procession extended for nearly six miles, and it was estimated that two hundred thousand men took part in it, an extraordinary number when the population of Dublin was less than a quarter of a million. The procession traversed the greater part of Dublin, and took three and a half hours to reach Merrion Square.

'Throughout all parts of Ireland the unexpected triumph of their leader produced an electrical sensation on the minds of the people', said the *Annual Register*. The news which spread like wildfire, was received

> with the most lively demonstrations of joy, such perhaps as no people but the Irish or the French would exhibit.
> The news arrived in Cork about noon...Some of the streets were so densely crammed with people that it was not possible to pass along. The whole place was alive with excitement; and before the news had been half an hour in town, processions of people were formed, parading the streets with green boughs and music...At night the whole country was illuminated...

MR. O'CONNELL, IN HIS TRIUMPHAL CAR.

Illustrated London News, 14 September 1844

On the Sunday following the liberation, a pontifical High Mass was celebrated in Dublin, in the church of the Conception, and a Te Deum offered for 'the deliverance of the beloved Liberator, and of his fellow martyrs, from their unjust captivity'. In his sermon, the Rev. Dr. Miley discoursed on the politics of Repeal and on the Divine intervention, at the instance of the Virgin Mary, on O'Connell's behalf.

The public rejoicings extended throughout Ireland. When Duffy and two companions made a leisurely journey through Kilkenny, New Ross, Waterford, Cork and Killarney, to visit O'Connell in his mountain retreat at Darrynane, by the Atlantic, they were greeted everywhere with bands, bonfires, triumphal arches, deputations and illuminated addresses.

O'Connell was a lavish host. In a letter to Davis, Duffy described breakfast as 'Homeric, or rather let me say Ossianic...a hot roast or two, grilled fowl, smoking potatoes, slim-cake, delicious fresh honey, home-made bread and baker's ditto...all the ordinary edibles and drinkables of a metropolitan table'. And O'Connell ate like a chieftain. 'Let no puny nibblers or toast of sippers of tea pretend to resist a Titan like this', Duffy wrote.

Despite his capacity for attacking Homeric (or Ossianic) breakfasts, O'Connell was a sick man. The strain of the State trials had told on him. 'O'Connell left Richmond Prison suffering under a mortal disease, aggravated by public and private troubles', says Duffy, and continues

> The slow retreat before the triumphant enemies from the Mallow Defiance to the sentence and the jail had tortured him. For a time he was disturbed by fears of a popular rising for which no preparations were made, and when these fears passed away, he had to bear the strain of a weightier responsibility in his new undertaking to conduct the cause to speedy success...stooping under the burthen of seventy years, no longer able to concentrate his faculties on a single point, his powerful will slackened, his great brain distraught, it is no wonder that he lost heart in the cause he loved.

The disease, from which he was to die three years later, was what the Victorians quaintly called 'softening of the brain'. The private troubles, according to Duffy, came from an unrequited love affair; O'Connell was 'labouring under the most distracting influence that can possess a man of his years, a passionate love for a gifted young girl who might have been his granddaughter'. Apparently the girl who was neither Irish nor Catholic, persistently refused to marry him.

'From the day he left Richmond prison', says Duffy, 'the leader of the people never took a step that was not in its design, or in its result, a step backwards'. According to Duffy, O'Connell when in prison had secretly decided to reconcile himself with the Whigs and to abandon the Repeal campaign. He had co-operated with the Whigs between 1835 and 1840, in the hope of gaining substantial reforms. 'It may well seem impossible that the adored leader of the Irish people could sell...his large honours for any Whig trash or boons of patronage', Duffy wrote. But he was 'old, infirm, and in the first stage of a disease which he sank under, and it may well be that he believed Repeal to be impossible'.

An Orange journal suggested that O'Connell had taken two featherbeds into Richmond Prison: one for himself, the other for Repeal.

A happy result of the State prosecutions was to attract many recruits to the Nationalist cause. The most important of these was the forty-year-old William Smith O'Brien. His father, Sir Edward O'Brien, a Protestant baronet, of Dromoland Castle, County Clare, was the head of the O'Brien clan which claimed direct descent from Brian Boru. Smith O'Brien was a product of Harrow and Cambridge, where he graduated Bachelor of Arts in 1826. Two years later, he was elected M.P. for the borough of Ennis, as a supporter of Sir Robert Peel. In 1832, he had energetically resisted Repeal, believing that Catholic Emancipation would give Ireland political equality and prosperity. But with the passing of the years, and the continuing distress and discrimination in Ireland, he had changed his mind. 'O'Brien's historic descent and stainless reputation made his junction an epoch', wrote Duffy: To the Celtic imagination, the new recruit was an historical personage, the representative of a house which for twenty generations had ruled territories, conducted negotiations and marshalled armies, and the lineal heir of a king...He was the incarnation of public duty'.

'O'Brien was not an orator in the rhetorical Irish tradition, nor a gregarious demagogue. His speech was precise and unemotional, and his manner, in Duffy's words, 'not genial or winning'. But he was a man of great integrity, with a rigid code of behaviour. Duffy quotes a current anecdote about him, when he was duelling, and the signal to fire was about to be given. O'Brien cried, 'Stop! No signal I pray'. His opponent's second was astonished, 'This is very irregular, sir', he said. 'Pray what do you want to say'? 'I want to call your attention to the fact that the gentleman opposite me has let the cap fall off his pistol', replied O'Brien.

Three

Carlyle

For many years, Thomas Carlyle, in his self-ordained role of prophet, had been solving the Irish problem. In *Chartism*, published in 1840, he had reduced it to a simple alternative: 'The time has come,' he wrote, 'when the Irish population must either be improved a little, or else exterminated'. England, he conceded, was to blame for Ireland's woes. 'We English pay, even now, the bitter smart of long centuries of injustice to our neighbour Island . . .' he wrote. 'England is guilty towards Ireland; and reaps at last, in full measure, the fruit of fifteen generations of wrong-doing'. As a consequence, the Irish character had become 'degraded' and 'disordered'.

> Immethodic, headlong, violent, mendacious: what can you make of the wretched Irishman? 'A finer people never lived', as the Irish lady said to us; 'only they have two faults, they do generally lie and steal: barring these' . . . ! A people that know not to speak the truth, and to act the truth, such people have departed from even the possibility of well-being.

Carlyle also deplored the fact that the Irish spoke 'a partially intelligible dialect of English' and that, as the fare across by steamer was only fourpence sterling, crowds of 'miserable Irish' darkened England's towns:

> He is the sorest evil this country has to strive with. In his rags and laughing savagery, he is there to undertake all work that can be done by mere strength of hand and back; for wages that will purchase him potatoes . . . he lodges . . . in any pighutch or doghutch, roosts in outhouses; and wears a suit of tatters, the getting off and on of which is said to be a difficult operation, transacted only in festivals and the hightides of the calendar . . . There abides he, in his squalor and unreason, in his falsity and drunken violence, as the ready-made nucleus of degradation and disorder.

As a young man of 25, Duffy had been moved by Carlyle's 'daring theories'. The historian William Henry Lecky commented

> It is curious to observe that Carlyle who detested and despised O'Connell, and who certainly had no great admiration for the Irish character or aspirations, found among the Young Irelanders some of his earliest and most enthusiastic disciples . . .

More than any other writer of his age, he appealed to the enthusiasm of the younger generation of his contemporaries, and at a time when he was very little appreciated in England his works were eagerly read and discussed in Young Ireland circles.

It is even more curious that Carlyle had a personal regard for many of the Young Irelanders, particularly Duffy. No more improbable association could be imagined than that between these two. Carlyle was an iconoclast in religion (he described Keble as 'a little ape', and said Newman had 'the intellect of a rabbit') and he regarded the Irish as little better than savages; Duffy was ever a practising Catholic and a dedicated Irish nationalist. Yet for thirty-six years, until Carlyle's death, they maintained a warm, and except for one brief quarrel, unbroken friendship.

Carlyle's *'Life of Cromwell'* on which he had been working intermittently for about six years was published in 1845, and was a great success. Mitchell reviewed it in *The Nation*, and Carlyle attributed the review, which he considered 'honest and manly', to Duffy. In January 1845 when he was preparing a new edition he wrote to Duffy 'I am about to do what to another kind of man than you I should myself regard as a very strange thing. I am sending you the *Curse of Cromwell* to get it *improved* for me!' He wanted Duffy to check on topographical errors, and the spelling of Irish names. At the same time, he tried to convince him that Cromwell *'was* a Hero full of manhood, earnestness and valour' and that 'the actual God's fact was that Cromwell in Ireland did not in any respect depart from the established rules of war', nor did he 'sanction or order the death of anyone not found in armour'.

Duffy returned the corrected sheets in March, and Carlyle, 'abundantly sensible' of the trouble Duffy had taken, continued his defence of Cromwell. 'I find on evidence . . . that the Wexford "200 women", the "massacre" at Iredale, and indeed any massacre at all on Cromwell's part — is indispensable *fable*, and can do nothing but *mischief* till it vanish from all heads and tongues'. He continued:

> You, I believe, are individually as far lifted above the rubbish of Papistry as I am above that of Protestantry — and might understand by much meditating, what it was that Cromwell . . . did *mean*, and the eternal *Heaven* along with him, in Ireland; if you cannot, there is no other Irishman yet born, I suppose, that can . . .

Some friendly critics, Carlyle continued, had upbraided him for not admitting the Irish to be a nation, 'Really and truly that is the fact', he wrote. 'I cannot find that the Irish were in 1641, are now, and until they conquer all the English, ever again can be "a Nation", anything but an integral constituent *part* of a nation — anymore than the Scotch Highlanders can, than the Parish of Kensington can . . .' Despite this persuasive pleading, Duffy continued to call his paper *The Nation*.

Duffy and Carlyle first met in April 1845. Carlyle, the son of a Scottish stonemason, was then forty-nine and had been married to Jane Welsh, the cultivated daughter of a prosperous Scotch doctor, for nineteen years. Since 1835, he had been living in a narrow, three-storied house in what Duffy described as 'a dingy little street off the Thames' — Cheyne Row. The house was ancient but roomy, and, Carlyle had been assured, harboured no bugs. The rent was £35 a year.

'Last night we had a novelty in the way of society, a sort of Irish *rigg*,' Jane wrote in her diary on 26 April. Frederick Lucas had arrived before tea 'with a tail consisting of three stranger Irishmen — red hot and live Irishmen, such as I have never before sat at meat with or met'. Lucas was an English Quaker who had been converted to Catholicism. He had been a writer for the *Times*, and was conducting a Catholic paper, *The Tablet*, in London. He was married to a sister of John Bright, the radical M.P. His 'red hot' Irish friends were John O'Hagan, John Pigot and Duffy, all of them in London to dine at an Inn of Court, so as to qualify for a call to the Bar. 'They came to adore Carlyle', Jane wrote, 'and also to remonstrate with him, almost with tears in their eyes, on his opinion, as stated in his *'Chartism*, that "a finer people than the Irish never lived; only they do lie and they do steal!"'

She described the youngest of the trio, Pigot, as 'a handsome youth of the romantic cast, pale-faced, with dark eyes and hair'. Of O'Hagan, she recorded only that in the emotion of their defence of Ireland, his nose 'burst out bleeding'. 'The third, Mr. Duffy, quite took my husband's fancy, and mine also to a certain extent', she wrote. 'He is a writer of national songs, and came here to "eat his terms". With the coarsest of human faces, decidedly as like a horse's as a man's, he is one of the people that I should get to think beautiful, there is so much of the power both of intellect and passion in his physiognomy'.

Jane poured tea and sided with the remonstrating Irishmen. And she delighted them by teasing Carlyle about his style and his opinions. After listening to the Master in attentive silence for about an hour, Pigot said: 'Now I am assured you are not in your heart so unjust to Ireland as your writing leads one to suppose: so I will confess, for the purpose of retracting it, the strong feeling of repulsion with which I have come tonight.' 'Then why in the name of goodness *did* you come?' asked Jane pertinently.

The conversation turned to the Devil and Hell. Carlyle, a chronic dyspeptic, said 'If the Devil had my stomach to chew with, I could not wish him worse, poor fellow!'

When Jane said 'Thomas tells me not to be afraid of Hell — there is no such place'. Lucas replied, 'I think all his principles lead logically to a belief in Hell'. 'In a certain sense that is true', said Carlyle enigmatically. The conversation moved from theology to politics, and Carlyle's visitors told him what was happening in Ireland, in the hope of persuading him to become their advocate 'before England and the world'.

A less controversial gossip session followed, and Jane said that Tennyson was unlikely to marry as no woman could live in the atmosphere of tobacco which he made about him. The talk went on till late in the night. Duffy and his colleagues were greatly impressed with Carlyle. They did not accept his specific opinions on almost any question', Duffy told Carlyle's biographer, David Alec Wilson, 'but his constant advocacy of veracity, integrity, and valour, touched the most generous of their sympathies, and his theory that under the divine government of the world, right and might are identical, as right infallibly became might in the end, was very welcome to men struggling against enormous odds for justice'. Duffy admitted that as he listened to Carlyle, he began to share this conviction. In the excitement of the symposium, the three Irishmen went off without their hats, and returned to look for them. Jane found O'Hagan's hidden under the sofa.

After the meeting, Duffy regularly sent *The Nation* to Carlyle, who read it constantly, and from time to time offered 'friendly suggestions'. Carlyle sent Duffy a copy of his *Past and Present*, and in an accompanying letter dated 25 October 1845, wrote:

> When one reflects how in the history of the world the noblest human efforts have had to take the most confused embodiments and tend to a beneficent eternal goal by courses they were much mistaken in — why should we not be patient even with Repeal. You, I will with little qualification bid persevere, and prosper, and wish all Ireland would listen to you more and more. The thing you intrinsically mean is that all good Irishmen and all good men must mean. Let *it* come quickly and continue for ever . . .
> When you come to London again, fail not to let us see you. If ever I visit Ireland yours is a house I will seek out.

Duffy sent Jane Carlyle a first edition of *The Ballad Poetry of Ireland*. In thanking him 'emphatically' for 'the beautiful little volume,' Jane asked:

> When are you purposing through the strength of Heaven, to break into open rebellion? . . . If you have not a set time for taking up arms, when at least are you coming again to 'eat terms' (whatever that many mean)? I feel what my husband would call 'a real, genuine, healthy desire' to pour out more tea for you.
> Success to all your wishes, except for the destruction of us Saxons.

About the same time, Duffy sent a copy of *The Ballad Poetry* to Macaulay. Thanking Duffy for his 'great courtesy', Macaulay wrote:

> Some of these songs I already know, and I have been much struck by their energy and beauty . . . But I cannot refrain from saying with how much pain the pleasure which I have received from their composition has been mingled. I would entreat you to consider whether genius be worthily employed in inflaming national animosity between two countries which, from physical causes such as no political revolution can remove, must always be either blessing or curses to each other.

Macaulay also begged Duffy to do him the honour of accepting some volumes 'which I have requested my publisher, Mr. Longman, to transmit to you'.

Carlyle had long diagnosed the Irish malaise from his Chelsea desk. He now decided to study it at first hand. In July 1846, he wrote to Duffy for advice about a projected 'short flight over to Ireland'.

> A swift steamer, I know takes one over any evening (or I believe morning!) with the mail bags: there is Dublin to be looked at for a day or two . . . then *you* are to be seen, and talked with, oftener than once if you like . . . this, if other

things go right, will abundantly suffice . . . I get nothing but pain out of noise and display; and insist, even at the expense of some breaches of politeness, remaining altogether private; strictly *incognito* . . . I cannot say any man's words that I hear from your side of the water gives me anything like an unmixed satisfaction, except, for most part, your own; there is a candid clear manfulness, simplicity and truth in the things you write for your people . . . which seems to me the grain of blessed unnoticed wheat among those whirlwinds of noisy chaff . . . !

Duffy had retreated to country lodgings in Dundrum on the northern slope of the Dublin mountains, to write a history of the Rising of 1641. His work, which was never completed, was interrupted by Carlyle's visit. Early in September, Carlyle arrived at Belfast ('cold stony town') and took the coach to Drogheda, noting on the way 'Potatoes all evidently rotten; everywhere the air poisoned with their fateful smell'. Duffy and Mitchel were to have met him at Drogheda, but missed him because the postmaster overlooked a letter they had left in the post office. So he took the train to Dublin, writing to Jane: 'Rolled into Dublin (to Imperial Hotel) by railway. After sunset, wandered far and wide about the broad pavements, listening to the wild memories and cries of Dublin (on a Saturday night), went tired to bed, and in spite of riotous sounds audible slept well enough'. In his notebook he wrote: *Vapid — inane* looking streets in this Dublin, along the quays and everywhere sad defect of waggons, real *business* vehicles, or even gentleman's carriages, nothing but an empty whirl of streetcars, hucksters' carts, and, 'trashery'.

Next day, Carlyle went to Dundrum and was entertained by Duffy at a large dinner party where he met 'Young Ireland almost in mass,' and the novelist William Carleton ('big vulgar kind of fellow, not without talent and plenty of humour'.) They talked, argued and drank 'liquids of various strength.' The Young Irelanders defended their cause fiercely, and Carlyle as fiercely poured scorn on it. Although, recounted Duffy, 'he was entirely pleased with some of them, and he won their respect and sympathy in no limited measure'.

In Dublin, Carlyle dined with 'big blonde' Mitchel, and ate 'the last truly good potato I have met with in the world'. Mitchel's wife, his Presbyterian mother and his 'frugally elegant small house and table', greatly pleased Carlyle

> as did the man himself [he wrote to Jane], a fine elastic-spirited young fellow with superior natural talent, I grieved to see rushing on destruction, palpable by 'attack on windmills', but on whom all my dissuasions were thrown away. Both Duffy and him I have always regarded as specimens of the best kind of Irish youth seduced (like thousands of others in their early day) into courses that were at once mad and ridiculous, and which nearly ruined the life of both, by the Big Begger-man, who had £15,000 a year (and *pro pudor!* the favour of English ministers instead of the pillory from them) for professing blarney, with such and still worse results.

'Poor Mitchel!', Carlyle afterwards recalled. 'I told him he would most likely be hanged, but I told him too they could not hang the immortal part of him'.

Duffy took Carlyle to Conciliation Hall, where the Liberator, wearing his green cap, was making his last public appearance, in Carlyle's words, 'haranguing his beggarly squad'. Carlyle had an inviscerate hatred of O'Connell, whom he variously described as 'Big 'Beggar-Man, the eminently despiceable and eminently poisonous professor of blarney, and the chief quack of the then world'. Carlyle wrote to Edward Fitzgerald that O'Connell was 'the hugest *palpable* humbug' he had ever set eyes on. Further, he told his brother that O'Connell in Conciliation Hall was 'the *most* disgusting sight in Ireland', adding charitably, 'he is sinking, I think; that is a good symptom'.

On the last day of Carlyle's six-day visit, Duffy and Mitchel took him for one of the most beautiful drives in the world, by the Dargle and Powerscourt, through the Glen of the Downs, to Bray. According to his biographer, James Antony Froude:

> Before entering the Dublin mountains, they crossed the low rich meadows of the old Pale, the longest in English occupation, a fertile oasis in the general wretchedness.
> I have heard that he said, looking over the thick green grass and well-trimmed fences and herds of cattle fattening there, 'Ah, Duffy, there you see the hoof of the bloody Saxon'.

After dinner Duffy and Mitchel saw Carlyle on board the steamer at Kingstown, and early in the morning of 10 September, he was smoking a quiet cigar in the house of Mr. Welsh, Jane's uncle, in Liverpool.

Carlyle was an improbable contributor to *The Nation*, but he sent Duffy a manuscript with an explanatory note, which read, in part:

> Dear Duffy — The enclosed blotch of writing is tumbling about my blotting books for a while past. I ought to burn it at once, but as penny stamps have come into the world, I prefer that *you* should have the pleasure of burning it . . . Do what you will, only *don't* (except to your own heart) speak of my mortal name in connection with it . . . Do as you like; only, you are sworn to silence deep as death, mind that . . .

Carlyle in his article advised Irishmen not to talk of dying for Ireland, but to think 'in how many quiet strenuous ways you might beneficially live for it.'. Every patriotic Irishman, for example, could plant at least one tree. Eight million trees would be an undoubtable acquisition for Ireland, 'for it is one of the barest, raggedest countries now known . . . a country that stands decidedly in need of shelter, shade and ornamental fringing'.

'What I probably wrote to him, would have been discourteous to print: that his pleasant little paper betrayed a fundamental unacquaintance with Irish affairs. 'Duffy said years later. 'It was hopeless to reforest a country where, if a tenant planted his seed or sapling, and tended it until it became a mature tree, the law declared it to be the property of the landlord, with a scrap of compensation to the man who reared it.'

Carlyle's anxiety to conceal his authorship of this innocent piece is hard to understand. But the shy cloak of anonymity was immediately torn aside by a perceptive writer in the *Spectator*.

Four

Old and Young Ireland Separate

WHEN Daniel O'Connell, in a letter to the Repeal Association, expressed a preference for a Federal union with England, which would give Ireland a limited autonomy, 'as tending more to the utility of Ireland and the maintenance of the connection with England than the proposal of simple Repeal', Duffy addressed an open letter to him in *The Nation,* challenging this view. The letter, widely reprinted in Ireland and abroad, gave great satisfaction to the English Tories, who hailed it as a sign of division among O'Connell's followers. Though O'Connell issued what was described as a recantation, the damage had been done.

The rift widened when Peel in an attempt to conciliate Ireland, proposed to increase the grant to Maynooth College, and to establish middle-class colleges in Belfast, Cork and Galway, at which Catholics and Protestants would study together. (Maynooth had been established in 1795 as an endowed seminary for the Roman Catholic clergy, whose loylty it was hoped thus to secure.) The Young Irelanders and the middle classes welcomed both proposals. *The Nation* commented,

> The objections to separate education are immense, the reasons for it are reasons for separate life, for mutual animosity, for penal laws, for religious wars . . . and we are in favour of mixed education, because it is consistent with piety and favourable to the union of Irishmen of different sects, for want of which, Ireland is in rags and chains.

But the 'Young Liberator', as John O'Connell was somewhat derisively called, denounced Peel's bill as 'an abominable attempt to undermine religion and morality in Ireland' and his father agreed that it was a 'huge scheme of godless education'. His primary purpose, according to Duffy, was to assist the Whigs by frustrating Peel. 'But he was equally influenced no doubt by the determination to make John his successor, and John knew that the only Association he could control was one that had resumed the old sectarian character of Corn Exchange agitation'.

The Catholic bishops, after due deliberation, rejected the scheme as dangerous to faith and morals, and suggested amendments which would make it acceptable. When the Repeal Association met, Daniel O'Connell in a speech lasting two hours, declared triumphantly that the bishops had condemned the bill which he denounced as a 'nefarious attempt at profligacy and corruption'. He was supported in a wild speech by a young man named Michael George Conway, who had known Davis in college, and had a personal reason for disliking the Young Irelanders. During this speech, described by Duffy as a 'tipsy rhodomontade', O'Connell cheered vociferously, waving his cap over his head. Davis who spoke next, referred goodhumouredly to 'the useful, judicious and spirited speech of my old college friend, my Catholic friend, my very Catholic friend, Mr. Conway'. O'Connell interrupted him sharply to ask if it was a crime to be a Catholic, and suggested that Davis was sneering at Catholics. 'No, sir, no' replied Davis:

> My best friends, my nearest friends, my truest friends are Catholics. I was brought up in a mixed seminary, where I learned to know, and, knowing, loved my countrymen, a love that shall not be disturbed by these casual and unhappy dissensions. Disunion, alas! destroyed our country for centuries. Men of Ireland, shall it destroy it again? Will you take the boys of Ireland in their earliest youth and deepen the differences between them?

O'Connell, despite his two hours of oratory, had sufficient stamina to reply in a second speech, ending in a peroration that became famous. The venerated and esteemed hierarchy, he said, had condemned the Bill, but it had been supported by Mr. Davis, and advocated in a newspaper *The Nation*, professing to be the organ of the Roman Catholic people of Ireland:

> The sections of politicians styling themselves The Young Ireland Party, anxious to rule the destinies of this country, start up and support this measure. There is no such party as that styled 'Young Ireland'. There may be a few individuals who take that denomination on themselves. I am for Old Ireland. 'Tis time that this delusion should be put to an end. 'Young Ireland' may play what pranks they please. I do not envy them the name they rejoice in. I shall stand by Old Ireland; and I have some slight notion that Old Ireland will stand by me.

This unequivocal attack on the Young Irelanders was received with consternation. O'Connell, in Duffy's words 'had commenced a war in which either by success or failure he would bring ruin to the national cause'. Smith O'Brien and Henry Grattan junior protested, and O'Connell rose yet again to withdraw the nickname of 'Young Ireland', as he understood it was disclaimed by the young men to whom it was applied. Davis replied immediately that he was glad to get rid of the assumption that there were factions in the Association. He and his friends were bound to work together for Irish nationality, and he was bound by a strong personal affection for O'Connell. At this point, the usually unemotional and undemonstrative Davis burst into tears, and O'Connell seized him by the hand and cried, 'Davis, I love you'. The Association enthusiastically applauded the reconciliation, but in Duffy's words, 'a blow was struck from which the Association never recovered'.

THE amended education Bill was passed, but much of the bitterness remained. 'How very long it will take to get over the ill effects of the education row, and the worse effects of the bigotry shown during and since it took place', Davis wrote in August. Throughout the month the discontent of the Young Irelanders grew. O'Connell was on holidays, and his son, who in Duffy's words 'united a stealthy ambition to a narrow intellect', was in charge of the Repeal Association. He was suspected of circulating the story that the Young Irelanders were the enemies of the Church, and of his father. This charge was taken up enthusiastically by the Press and accepted by most of the Catholic clergy. The sales of *The Nation* suffered badly as a consequence.

Reports of John O'Connell's dictatorial and sectarian behaviour reached Duffy, who was touring Ulster. 'John O'Connell is the most mischievous public man in Ireland', MacNevin wrote to Duffy. 'The Association is now merely a Catholic Association. Repeal or any high or honourable principle of nationality is never heard there . . .'.

IN the autumn of 1845, Duffy made an excursion to his native Ulster, with John O'Hagan, John Mitchel and John Martin. It was a sentimental journey into history. At Drogheda, map in hand, they fought the battle of the Boyne over again, then on to Faughart, where according to tradition, Robert Bruce's brother Edward, the conqueror of Connaught, was buried. Then by way of Dundrum, the site of one of the castles erected by the great Norman soldier John de Courcy, to Downpatrick and the churchyard where the British ex-army officer, Thomas Russell, Wolfe Tone's friend and Robert Emmet's ally, lies; and from Downpatrick to Ballynahinch. Here one of the surviving pike-men guided them to the battlefield where in 1798 United Irishmen, Catholic and Presbyterian, fought and lost a pitched battle, Irish pike against British artillery, for six hours. And so by way of Armagh and Enniskillen to Donegal.

On the journey, the travellers usually finished the day with what Duffy described as 'Tea and Thomas' — Thomas being Carlyle, 'the philosopher of Chelsea', Duffy wrote, 'whom we all loved for having taught so well to scorn pretence and hold by truth and duty, without sharing in one in twenty of his opinions on men and events'. While they sipped their tea, one of them would read aloud from *Sartor Resartus*.

At Donegal a letter awaited Duffy with alarming news of his wife's health. He hurried back to find that all immediate danger was over; but the reprieve was short-lived.

TWO weeks after his return to Dublin, Duffy received a scrawled and tremulous note from Davis, who had been editing *The Nation* in his absence. It said: 'My Dear D. — I have had an attack of some sort of cholera, and perhaps have a slight scarlatina. I cannot see anyone and am in bed. Don't be alarmed about me; but don't rely on me being able to write'.

Duffy was not alarmed and replied banteringly: 'John O'Hagan says you have an opportunity of rivalling Mirabeau by dying at this minute'. In a similar vein, MacNevin reproached Davis for catching such an unpatriotic disease as 'English cholera'. But a week later, Duffy was summoned to Davis' house in Baggot Street to look upon his dead body.

'To me the spectacle . . . was like the light suddenly gone out of the sky', Duffy wrote.

Looking back a generation later, 'when years and communion with the world' had 'tempered the exaggerations of youthful friendship', Duffy could confidently say he had not known a man so nobly gifted, so modest and unselfish as Davis:

> He brought to political controversy a fairness previously unexampled in Ireland. In all his writings there will not be found a single sentence reflecting ungenerously on any human being. He had set himself the task of building up a nation, a task not beyond his strength had fortune been kind . . . During his brief career, scarcely exceeding three years, he had administered no office of authority, published no books, or next to none, and marshalled no following; but with the simplest agencies, in the columns of a newspaper, in casual communication with his friends and contemporaries, he made a name which, after a generation, is still recalled with enthusiasm or tears . . .

In his unstinted praise of Davis, Duffy often underestimates his own achievements, particularly the part he played in rescuing Davis from comparative oblivion, and in recognising his great contribution to Irish nationalism. 'While it is the figure of Davis that makes the noble monument for the period and gives the days of the Young Irelanders a life that goes on forever', wrote Brinsley MacNamara in a centenary tribute to Davis, 'it is Gavan Duffy who was the real founder of their movement and the one who gave us Davis greatly to remember'.

Nearly a hundred years before — in 1849 — Thomas D'Arcy McGee had written: 'Duffy was the projector and philosopher of the circle of which Davis was the spirit and organiser'.

Within a few days of Davis' funeral, Mrs. Duffy died, following the birth of her second child, John. She had been suffering from what was called 'a slow consumption'. Compounding his personal grief, Duffy was now faced with disintegration in *The Nation* office. John Dillon had ruptured a blood-vessel and had been ordered to winter in Madeira, under penalty of speedy death. Thomas MacNevin was suffering from an unknown disease that was soon to kill him. And John O'Hagan and John Pigot were in London, studying law. But despite his many troubles, and his own ill-health, Duffy finished his law studies and in the Michaelmas term, beginning in November, was admitted to the Irish Bar. At that time Catholic barristers had to take an additional oath and pay an additional fee. Duffy took the oath ('some absurdity about the Pretender') but refused to pay the half-a-crown fee, which he regarded as a remnant of the penal laws.

DUFFY set about organising a new editorial team for *The Nation*. Among the recruits were Thomas Francis Meagher, John Mitchel, Thomas D'Arcy McGee, and Thomas Devlin Reilly. Meagher, who was twenty-two, was the son of a Waterford merchant, the popular Mayor of the town. He had been educated at two Jesuit institutions, Clongowes Wood in Kildare, and Stonyhurst in Lancashire. His English education had given him a misleading manner. 'To the common eye . . . the new recruit was a dandified youngster', Duffy wrote, 'but this was a vulgar error. Nature had made him a great orator, and training had made him an accomplished gentleman'. Meagher had published some undistinguished verse in *The Nation,* and offered his services to Duffy when he heard of Davis' death.

Mitchel, a Trinity College graduate, was the son of an Ulster Unitarian minister, who had been a United Irishman. Duffy had known him in Belfast. He was practising law in Bannbridge when Duffy induced him to come to Dublin to work full time on *The Nation.* He had written one or two slight pieces for it, and a life of Aodh, Prince of Ulster, for the 'Library of Ireland'. He was then thirty, a year older than Duffy. 'He was a man of prompt and receptive intellect and lively fancy', Duffy wrote. But he lacked one important faculty — 'the gift ordinarily called judgment — a capacity of estimating justly the relative momentum of forces . . .'.

Thomas Reilly, who was seven years younger than Duffy, was the son of a country attorney. He was born in Monaghan, and like Duffy, attended the Rev. Bleckley's classical academy, though not at the same time. His education was completed at Trinity College. 'He was a big, clumsy, careless, explosive boy in appearance', wrote Duffy, 'but he possessed a range of ideas and a vigour of expression which made him a companion of men'.

McGee was born in Carlingford, County Down, the son of a Catholic Customs officer. At the age of eighteen, after his mother's early death, and his father's remarriage, he emigrated to the United States, with no assets but a school prize, which he sold to buy food. He got a job as a clerk on an Irish journal, the *Boston Pilot,* and rose from contributor to editor. One of his articles caught the eye of Dr. Gray, proprietor of *Freeman's Journal,* who offered him the position of London correspondent. After a disagreement with Gray over some contributions McGee had made to *The Nation,* he accepted Duffy's invitation to join its staff in Dublin. He was then only twenty.

He had what Duffy described as 'a face of almost African type' and a curiously dark complexion, which inevitably earned him the nickname of 'Darky' McGee. His dress was slovenly, but Duffy soon found he had a fertile and original brain. 'No one but Thomas Davis brought such splendid faculties to the Irish cause', Duffy wrote. Sir Samuel Ferguson considered he was the greatest of the Young Ireland poets.

McGee had first met Duffy crossing Carlisle (now O'Connell) bridge, in the summer of 1845. 'He struck me as of a dyspeptic constitution', McGee wrote, without explaining how he arrived at this diagnosis, 'and his middle size deceived me — we always expect a great man to stand six feet tall. His manner was frank, short and decided, like that of general when the campaign has begun'. And McGee recalled that Ireland's greatest general, Owen Roe O'Neill, and her first orator, Henry Grattan, were also invalids.

A modern historian, Professor Edward Norman, has noted a 'curious bond' of ill-health linking many of the Young Irelanders. He points out that Thomas Davis and a later supporter, Fintan Lalor, were too frail as children to participate in normal games, and both died young; that Reilly

Thomas Francis Meagher

suffered from nervous pains in the head and Mitchel from chronic asthma. 'These were a strange group of men to find glorying in the military virtues of the Irish race', he comments. But he sees the paradox as a familiar one, with contemporary parallels. 'Young intellectuals, of advanced political and cultural theories . . . and impatient with their own numerical and physical weakness, quite often attach themselves to romantic cults of violence', he writes. Believers in this valetudinarian interpretation of history might find further confirmation in the case-histories of Dillon and MacNevin.

THROUGHOUT 1845, the Young Irelanders drifted further away from O'Connell. Their differences were exacerbated by the publication in *The Nation* of a contribution which became known as 'The Railway Article'. When Duffy retired to Dumdrum, he had left Mitchel in charge of the paper. Commenting on food riots in Ireland provoked by the threat of famine, a Government organ, the *Morning Herald,* urged the Government to shut up 'Sedition Hall', and to declare that agitation for Repeal was high treason. It pointed out that the new railways in Ireland, which had brought every part of the country 'within six hours of the garrison in Dublin', would make it easy for the Government to suppress any resistance.

Mitchel replied with a spirited article: 'It might be useful', he wrote, 'to promulgate through the country to be read by all Repeal wardens in their parishes, a few short and easy rules as to the mode of dealing with railways in case of an enemy daring to make hostile use of them'. He explained in some detail how railways could be put out of action. It was easy to lift a mile of rail, or fill a perch or two of cutting, or break down an embankment. And the rails and sleepers could be used for making pikes and barricades. The article ended: 'But 'tis a dream. No enemy will put us to realise these scenes. Yet all understand what a railway *may* and what it may *not* do'.

A few days later O'Connell called at *The Nation* office to protest against the dangerous conjunction of Repeal wardens with guerilla warfare. 'It was somewhat surprising' Duffy later wrote, 'that the orator who had . . . promised that any attempt to suppress opinion by force — the identical thing here threatened — would be made over his dead body should have become so squeamish; but he was the leader, and we complied'. (An amusing footnote to the railway story is that Duffy had invested nearly all his savings in Irish railways!)

In the next issue of *The Nation* Mitchell mentioned O'Connell's remonstrance and pointed out that *The Nation* 'had neither connection with nor control over Repeal wardens', and that the views expressed in *The Nation* were not those of O'Connell.

Soon afterwards, Duffy, as proprietor of *The Nation* was charged with seditious libel for publishing the railway article and O'Connell issued strict instructions that no reference to the prosecution should be made in Conciliation Hall. Duffy, in a letter published as a leader in *The Nation,* 'examined, explained and justified' the article, and defended Mitchel. O'Hagan reported from London that Thomas and Jane Carlyle strongly sympathised with Duffy 'about this prosecution affair and liked your letter extremely'. And despite O'Connell's instructions, Duffy was supported in the Association by prominent members, including Smith O'Brien, who declared that Mitchel's article was morally and legally justifiable.

O'Connell's next move was to demand from Duffy and Mitchel, under threat of economic sanctions, an assurance that *The Nation* would not oppose the decisions of the Repeal Association. It was the practice of the Association to buy large numbers of *The Nation* for free distribution to Repeal reading-rooms. This was worth more than £1,000 a year to Duffy. When Duffy refused to give the required assurance, O'Connell gave orders to discontinue the distribution.

The Nation by then had acquired such influence that the ban seems to have done it little harm. Many of the 1,200 reading-rooms subscribed to it at their own cost, and Duffy's stand brought him fresh allies, including the vigorous and scholarly Father John Kenyon, parish priest of Templederry, in Tipperary.

In view of O'Connell's attitude towards the Young Irelanders, it is hard to understand a paper which he sent from London to be read out at the weekly meeting of the Repeal Association on 25 May 1846. 'Dissension has ever been the bane of Ireland and her destruction', he wrote. 'It has often afflicted our friends and given comfort to our enemies. But, with the assistance of Smith O'Brien, we are certain it shall never again rear its hideous head amongst the Irish popular party'. The imperative necessity, he said, was to prepare for the ensuing elections. Sixty or eighty Repealers in the House of Commons would, in the present state of the parties, render Repeal certain.

While Duffy was awaiting trial, Denny Lane offered him some good advice in a flippant wrapping: 'You are greatly in want of physical exercise', he wrote.

> Your amusements are too intellectual; you ought to ride, play billiards, hunt, shoot and kick up shindies. Cultivate the society of O'Gorman; he has what you want — the intense enjoyment of physical exercise. He would want, as I told him, to be put upon Tennyson and soda-water for half a year, while on the other hand your regime ought to be beefsteaks and porter, fox-hunting and a main of cocks. Acquire low tastes and gratify them, and you may defy Blackburne and all works'.

Blackburne, described by Duffy as 'one of the most subtle, skilful and vindictive of the Crown lawyers', had succeeded Pennefather as Chief Justice, and would preside at Duffy's trial. A few days before it began, Lord John Russell, declared in the House that *The Nation* was the organ of a party which excited 'every species of violence, which looked to disturbance as its means, and regarded separation from England as its end'.

SIX months after he had been granted bail, Duffy appeared in Green Street court to answer the charge of having published 'a false and defamatory libel' against Her Majesty's Government, etc. It seemed certain that he would be convicted. But the Crown had underestimated the powers of Duffy's principal counsel, the venerable Robert Holmes, the doyen of the Irish bar, then approaching his eightieth year. 'If ever assent was wrung from the consciences of unwilling jurors by the passionate conviction and personal eloquence of an advocate, it was in this case', Duffy wrote.

Holmes based his defence on the fact that Ireland had been all along, and was at that hour, treated as a conquered country. The people of a country so treated had certain natural rights, which were precisely the rights insisted upon in the prosecuted article. The real meaning of the article was that if the sword should be employed to put down opinion, and the railways used to facilitate the conveyance of troops for that purpose, resistance would be justifiable. Holmes justified this defence by an appeal to history and constitutional law, alternating dispassionate fact with impassioned oratory.

In his magnificent peroration, he recalled how Grattan's parliament, which had given Ireland some measure of prosperity, had been destroyed by an Act of Union, imposed by bribery and intimidation:

> It is not the sword which destroys the body, as much as the policy that lays waste the mind, which Ireland has reason to deplore. A light once shone across the gloom, bright and glorious, but transient, only serving to show the darkness that had gone before and the darkness that followed. That light was extinguished by the foulest means that fraud or tyranny ever practised, and now it seems any attempt to rekindle it is to be treated as sedition, and the sentence of degradation and dependence pronounced against Ireland to be confirmed and made perpetual. Against this sentence, my client has raised his voice; and not only on my client's behalf, but on behalf of an injured and insulted country, I exhort the jury to avert the sentence. I do not ask their verdict as the boon of mercy, or the safety-valve of doubt, but as the unequivocal expression of their regard for the rights of nature and the welfare and honour of their native land.

'The effect of this speech', wrote Duffy, 'was like an experiment in electricity; a dull inert mass was kindled with sudden fire'. The Chief Justice, in advising the jury to put the speech out of their minds, described it as one 'which had never been surpassed in a court of justice'. But he told them that as the publication of the article was clearly a seditious libel, all the jury had to decide was whether Duffy had published it with all or any of the intents charged in the indictment. After being locked up for twenty-four hours without food, drink, fire or light, the jury still could not decide, and Duffy was discharged. The news, he wrote, was received throughout the country 'with paroxysms of joy'.

Holmes' great speech was widely acclaimed. O'Brien wrote to Duffy: 'I wish we could hear such language in Constitution Hall as Mr. Holmes was not ashamed to utter in the Queen's Bench'. But O'Connell did not join the chorus of acclamation, and would not allow the Repeal Association to reprint the speech as a pamphlet. However, this was done by the '82 Club, and Lord Brougham told the House of Lords that he had read it 'with the greatest admiration' for Holmes' 'great ability and learning'.

William Smith O'Brien

O'CONNELL continued his efforts to form an alliance with the Whigs, who he still thought might be induced, if they came to power, to do something for Ireland. He told Smith O'Brien in December 1845, that he could 'squeeze out' of them a great deal of good for Ireland. Meanwhile the Repeal issue was discreetly shelved.

This did not please the Young Irelanders. They continued to denounce O'Connell's flirtation with the Whigs, whose leaders, they believed, were fundamentally as intransigent on the question of Repeal as the Tories. There were continuous disagreement about this between O'Connell and the Young Irelanders. Duffy, writing in *The Nation*, rejected the idea of an alliance which he thought might lead to Repeal being bought off with a few minor reforms, and O'Brien wrote that he feared 'more danger to Repeal from the subtle influence of a Whig administration than from the coercive measure of a Tory one'. Another cause of disagreement was the future of the Corn Laws. O'Connell advocated their repeal. *The Nation* argued that repeal would damage Ireland's biggest industry — agriculture. The squabbles in the Association continued. Smith O'Brien said with some humour, 'I am neither Old Ireland nor Young Ireland; I am Middle-Aged Ireland'.

The final breach between Old and Young Ireland took place on 28 July 1846, when John O'Connell, in his father's absence, gave the Young Irelanders the option of renouncing physical force absolutely, or leaving the Association. He was determined to drive them out. The Young Irelanders declared that they did not advocate force as a solution of Ireland's difficulties, but they would not condemn its use under all circumstances. O'Connell said the Association was convinced the conductors of *The Nation* had contemplated physical force and treasonable designs. Meagher jumped to his feet and said there had been some condemnation for the man whom he was proud to call his friend — the 'conspirator', Charles Gavan Duffy. He would gladly defend a journal that had attained European fame, and he did not believe the people would ratify the censure that had been pronounced on it (tremendous cheers). He then, at great length, while repudiating resort to physical force in the case of Ireland, referred to events in ancient and modern history where appeals had been made successfully to the sword, and declared he could never condemn those means.

Addressing the Lord Mayor, he cried:

> Abhor the sword and stigmatise the sword? No, my lord, for in the cragged passes of the Tyrol it cut to pieces the banner of the Bavarian, and won an immortality for the peasant of Innsbruck. Abhor the sword and stigmatise the sword? No, my lord, for at its blow a giant nation sprang up from the waters of the Atlantic, and by its redeeming magic, the fettered colonies became a daring, free republic. Abhor the sword and stigmatise the sword? No, my lord, for it scourged the Dutch marauders out of the fine old towns of Belgium, back into their own phlegmatic swamps . . . .

How many more historic swords Meagher might have unsheathed is impossible to say, for in the midst of his peroration, he was interrupted by John O'Connell who called him to order sharply, declaring that his language was dangerous to the Association.

Smith O'Brien protested that Meagher's argument was perfectly legitimate. If it were his last act in the Association, he was delighted to have the opportunity of protesting against the attempt to put Mr. Meagher down. He then picked up his hat and cloak, bowed to the meeting, and left the Hall, followed by Meagher, Mitchel, and the rest of the Young Irelanders. In the street, they were loudly cheered. Those remaining in the Hall raised a triumphant shout which continued for some minutes. John O'Connell, having precipitated it, said he felt nothing but pain, heartburning, and grief at the event.

Five

Famine and Epidemics

THOUGH the wrangles between Old and Young Ireland loomed large in Conciliation Hall or *The Nation* office, they were overshadowed in the summer of 1845 by the onset of the most catastrophic famine in Ireland's history. Ireland's population was then about eight millions (some estimates put it as high as nine millions), most of them desperately poor and utterly dependent for survival on the potato, the only crop they knew how to cultivate. With huge unemployment and a rapidly increasing population, Ireland was constantly on the brink of disaster, a condition which many Englishmen, with Carlyle, attributed to the improvidence and laziness of her peasantry. As that wit and worldly clergyman, the Rev. Sydney Smith wrote: 'The moment the very name of Ireland is mentioned, the English seem to bid adieu to common feeling, common prudence and common sense, and to act with the barbarity of tyrants and the fatuity of idiots'.

IN 1844, a hitherto unknown disease attacked the potato in North America. The blight soon crossed the Atlantic, and in August 1845 reached Ireland. 'The crops about Dublin are suddenly perishing . . .' wrote the eminent horticulturist, Dr. John Lindley. 'Where will Ireland be in the event of a universal potato rot'? His forebodings were well founded. The blight swept across the country, the potato crop failed, and millions faced starvation.

At first, the Government acted wisely and generously. Peel, without consulting Treasury, imported Indian corn from the United States to retail in Ireland at one penny a pound. The Corn Laws, which kept up the price of home-grown grain, were repealed so that Ireland could get cheap wheat — a bold *volte-face* by a Tory leader. ('Rotten potatoes have done it all', grumbled the Duke of Wellington. 'They put Peel in his damned fright'.) And a huge sum — between eight and ten million pounds — was advanced for an unprecedented programme of public relief works on which starving men, if they were strong enough, could earn ninepence or a shilling a day. 'Not enough was done considering the size of the catastrophe', says Miss Woodham Smith. 'But it is doubtful if any Government in Europe would have done more'.

In 1847, however, while the Great Famine still raged, the Government, faced with a financial crisis at home, changed its policy, and transferred responsibility for famine relief to the Union workhouses, administered under the degrading Poor Relief Act of 1838. Most of the workhouses were in a deplorable condition, bankrupt, insanitary, understaffed and ill-managed, and situated in districts where destitution was at its worst. Yet thousands of wretched men, women and children were thrown upon their meagre charity. Duffy described the scene of 'piercing woe' in a Munster workhouse, 'with hundreds of once frank and gallant yeomanry turned into sullen beasts, wallowing on the floor as thick as human limbs could pack'.

The Illustrated London News commented on Ireland's huge workhouse population: 'We have peopled North America, civilised India, taken possession of Australia, and scattered the Anglo-Saxon name and fame, language and literature, religion and laws, ideas and habits, over the fairest portion of the globe. Yet, with all this, we maintain in unproductive idleness, no less a number than one million and a half paupers'.

TOWARDS the end of 1845, Charles Dickens, planning his paper, the *Daily News* offered the job of Special Commissioner in Ireland to his friend Richard Henry (later self-styled 'Hengist') Horne, a versatile but eccentric man of letters who had collaborated with Elizabeth Barrett, and published his impressive epic *Orion*, at the price of one farthing, to mark the contempt into which epic poetry in England had fallen. 'What do you think of eight guineas a week and travelling expenses — as a point to start from'? Dickens suggested. It was a handsome offer. The standard weekly rate for reporters was five guineas.

Horne accepted and set up Dublin headquarters at 9 Lower Sackville Street, with a sub-editor, reporters, and 'unlimited credit'. Horne, himself a first-rate reporter, travelled to Limerick along the south-west coast of Clare, into Galway and 'the wilds of Connemara,' sending vivid and sympathetic accounts of the famine. He remained with the *Daily News* for more than a year, most of which he spent in Ireland.

In his first despatch from Dublin, he expressed surprise at the elegance of Conciliation Hall. He had pictured it as a 'shabby, ramshackle, misshapen building, half-hall, half- barn . . . crowded with . . . thousands of the lowest and raggiest class of the Irish poor . . . red-headed paddies in ragged coats and frocks, with shillelaghs and forks, and potato spades, with whisky bottles with the genuine *poteen*'.

He found 'a large new building . . . quietly elegant and commodious . . . lit by twelve bronze candelabra . . . and a row of thirteen more . . . extending round the wall above the gallery'. Upon the ceiling were 'three very large and beautiful rosettes of pale gold and containing the shamrock in low relief, with a harp. In . . . the centre, and in front of the ladies' gallery hung a green silk banner, inscribed in gold letters with the words of Daniel O'Connell: 'The Man who Commits a Crime gives Strength to the Enemy'. And Horne reported that the week's Repeal Rent was £367.3.11d. In a later despatch, he quoted approvingly from an article written by William Howitt in *Tait's Magazine:* 'It is for Irishmen to seek Justice through Repeal and for us Englishmen to render Repeal unnecessary'.

Horne saw many heart-rending evictions. He gave the account of some in which soldiers had participated:

> It was disgusting to observe with what recklessness the bailiffs dragged out every little article of furniture which belonged to the wretched inmates of each hovel they visited, and, in some instances, threw out the miserable remnants of rotten potatoes which they had for subsistence. 'I have been in the army for 27 years, and, by God, I would rather face an enemy than witness what I have seen today', said one of the soldiers.

At times Horne's compassion found expression in verse. After attending the inquest on a woman found dead in a ditch from destitution and hunger, he wrote 'A Wake in Clare', which began:

> *Bones starting through the skin;*
> *High knees and lifted chin,*
> *All the rest fallen in*
>   *Grim every feature;*
> *Ghastly despair is here!*
> *Horror 'wakes' round thy bier —*
> *Once thou were very dear,*
>   *Lost fellow creature.*

And when he heard of a poor woman in Limerick who died of hunger and was carried three miles to her grave by three women and a blind son-in-law, he wrote 'An Irish Funeral', which began:

> *An old door's the hearse,*
> *Of the skeleton corpse*
> *And three women bear it*
> *With a blind man to share it,*
>   *Over flint, over bog,*
>   *They stagger and jog . . .*

As an objective historian such as Miss Woodham Smith has pointed out: 'The 1840's must not be judged by the standards of today; and whatever parsimony and callousness the British Government displayed towards Ireland, was paralleled seven years later by the treatment of their own soldiers . . . in the Crimea . . .'. *The Times* expressed a somewhat similar view when, in September 1846, it said that 'all classes of Irish society' should be told there was 'nothing so peculiar, so exceptional, in the conditions which they look on as the pit of utter despair'; and it asked philosophically, 'Why is that so terrible in Ireland which in England does not create perplexity and hardly moves compassion'?

Had they been able to read *The Times,* this counsel would no doubt have greatly consoled the starving Irish. Miss Woodham Smith, drawing on census and emigration figures, estimates that about one million and a half people perished during the famine, of hunger, diseases caused by hunger, and fever. She adds cautiously, 'The figures available, however,

must be regarded as giving only a rough indication . . . no record was kept of deaths, and very many people must have died and been buried unknown'.

Thousands were thrown, uncoffined into mass graves. An ingenious improvisation was the 'trap coffin'. The bottom was supported by hinges on one side, and a hook and eye on the other. By releasing the bottom, the body fell into the grave, and the coffin was used over and over again.

Crimes of violence, midnight assaults on people and property, were increasing in Ireland. Houses were burnt down. The peasants were buying arms. Famine riots were breaking out. A Clonmel correspondent reported: 'We have cannon at either end of the town and the streets are full of soldiers and police. This morning the mob broke into every baker's shop . . . and took out all the food they could lay their hands on'.

In January 1846, Peel agreed to bring in a 'Bill for the Protection of Life in Ireland' which Lord George Bentinck called 'the Anti-Murder Bill', but which was better known as the 'Irish Coercion Bill'. It was not the first or last Bill of its kind. It suspended Habeas Corpus and enabled the Lord Lieutenant to put any district under martial law. Arrests could be made on suspicion alone, and the possession of any firearm became a criminal offence. A man who ventured out of his house in a proclaimed district between sunset and sunrise could be transported for fourteen years. Likewise treated was any person found in a public-house in such a district unless he were an inmate or traveller. About this state of affairs Horne wrote:

> Can the Government really coerce a populous country . . . so that tens of thousands or hundreds of thousands, or millions, may be compelled to become prisoners in their cabins from sunset till sunrise? The thing cannot be done . . . There is no power in the machinery or the law to enslave the spirit of man . . . You might as well attempt to seize the soul by its immortality, and put it in a soldier's tin canister . . .

The Bill was introduced into the House of Lords on 24 February, and passed without objection by Whigs and Tories alike. 'To what lunatic degree of patient forbearance do the mad rulers of Ireland imagine the people ought to arrive at and maintain'? asked Horne. Families, he reported, were living on sea-weed and rotten potatoes. O'Connell, addressing a meeting convened at the Crown and Anchor tavern in London to discuss 'the atrocious' Bill, declared: 'They might as well apply a blister to the King Charles' horse at Charing Cross as this Coercion Bill to the people of Ireland. If justice were refused to Ireland, he said, 'Woe to England!'

In the Commons, Disraeli opposed the Bill, and on the night of 25 June, it was defeated by 73 votes. What the Duke of Wellington described as 'a blackguard combination' of Whigs, Radicals, and Irish had turned Peel out of office for ever.

PROTESTANT churches throughout the United Kingdom offered up the 'Dearth and Scarcity' prayer for the Irish at morning and evening services each Sunday, and appropriate prayers were offered up in all synagogues. Nor was there a lack of inspired suggestions to relieve Ireland's distress.

The Duke of Cambridge believed that a mixture of diseased potatoes and grass would provide excellent food for the starving millions. Equally imaginative was the proposal of the Duke of Norfolk that the Irish should acquire a taste for curry powder mixed with water. He seemed to think this was the staple diet of the population of India. Another suggestion was that the daily ration of corn enjoyed by the twelve thousand army and police horses in Ireland should be reduced from ten to five pounds, thus providing an extra sixty thousand pounds a day to feed the people. More practically, the eminent French chef of the Reform Club, August Soyer, — of whom it was said that he had found the Club *'aux gigot* and left it *aux bechamel'* — set up huge soup kitchens in Dublin, where he dispensed an economical soup — two gallons cost sixpence, including one pennyworth of meat. But Soyer warned philanthropists against putting spices in food designed for the poor, for these only 'flattered the appetite' and stimulated it.

While Irish peasants were still dying by the thousands, or struggling to survive on a ration of one pound of Indian meal a day, The *United Irishman* in its second issue (19 February 1848) carried a conspicuous and titillating advertisement from a Dublin merchant, Mr. John Hughes, who announced that

FOREIGN FRUIT OF EVERY DESCRIPTION

Never was *Finer* or *Cheaper than at the present time, owing to the immense arrivals from Liverpool, from which port he had received 'the largest and best selected stock that can be possibly piled together in any one establishment'.

Prime Almeria Grapes (large Amber)
Ditto Malaga, ditto (Green, moist, tender)
Large Black ditto.
Sweet St. Michael and China Oranges.
Fine Large Bitter Seville ditto (for preserving)
Ditto, do Messina Lemons.
American Newtown Pippin, and other Apples
New Spanish Chestnuts
Ditto French Walnuts.
Kent Cobb Nuts and Filberts.
Extra Large Figs (from the London Markets).
Fancy Cartoons and Boxes — French Plums.
New Barbary Dates (Abd-el-Kader's favourite).
Crystallised Fruits (in basquets assorted).
The finest Muscatel Raisins (Layers) in packages from 3 lbs. to 26 lbs. each.
New Jordan, Valencia, and Bitter Almonds.
Ditto, Soft Shell Ditto.
Very large Spanish and Portugal Onions etc., etc., with a great Variety of well-known genuine Old Liqueurs.

Mr. *Hughes also offered 'a constant supply of beautiful Camelia Bouquets* from the best Green Houses in the vicinity of Dublin'.

In the same issue the Rev. Peter Fitzmaurice reported from Clifden that some of his parishioners had been living on horse and dog flesh 'until death put an end to their sufferings;' the *Sligo Champion* reported that most of the inhabitants of Kilura were living on turnips, and a report from Roundstone, Galway, described how a number of dead bodies had laid for days 'over-ground . . . until the dogs had destroyed the body of an old man, the flesh off the back 'being entirely taken away'.

The paradox of the famine years is that while the Irish were starving, huge quantities of wheat were being exported from Ireland. This was seen by the Repealers as a further proof of England's villainy. But the landlords who exported the wheat were often themselves in a precarious position. They were heavily taxed, and their land was often mortgaged, and subject to enormous rent-charges. They had to export to survive. And, as modern historians point out, when the famine was at its worst, four times as much wheat came into Ireland as was exported. It was an extraordinary situation, and the furious and widespread indignation of the Irish is understandable. Duffy cried out that the famine was nothing less than 'a fearful murder committed on the mass of the people'. Mitchel uttered a similar indictment.

The Irish have long memories and there are people in the Republic of Ireland today who believe that England somehow contrived the famine, either to subdue the Irish, or to force them into the factories of the Industrial Revolution. Such beliefs, of course, belong to folklore.

The *Annual Register* of 1847 offered pious comment on the state of Ireland. 'The condition of this unhappy land during the past month [November] has been even more shocking than hitherto', it wrote. But during the fearful visitation of the famine, when the peasantry were dying by hundreds, there was yet this consolation:

> that the evil was from the hands of the Almighty in the exercise of His wisdom, and that man could but bow himself in humility to the stroke — and this dire affliction further exhibited the noble spectacle of nations hastening to the relief of their fellow creatures, all selfish and angry feelings forgotten. We have now, however, to contemplate the wickedness of man; the people, but so recently relieved from their sufferings, so recently the objects of unbounded generosity, turn upon their benefactors, and all gratitude to God and man forgotten, turn their beautiful and fruitful land into an Halcedana.

Punch made a similar comment on Ireland's 'ingratitude'. 'What can be done with Ireland'? it asked. 'Kindness, judging from the speeches of Young Ireland, is thrown away on her. Every sympathy is shown to her distress, that charity can devise, and money execute, but it all goes for nothing . . . Instead of saying "Thank you", it does nothing but heap abuses on the hand that relieves her'.

THE famine was followed by epidemics of cholera, dysentery and opthalmia. In September 1849, the *Illustrated London News* reported that cholera was still claiming many victims, not only among the poor, but 'in the better classes'. Its incidence was so great that Catholics were given permission to eat meat on Friday. In January 1847 when the horrors of the famine were daily multiplying, the Young Irelanders formed a new association, the Irish Confederation. Its purpose was in Duffy's words, 'to arrest the ruin of the national cause . . . For twice twelve months, there had not been a step made towards self-government; nothing effectual had been done to counteract the famine; the mass of the people were bewildered and helpless; the best of the middle class were falling into apathy and despair'.

Though Duffy claimed no pre-eminent role in the establishment of the Confederation, according to D'Arcy McGee, he was its virtual creator. 'Duffy projected the Confederation . . .' wrote McGee. 'He not only founded but he *made* the Confederation. He invented the Clubs. He won over all the considerable men who joined it, *one by one*, by dint of argument and exhortation; he gave it its impulses and policy. He *was* the Confederation'. As Chairman of the Committee of Organisation, Duffy drew up the 'Instructions for the Formation and Government of Confederate Clubs', and defined their objectives:

> The first object is *organisation* for the Repeal of the Union — spreading the principles and increasing the numbers of the Confederation.
> The second object is *conciliation* — spreading the doctrines of toleration and brotherhood, overcoming prejudices, and healing up ancient animosities.
> The third object is *education* — to teach the Members to know and maintain their rights, and perform their duties as Irishmen.

At the initial meeting, on 13 January, Duffy and Pigot were appointed Inspectors of Clubs for Leinster; Smith O'Brien and Meagher for Munster; and Martin and Mitchel for Ulster. A member appointed to the Council was Major Bryan, a Tasmanian squatter who had returned to Ireland to enjoy the 'modest competence' he had acquired in the Antipodes. Duffy describes him as 'an honest, resolute, passionate patriot, who, when things were not going to his satisfaction in Conciliation Hall, was accustomed to blow his nose in 'a loud and menacing manner'. After the Young Irelanders seceded from Conciliation Hall, they held reunions in the Major's house, Raheny Lodge.

Six months after its foundation, Duffy reported that the Confederation had enrolled ten thousand members. It had been founded upon independent principles new in Irish politics, 'demanding no systematic pecuniary support from the people, attempting no extensive organisation and little direct action'. But now the time for these had at length arrived. Reunion with Conciliation Hall was no longer desirable or possible. O'Connell's organisation of 1840 had no well-digested and intelligent policy. 'It had committed the fatal error of rushing at one time to the verge of insurrection and retreating at another to the most slavish professions of eternal submission'. To its followers it had given no higher pursuits 'than the mere gathering of money and attending public meetings'.

Clubs, Duffy wrote, should be established in every town and parish in Ireland. Town Clubs had special duties, including to encourage the use of Irish manufactures, to promote a knowledge of the history and resources of Ireland, to work for the extension of the popular franchise, and to procure signatures to addresses to the Queen, calling for the reassemblage of the Irish Parliament. The special duties of the Country Clubs included to procure protection for the rights of the tenant-farmer, to encourage the diffusion of agricultural knowledge, and to discourage secret societies of all kinds. And in an address to the Club of which he became president, Duffy repeated his plea for unity and tolerance:

> When you ask Protestants to help you, if you do not mean to protect the religious liberty of Protestants, in all contingencies, as zealously as you would protect your own, you are hypocrites, unworthy of liberty. When you invite the co-operation of the gentry, if you do not intend to maintain all their just rights — by which I mean their rights to their estates and a fair rent, not any assumed right over the conscience or property of their tenants — you deserve to fail, and you will get your deserts. To speak the truth is wisdom and policy.

SMITH O'Brien was in Clare, delicately keeping out of the way until the Confederates had decided on their policy. Duffy urged him to return without delay: 'The Old Irelanders seem ripe for reconciliation . . . There will be an outburst sooner or later, be sure of that. But unless you provide against it, it will be a mere democratic one, which the English Government will extinguish in blood . . .' ('Democratic' then had some of the explosive connotation that 'communist' has acquired in our time.) If 'by a miracle' this outburst succeeded, Duffy continued, it would mean death and exile to the middle as well as the upper classes. He saw but one safety for Ireland:

> . . . a *union* of the Old and Young Irelanders, an arraying of the middle class in the front of the millions, and a peaceful revolution, attained by watching and seizing our opportunity. By peaceful I mean without unnecessary or anarchical bloodshed. It may be won without a shot being fired. But trust me, if there is no such junction, and if things are let to take the course they are tending towards, we will see the life of the country trampled under the feet of English soldiers, suppressing a peasant revolution; or you and I will meet on a Jacobin scaffold ordered for execution by some new Marat or Robespierre . . . It is the fixed and inevitable course of revolutions when the strength of the middle classes is permitted to waste in inaction . . . History reproduces itself. We may have a peaceful, and happy revolution, and Ireland's opportunity is coming fast; but much depends on you . . .

Daniel O'Connell was a broken old man when he addressed the House of Commons for the last time in February 1847 to make a final plea for Ireland. In a few almost inaudible words he whispered, 'Ireland is in your hands, in your power. If you do not save her, she cannot save herself'. Disraeli, despite their past differences, was among the many who were greatly moved. 'It was a strange and touching spectacle to those who remembered the form of colossal energy, and the clear and thrilling tone that had once startled, disturbed and controlled senates', he wrote. 'To the House generally it was the performance of dumb-show, a feeble old man muttering before a table . . .' But the dying giant was listened to with silent, respectful attention. He had hoped to end his days in Rome, but he died on the way, at Genoa, on 15 May 1847. His heart, as he had requested, is preserved in Rome. His body was taken back to Dublin.

A month after the founding of the Confederation Clubs Duffy married his first cousin, Susan Hughes. She was the sister of Terence McMahon Hughes, and of Mrs. Margaret Callan. (It was the third intermarriage between the Duffys and the Hughes). Susan was a cultivated woman and a very fine pianist, who had studied under Chopin and Lizst. After her marriage, she gave up the piano because Duffy did not like music. But she was the 'sweet Sybil' of his songs.

> *Sweet Sybil! sweet Sybil! my heart is wild*
> *With the fairy spell that her eyes have lit;*
> *I sit in a dream where my love has smiled —*
> *I kiss where her name is writ!*

Carlyle was delighted to hear of Duffy's 'good fortune', and of his new home. He hoped to 'see with satisfaction what a Temple of the Muses and stronghold of Heroisms and Veracities you have made of it, even in these sad times' he wrote in March 1847. But he predicted

The world, mainly a wretched world of Imposture from Zenith to Nadir, seems as if threatening to fall rapidly to pieces, in huge ruin about our ears. It seems as if in this loss of the poor Irish potato, the last beggarly film that hid the Abyss from us were snatched away, and now its black throat lay yawning, visible even to fools.

How was one to demean oneself in these new circumstances? His advice to Duffy was *Bocca stretta, occhi sciolti* ('mouth shut, eyes open').

WHILE the Seceders were seeking a clearer definition of their policy, Duffy received from an unknown correspondent 'a letter of singular originality and vigour' that was to become 'the root of . . . many unexpected changes'. The writer was James Fintan Lalor, eldest son of Patrick Lalor, and brother of Peter Lalor, who, seven years later, was to make Australian history by leading an insurrection of miners at the Eureka Stockade, in Ballarat, Victoria.

Patrick Lalor, known as 'Honest Pat', was a gentleman farmer of Tinaskill, who had fought in the bloody tithe war of 1831, and represented Queen's County in the House of Commons. He had ten sturdy and vigorous sons. James Fintan was a painful exception; he was deaf, near-sighted, and ungainly from a spinal deformity.

But he was an intense and original thinker who had brooded long and deeply on Ireland's wrongs. In his letters to Duffy, he declared that he was once a Repealer, but had never joined the movement because its leaders and methods were 'essentially vile and base', and its 'craven crew' had 'a sworn dastard and forsworn traitor at the helm'. Nor would he join the projected Confederation if, even though honest, it were 'just as feeble, inefficient and ridiculous'. But Repeal was no longer the sole and important issue. A mightier question was in the land, one which dwarfed

Repeal into being 'a petty parish question . . .'

He was scornful of the pledge which Mitchel and many of the Young Irelanders had given to abstain from anything but moral force:

> I am quite willing to take such a pledge, if, and provided, the English Government agree to take it also; but 'if not, not'. Let England pledge not to argue the question by the prison, the convict-ship, or the halter; and I will readily pledge not to argue it in any form of physical logic. But dogs tied and stones loose is no bargain. Let stones be given up; or unmuzzle the wolf-dog. There is one at this moment in every cabin throughout the land, nearly fit already to be untied, and he will be savager by and by . . .'

Lalor ended his impassioned letter with a tribute to Duffy: 'I owe to you some gratitude', he wrote. *'You have given me a country*. Before your time I was an alien and an exile, though living in my own land. I hope you won't make me one again'.

Duffy immediately invited him to elaborate his views in the columns of *The Nation*. Lalor replied with three letters. The first, addressed to the landlords of Ireland, urged them to do justice to the tillers of the soil. The future of Ireland lay in possession of the land. A fight for the land would unite North and South, he argued. In another letter, he said he did not advocate an insurrection against an army of occupation. The small farmers and farm labourers — the only martial population Ireland possessed — were sick of 'bloodless agitation', and would never wield a weapon in favour of Repeal. But they could carry out what he called 'Moral Insurrection' [we would call it 'civil disobedience' today] by disobeying selected laws, beginning with a refusal to pay rent; 'By one move alone you can meet and match — and by that same move you will checkmate England'.

Lalor explained his principle explicitly to D'Arcy McGee: 'The entire ownership of Ireland, moral and material' was 'vested by right in the people of Ireland'. Only they and none but they were 'landowners and lawmakers'. All laws not made by them were null and void . . . "And he elaborated this argument in a Letter to the Landowners of Ireland, a letter that Karl Marx would have approved: 'Political rights are but paper and parchment', he wrote. 'It is the *social constitution* that determines the condition and character of a people, that makes and moulds the life of man'.

There was nothing fundamentally new in Lalor's call for an agrarian revolution, but what Duffy called his 'passionate, persuasive rhetoric' made an intense impression on some of the Confederates, particularly on Mitchel, Father Kenyon, Doheny and Reilly. Doheny after calling on Lalor, wrote to Duffy: 'I could not be persuaded that I had before me, in the poor, distorted, ill-favoured, hunch-backed little creature, the bold propounder of the singular doctrines in *The Nation* letters'.

Smith O'Brien and Duffy considered Lalor's policy impracticable, but Mitchel, after some doubts, was persuaded by Lalor and Kenyon to accept it in its entirety — as completely, Duffy later wrote, 'as a man adopts a new religion, or puts on a new suit of clothes'. But Duffy considered it 'a fantastic dream'. Lalor's . . . angry peasants, chafing like chained tigers, were creatures of the imagination — not the living people through whom we had to act. Famine, suffering, the servile doctrine of perpetual submission, had made them incapable of spontaneous self-assertion . . .'

Lalor's theory that Ireland would regain her freedom by abandoning the thinking and educated classes, and relying on the peasantry alone, seemed to Duffy 'the maddest absurdity that had entered a human brain'. In Lalor's case 'it was the monomania of a recluse'. In Mitchel's, 'it was founded on complete ignorance of the peasantry'. 'The people of Munster', Meagher wrote to Duffy, 'know as little of Mitchel as of Mahomet'.

Mitchel wanted *The Nation* to support Lalor's proposals editorially. This Duffy refused to do while conceding the right of Lalor, Mitchel and Kenyon to advocate them in signed letters. The irreconcilable differences between Duffy and Mitchel reached a climax when Duffy rejected two unsigned leading articles Mitchel had written for *The Nation*, defending negro slavery and denouncing the emancipation of the Jews, doctrines borrowed from Carlyle which Duffy thought 'unsuited to a spokesman of Irish liberty'.

In a letter to Lalor dated 4 January 1848, declaring his conversion to Lalor's theories, Mitchel wrote:

> *The Nation*, I fear has fallen into merest old-womanly drivelling and snivelling, and the people are without a friend at the press. In truth I fear it is but a lost people. I see nowhere any gleam of spirit, or spark of vitality in it . . . Yet it is not, I say, to be abandoned in despair.

He had been urged to return quietly to his profession of attorney, but had chosen to try a fall with the enemy 'on some ground or other', and convinced that a rising was imminent, was looking for an opportunity to get hold of a newspaper:

> As for the Confederates, it seems likely soon to go smash upon the very same rock that broke up *The Nation*, and I have determined to change its milk-and-water course, or else destroy it as a nuisance . . . The outlook before us is certainly dismal and black, but in any kind of storm or earthquake there is hope. Anything that may awaken the apathetic somnambulism in which the people walk . . . It is better to reduce the island to a cinder than let it rot into an obscure quagmire, peopled with reptiles.

Inevitably, at the end of January, Mitchel left *The Nation*. 'We parted without ill-will', Duffy wrote. And Mitchel gave formal notice of his retirement in a letter which, in view of his later attitude towards Duffy, has particular interest:

> I do not blame you *in the slightest particular;* and moreover I am quite certain I could not have worked in subordination to *any other man alive* near so long as I have with you. And lastly, that I give you credit in all that is past for acting on good and disinterested motives, with the utmost sincerity, and also the uniform kindness to me personally.

After trying to buy a Cork newspaper, the *Southern Reporter*, Mitchel launched his own paper *The United Irishman*. The first issue appeared on 12 February 1848.

NEWSPAPER history was made on 14 May 1842, when Herbert Ingram, a former Northampton newsvendor, launched his *Illustrated London News*. It was a politically uncommitted weekly presenting a lively and comprehensive cover of world news, illustrated with well-executed woodcuts — an innovation which Wordsworth condemned in a sonnet as 'a backward movement . . . back to childhood'. Despite the disapproval of the bard, the paper was an immediate success, and within a year claimed the astonishing circulation of 230,000 — more than four times the circulation of England's leading daily, the thunderous *Times*.

The Illustrated London News reported Irish affairs with admirable objectivity, and its illustrations brought home to thousands of English readers the horrors of the famine and its aftermath. But when events were moving to a crisis in 1848, it vigorously condemned 'the O'Briens, the Meaghers, the Mitchels, and all the raving democrats' for their 'noisy declarations . . . brutality of feeling . . . disregard for truth . . . scorn for justice . . . contempt for commonsense' and appeals to 'Irish passion and ignorance'.

'We know nothing in history more deplorable and disgraceful, more painful and disheartening, than the conduct of the physical force agitators in Ireland since their first split with the late Daniel O'Connell' it said on 19 July 1848. 'Self-glorification at the expense of the pockets of the people may have been the fault of that great leader; but he never indulged in self-glorification at the hazard of their blood'.

PUNCH AND PADDY.

"PUT AWAY THAT NASTY THING, AND LET'S HAVE A MERRY CHRISTMAS."

Punch, 1848

Six

Rebellion and Imprisonment

EIGHTEEN forty-eight. The year of the *Communist Manifesto*. The year of revolution and unrest. In England, Chartists demonstrate in their hundreds of thousands. In Europe, despotic regimes topple. An insurrection in January forces the King of Sicily to grant a constitution. Revolution sweeps through Rome, Florence, Turin, Vienna to Paris, where on 22 February, a bloodless coup ends the monarchy of Louis Phillippe. A republic is proclaimed with the distinguished poet, historian and orator, Alphonse de Lamartine, as president, and the left-wing radical, Alexandre de Ledru-Rollin, Minister for Foreign Affairs.

England becomes a sanctury of the deposed. Early in March, Louis Phillippe, grotesquely disguised as an Englishman ('Mr. Smith') in enormous goggles, and a rough pea-jacket, with a red-and-white comforter round his neck, and a newly sprouting beard, lands at Newhaven, and moves into an uncomfortable Surrey villa. His Prime Minister, Guizot, occupies a small house in Brompton, and the reactionary Austrian chancellor Metternich, is living as Herr von Meyer in a Hanover Square hotel.

Carlyle, who strongly disapproves of the spread of revolution in Europe, later writes: 'Everywhere immeasurable democracy rose, monstrous, loud, blatant, inarticulate as the voice of Chaos. Such was the history from the Baltic to the Mediterranean. Since the destruction of the old Roman Empire by the northern barbarians, I have known nothing similar'.

The French Revolution was welcomed with wild enthusiasm in Dublin. The Young Irelanders were swept up in an intoxicating spirit of revolt. Wordsworth's acclaim of the first French Revolution: 'Bliss was in that dawn to be alive, but to be young was very heaven'. [he was 28[was echoed by Duffy's: 'To young eyes, the New Commonwealth looked like a better Utopia — the golden age of human liberty and progress'. [he was 32]. 'The French news has fallen here like fire upon powder', he wrote to Smith O'Brien in London. Lalor asked: 'Will Ireland perish like a lamb, or will she turn as turns the baited lion'? And to Mitchel, the Revolution confirmed his belief in armed revolt.

Bonfires in many parts of Ireland flared a salute to France's new freedom, and banners inscribed 'Honour to France' and 'Despots beware', fluttered in many streets. A lighted transparency in Cork read: 'France is free — an example to the world'. Mangan contributed a translation of the *Marseillaise,* more passionate than poetic:

To ARMS *then citizens, all woes*
All curses on the coward that yields
The impure blood of our tyrant foes
Shall flow like rain upon our fields

Dublin booksellers advertised 'A Full Account of The Glorious Revolution in France', and the enterprising Mr. P. Rogers, 2 Upper Ormond Quay, announced on the front page of *The United Irishman:*

PROCLAMATION
A Republic for Ireland
Fellow Countrymen

A retrograde movement is now rendered impossible by the Intelligence and Public Spirit of the Citizens.
For centuries ye have groaned under the weight of high Prices and Inferior Articles relentlessly imposed by the Clothiers of Dublin. A REVOLUTION has been effected.
A PROVISIONAL GOVERNMENT, at the Call of the People, has been charged with the care of organising and securing National Pre-eminence in Dress.

President — High Fashion
Vice-President — Good Taste

Committee

Citizen Prompt Attention
Citizen Great Civility
Citizen Sterling Integrity
Citizen Sure Punctuality

Ordered

That the People henceforth are to pay for no more cloth than
they consume.

THE news of the revolution reached Dublin on the eve of a meeting of the Confederates. Duffy's principal colleagues had not returned from electioneering at Waterford, so, despite his dislike of public speaking and 'the hysterics of popular oratory', he was obliged to address the meeting. The chairman was Lord Wallscourt, son of a Union peer, a man of advanced social views, who believed in a partnership of capital and labour, and welcomed the French revolution as the harbinger of a better deal for the Irish worker.

Duffy told the meeting that the rise of the French republic gave the Irish people a great opportunity which would never come again in their lifetime. But to turn it to account they must forget their differences. The Confederates had recently declared that they would joyfully embrace any chance of fighting for Ireland in which not a class but the country could unite. Old and Young Ireland must be reconciled. The meeting vehemently agreed, though Lord Wallscourt, who had been a soldier, expressed a cautionary belief that when it came to blows, 'undisciplined peasants could never be got to stand shoulder to shoulder'.

In the pages of *The Nation,* Duffy was more rhetorical:

Ireland's opportunity — thank God, and France — has come at last! Its challenge rings in our ears like a call to battle, and warms our blood like wine . .
We must answer it if we would not be slaves forever. We must unite, we must act, we must leap all barriers but those which are divine; if needs be, we must die, rather than let this providential hour pass over us unliberated.

What did the Irish people want? 'An Irish Parliament, a native Privy Council, an Irish flag, a National Guard, social security and protection, and the control of all offices, taxes and public institutions in their own country; the rule and sovereignty of this Irish land.' And they desired that this might be won, if possible with the concurrence of all classes of Irishmen; but won it ought to be, 'at any price which might prove needful'. Duffy, then, did not rule out the possibility of bloodshed.

On 15 March 1848, an immense meeting of Confederates was held in the Music Hall, Abbey Street, Dublin. Smith O'Brien again urged the union of all parties to achieve the great end for which they were confederated. He warned that discretion was indispensable: 'If an outbreak took place at present, the Government could put it down in a week; or if it won a temporary success, they could starve the country by stopping the supplies of food obtained from abroad'.

But he invited all classes who desired the legislative independence of Ireland to enrol for service in a National Guard, and to fraternise with the millions of English Repealers [that is, Chartists] and above all with the people of France. The Confederates would probably send a deputation to the United States and recommend the formation of an Irish Brigade there, which would serve as the basis of an Irish army:

He had recently deprecated the advice that the people ought to be trained in military knowledge, but the circumstances were entirely altered, and he now thought that the attention of intelligent young men should be turned to such questions as how strong places can be captured and weak ones defended. More than a third of the British army consisted of Irishmen, and there were ten thousand of their countrymen serving in the Constabulary; with both these forces the people ought to cultivate friendly relations.

Meagher followed this plan of action with a 'passionate incitement' to give it effect as soon as was practicable. Once more, he soared into dizzy heights of rhetoric:

If the Government of Ireland insist upon being a Government of dragoons, and bombardiers, of detectives and light-infantry — then up with the barricades and invoke the God of Battles! Oh! think of the joy, the ecstasy, the glory of this old Irish nation, which in that hour will grow young and strong again. Should we fail, the country will not be worse than it is now. The sword of famine is less sparing than the bayonet of the soldier.

The meeting adopted an address to the French Republic, congratulating it on its success, and its respect for religion, private property, and public order. O'Brien, O'Gorman and Meagher, with a silk-weaver named Holywood, representing the workers, were appointed to carry the address to Paris.

Five days later, an open-air meeting was held in the fields ('a piece of reclaimed slob', according to the *Daily News*) adjoining the Hibernian tavern, near the North Wall. Duffy was among the great crowd (variously estimated according to the politics of the reporter, at 'only 3,000' and 'not less than 15,000'), which again acclaimed the French Revolution. On the platform with him were Smith O'Brien, Thomas Meagher, Thomas Devlin Reilly, Richard O'Gorman, Edward Brennan — and despite the separation — John Mitchel.

On St. Patrick's Day Meagher, who had attended a meeting of 15,000 Chartists in Manchester, assured the crowd that the English people would support them. He owed it 'as a loyal subject of the Queen' to announce that if one drop of Irish blood was shed by the armed Government, there would be ten thousand shed in England, and the workhouses of the chief cities of England would be burnt to the ground in revenge. (Loud cheers were given for the English people.) Reilly hinted that a National Guard would soon be formed. He knew no franchise like the possession of a gun (loud cheers). He would rather give the peasant a gun and teach him how to use it than give him the right to elect a Poor Law guardian. McGee urged them to wait a little longer — until Britain was engaged in a foreign war. They should wait until French steamers were letting off their steam in Falmouth and Portsmouth. Then, when their opportunity was ripe, if the Irish people did not grasp it, he would say, may they be slaves forever.

Introducing another address, from the citizens of Dublin to the citizens of the French Republic, Mitchel demanded:

> Who amongst us did not feel his heart bound stronger and his blood run quicker, when he heard of the mighty and generous nation arising in her majesty and, at a single effort, flinging off the strongest tyranny in Europe, with its endless chains of fortresses, barracks and batteries, like dew-drops from the lion's mane?

Loud cheers greeted this poetic query. The Address began: 'As slaves should address freemen — as a land which has yet its independence to assert, and its social freedom to attain — should address a sovereign state and a republic, we address you citizens'! It was decided that it should be presented by Smith O'Brien and O'Gorman, representing the citizens of Dublin; Martin MacDermott, representing the Confederates of Liverpool; Meagher, representing the Repealers of Manchester; and Holywood, again representing the workers. The meeting ended quietly, but a crowd marched to the closed and guarded gates of the Castle, and serenaded Clarendon with loud and prolonged groans.

The following day Smith O'Brien, Meagher and Mitchel were arrested. O'Brien and Meagher were charged with having made seditious speeches and Mitchel, with having published seditious articles. All were immediately released on bail, and O'Brien and Meagher set out for Paris. The night before he left London, O'Brien wrote to Duffy, expressing his concern for the future of the cause, which he feared might be wrecked by the excesses of Mitchel and his followers. (An article in the *United Irishman*, attributed to Reilly, recommending that vitriol should be thrown on soldiers if a rising took place, had been widely quoted in the English press.'

ONE of the fiercest rebel voices was that of Father Kenyon of Templederry. Addressing a meeting at Templederry on the borders of Tipperary and Limerick, he referred to the prosecution of O'Brien, Meagher and Mitchel; 'These brave men are determined to fight the Government — and conquer the Government', he told the cheering crowd. He then asked: 'Are you ready to die for Ireland'?

Several voices: 'Yes, yes, all ready to die this minute'.

Kenyon: 'Do you fear death, you starved and whipped and lashed wretches — do you fear death'? (Cries of 'No, no').

Father Kenyon then said that if things went on as they had gone, another million would die within a year and slavery would be innate in their race. No great revolution was ever brought about by mere moral force, he continued. Physical force was the only thing to right a nation. They ought to prepare for the fight, they ought to get arms privately, and when the moment came, arise and do battle bravely.

Another fire-breathing cleric, Father Bermingham, of Borrisokane, wrote to *The Nation*: 'First make your peace with God. Secondly, arm quietly and without tumult . . . Recollect that England's necessity is Ireland's opportunity. Wait for it. Bide your time'. The Bishop of Killaloe, the Right Reverend Dr. Kennedy, passed sentence of suspension on Kenyon and Bermingham until they retracted their recent speeches and letters.

Before the Irish delegation reached Paris, the Foreign Secretary, Lord Palmerston, had warned Lamartine, through the British Ambassador, Lord Normanby, not to interfere in England's domestic affairs, 'such as Catholic Emancipation, Irish agitation, Repeal of the Union, and other matters with which no foreign Government has any right to meddle'. If France did so, Britain might withdraw its Embassy.

The warning had the desired effect. Ledru-Rollin favoured giving Ireland immediate assistance (in 1843, at a public dinner in Paris held to express sympathy with the Irish cause, he had said: 'Let England understand that if she attempts to overcome legitimate rights by violent and coercive measures, France is ready to lend an oppressed people . . . experienced heads, resolute hearts, and sturdy arms'.) But Lamartine now offered the delegation flowery expressions of goodwill — and nothing more. 'We are not astonished to see today a deputation from Ireland', he declared:

Ireland knows how deeply her destinies, her sufferings, and her successive advances in the path of religious liberty, of unity, and of constitutional equality with the other parts of the United Kingdom have, at all times, moved the hearts of Europe. Rest assured, therefore, that you will find in France, under the Republic, a response to all the sentiments that you express . . .

Then rhetoric gave way to realism: 'As regards other encouragements, it would be neither expedient for us to hold nor for you to receive them . . . We are at peace and we are desirous of remaining on good terms of equality, not with this or that part of Great Britain, but with Great Britain entire . . .'

According to the embittered Mitchel, the 'foolish old poet', having made up his mind that the Irish would be seeking armed aid from France, had prepared his reply before the address was presented. (Lamartine had an English wife, which immediately made him suspect in Ireland.) The British Government considered the reply salutary reading for the Irish. It reprinted the text in full and posted it up on all the police-stations in Ireland.

Smith O'Brien was not discouraged. He told a deputation of Irish residents in Paris: 'We have seen and heard enough to feel that, were Ireland to demand assistance, France will be ready to send fifty thousand of her bravest citizens to fight for her liberty'.

O'CONNELL's death had exacerbated the conflict between Old and Young Ireland. Most Irish Catholics still followed the dead leader. The Young Irelanders were accused of having murdered him. 'The physical force men, whenever they meet for spouting have to be escorted home by two or three hundred police', Clarendon wrote to Henry Reeve, 'or not one of them would escape alive from the moral persuasion party . . .' Nearly a year after the death of the Liberator, a Limerick mob gave a violent demonstration of this.

After Smith O'Brien returned to Dublin from Paris, an enlistment form for a National Guard was prepared, and plans for a Council of Three Hundred went ahead. Each member of the Council was to have, if possible, a constituency of a thousand enrolled men, and to contribute at least £100 to a national treasury. This would ensure a nation-wide movement, organised with authority.

O'Brien and Meagher arranged to visit the chief towns of Munster, beginning with Limerick, to review the Repealers and assess the spirit of the people. Ignoring the emphatic appeal from O'Brien to keep away, Mitchel insisted on participating. He had recently offended the Old Irelanders by savagely attacking O'Connell in the *United Irishman,* and when he reached Limerick on his own, a crowd jeered and hustled him as he alighted from his coach. He hastened to his hotel and shut himself up. That night, the Old Irelanders paraded the streets, bearing an effigy of Mitchel and placards inscribed: 'Mitchel the calumniator of O'Connell' and 'Mitchel the slanderer of the Catholic religion'. Next day, Smith O'Brien and Meagher arrived to speak at a soiree attended by about three hundred men and some women. What followed was described exuberantly in the *Spectator:*

> The speeches had scarcely begun when a shower of stones came through the windows into the room — a mob had assembled, and was preparing to burst into the house. The window-shutters were closed, and boards were nailed up; the door was strengthened with planks fastened athwart. Some of the men were struck by the stones, but the females behaved with courageous self-possession. The speakers resumed, and had gone on for nearly an hour, when signs appeared of desperate doings without. Smoke curled through the shutters of the windows — a blazing tar barrel had been raised against them outside; and the door began to yield under tremendous shocks — a score of men were battering it with a huge beam of timber. The females having been conveyed into safer rooms, those of the men who had pistols, pikes and daggers, got them ready. A sally was resolved on. As the door was loosened, the mob pressed in. The first man who entered was shot in the thigh, and fell. This staggered the assailants, and they receded somewhat. Mr. Smith O'Brien raised a cry of 'Repeal'! but was answered by shouts of 'Death to Mitchel'! A vigorous Irish row was waged in the streets for some time; the weapons of the Confederates giving them much advantage. Cries of 'Don't hurt O'Brien'! or 'Don't hurt Meagher'! were heard, but no practical distinctions were made, and Mr. O'Brien was at last borne off the field, wounded and bleeding.

When O'Brien appeared in Court next day, to answer the sedition charge, his head was strapped and bandaged over and it was said that some of his ribs were broken, and four of his teeth knocked out. He announced his intention of retiring from public life until the Irish forgot their senseless divisions. After much persuasion, he agreed to continue as an active member of the Confederate on condition that he never be made responsible for Mitchel's opinions. Mitchel and Reilly then left the Confederation, stating their reasons in letters which were made public.

The news of the attack on O'Brien was received in London with great satisfaction. The Funds rose, as though England had won a great victory, and the Press, especially *Punch,* was jubilant. Thackeray filled a whole page with a satirical account of 'The Battle of Limerick'. Other contributors seized on the amusing story, and *Punch* published 'English Definitions For An Irish Dictionary', in which two entries read:

> *Moral Force* — Brick-bats, fruit in an advanced state of decomposition, blazing tar-barrels, and shillelaghs.
> *Physical Force* — Threatening to use pikes, and running away from them when used by others.

T HE *United Irishman* took its motto from Wolfe Tone: 'Our independence must be had at all hazards. If the men of property will not support us, they must fail; we can support ourselves by the aid of that numerous and respectable class of the community, the men of no property'. Under the general heading, 'The War Department', Mitchel conducted a series of homely articles on guerilla warfare. 'Our great strength', said one, 'lies in the fact, that we oppose to disciplined troops a system of warfare to which they are wholly unaccustomed'. Explicit instructions were given on the use of the pike, which Emmet had described as 'the weapon of the

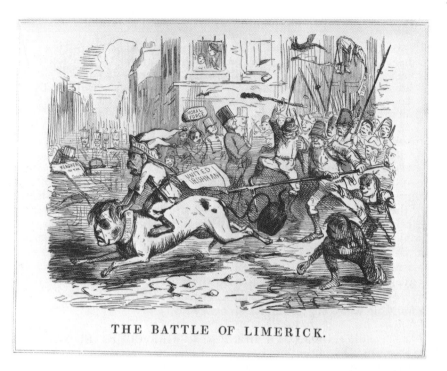

THE BATTLE OF LIMERICK.

Punch, 1848

brave'. The first business of pikemen was to learn to charge in line:

> This should always be done in a trot. The pike should be grasped with both hands — the right hand resting on the right hip, the hands from two to two feet six inches asunder, and the shaft quite horizontal. The files of pikemen accustomed to act together should be as nearly as possible of equal height, the line in charging should be kept with the most perfect precision, and the points all brought to bear on a right line, and simultaneously. This is the perfection of a pike charge . . . If the thing be rightly done, as we have explained, no column of infantry can resist for an instant.

There were also do-it-yourself hints, based on the experience of Parisian revolutionaries, on the construction of barricades from iron railings, lamp-posts, carts, felled trees, furniture, stones, mud and rubbish, and on the harassment of troops in city streets by dropping window-pots, brickbats, logs of wood, chimney-pieces and heavy furniture on them from the security of roof-tops, an operation which 'ladies or chambermaids' could perform as effectively as men. 'Bottles, delph and such missiles mixed with these not only knock down and wound infantry, but render the streets impassible to cavalry and artillery. A horse may dance on eggs, but no squadron can charge over broken bottles'. These 'admirable weapons' abounded in every house,

> and if any engineering urchin take a soda-water bottle, or small flask of thick glass, dry inside, filled with bits of stone, or iron, or metal of any sort — nails, for instance — and with coarse gunpowder thrown into the interstices — cork it tight (the cork being perforated), and then attach a judiciously adjusted fuse, he will possess a domestic bomb or grenade by which he can either blow his arm off, or act with deadly effect against cavalry or infantry below — especially cavalry. To these missiles, from windows and house-tops, revolutionary citizens add always boiling-water, or grease, or, better, cold vitriol, if available. Molten lead is good, but too valuable — it should be always cast in bullets, and allowed to cool.

By following these simple procedures, the *United Irishman* pointed out, every street could be made a defile. Even more ingenious was the advice addressed to female insurrectionaries. They should procure a number of hoops [presumably extracted from their crinolines] and a basin filled with oil of turpentine, or tar, into which the hoops were dipped:

> When thus prepared, the hoop would be fit for the last operation — namely, setting fire to it and throwing it horizontally on the red coats, whose bayonets would very conveniently serve to catch it, and thus allow it to pass over their necks, where it would do its business. The great advantages of large hoops over smaller ones is quite apparent, as the former would promote fraternisation between two or more of the enemy by encircling them.

Writing anonymously in *Punch* under the heading 'From the United Irishwoman', Thackeray offered female street fighters additional suggestions:

> A grand piano sent down upon a troop of hussars will play such a sonata over their heads as the scoundrels never marched off to . . . A guardsman won't

look well with a copper coal scuttle for a helmet . . . A hot saddle of mutton, flung by cook into the face of a bawling Saxon Colonel, will silence him . . . Old port makes excellent grape-shot; and I don't know any better use you can make of a magnum of Latouche than to floor an Englishman with it . . . A good large cheese would be found rather indigestible by a Saxon, if dropped on his nose . . . There is a lady in Leeson street who vows to fling her Angora cat and her pet spaniel at the military . . . You will, of course, empty the china closets on the rascals, and all the bedroom foot-baths and washing-basins. Have them ready, and the chest-of-drawers balancing on the windowsill. . .

But the Government, unlike Mr. Thackeray, did not treat Mitchel with derision. The Lord Lieutenant, Lord Clarendon, was convinced that the inflammatory writings in the *United Irishman* portended an imminent uprising. Once more, the Duke of Wellington, then in his seventy-ninth year, answered the call of his country. Under his command, troops, arms and ammunition poured into Dublin. Soldiers occupied the University, the Old Parliament House and the Customs House, the Royal Barracks, the Portobello Barracks, the Royal Military Hospital, and other strategic positions and, in Duffy's words, 'the striplings of Trinity College, the elderly antiquities of the Royal Dublin Society, and the clerks in the Bank of Ireland', were invited to take up arms. Similar precautions were taken in other towns. Northern Irishmen were armed, and told to prepare for civil war. Ordanance pieces were brought into the Castle, and the fleet, which had been off Lisbon was ordered to the Cove of Cork. 'I think things are in a very ticklish position,' wrote Sir Charles Napier to the Admiralty on 5 April.

IN May 1847, George William Frederick Villiers, fourth Earl of Clarendon, had succeeded Lord Bessborough as Lord Lieutenant of Ireland. Duffy's picture of him is not flattering. 'His training in public affairs had been acquired in various subordinate employments in Ireland and Spain' Duffy wrote,'. . . and his good-natured friends affirmed that his intellect was ruined by his long apprenticeship to the petty arts of diplomacy, and his nerves shattered by eternal tobacco. He was fit enough, however, for his post — which, in quiet times, might be filled by a lay figure — till the French revolution came to disturb his tranquillity'.

But Miss Woodham Smith writes: 'He was universally agreed to be the best man for the post, and O'Connell, with whom he had been on good terms, had regarded him as a desirable Lord-Lieutenant. He was noted for charm and tact . . . he was industrious, and both a liberal and an aristocrat'.

Clarendon was not happy about what he described as 'the terrible task imposed on me'. Soon after his appointment, he wrote: 'I go to Ireland without making myself the smallest illusion as to the more than probability of failure that awaits me . . . Moreover I fear that the distress next autumn and winter will be greater than the last . . .' 'The real difficulty', he told his friend Henry Reeve of *The Times*, 'lies with the people themselves. They are always in the mud . . . their idleness and helplessness can scarcely be believed'.

To Mitchel, Clarendon was 'Her Majesty's Executioner-General and General Butcher in Ireland'. He denounced 'those drivelling doctrines of "legality" and "constitutional agitation" which were preached for forty years by your late ally, Daniel O'Connell':

> Ireland, if I can help it, will not much longer endure talk of *law*, when there is no law but rope and steel — or peace, when there is no peace but the grave, or *patience and perseverance* when human beings are daily, hourly, withering and perishing for want of food, in the midst of abundance.

A fortnight later he advised a gathering 'for the love of God to get themselves guns . . . a very good serviceable rifle could be had for £3 . . .' And he referred to events in Europe. 'The King of France has run away from Paris, the King of Prussia is hiding in Potsdam, the Emperor of Austria is packing his portmanteau to run from Vienna, but Lord Clarendon still sits in Dublin Castle'. He (Mitchel) meant to call on them, 'if they would not remain slaves for ever, to rise up . . . at an early day, or perhaps an early night, and smash through the Castle of Dublin or tear it down'. The audience responded with deafening cheers and cries of 'Pikes!' 'Pikes!' At the Castle Clarendon found the situation nerve-wracking. On 30 March he reported to Lord John Russell that he received so many assassination threats that he only went out in the carriage or a short walk in the Park, 'which makes me nearly a State prisoner . . . the life I lead is hardly endurable'.

According to Duffy, Clarendon 'was persuaded Mitchel would not have employed the language of menace and exasperation he used week after week unless an insurrection was ready to break out. He had assumed, indeed that St. Patrick's Day (17 March 1848) was fixed for rising in Dublin'.

At the end of March, Clarendon wrote to the Home Secretary, Sir George Grey, that 'the time to suppress the public preaching of sedition had come', but a week later, on 4 April, the Marquis of Londonderry reassured his fellow-peers that he was not one who felt alarm at the present state of Ireland; and as to the conduct of Mitchel and other persons who were endeavouring to excite the population, it was an extraordinary specimen of Lord Clarendon's prudence to let them take their own course 'until he was ready to put his hand upon the miscreants'.

Mitchel's exhortations reached a crescendo of violence. 'I have a mission to bear a hand in the final destruction of the bloody old "British Empire" . . .' he wrote in April. 'Against that Engine of Hell, a thousand ghosts of my slaughtered countrymen shriek nightly for vengeance . . . Thank God they are arming. Young men everywhere in Ireland . . . cherish their rifles as the very apple of their eyes'. The ghosts may have numbered thousands, but the young men who cherished rifles, or any arms, were few. To assist them, Mitchel offered advice on the organisation of guerilla warfare clubs, where arms could be bought on easy weekly instalments — two shillings a week for riflemen, one shilling for musketeers, and only threepence for pikemen. When bayonets were not available, he recommended a 'strong English reaping hook, straightened, with a saw-edge ground sharp, and rounded, and a socket-hilt welded to the tang . . . attached to a duck gun or fowling piece'. And a scythe blade fixed to a long shaft was as deadly as a pike. *The Times* Dublin correspondent reported that 'the run for pikes' was on the increase; to meet the demand, very inferior weapons were on sale, at prices ranging from 8d to one shilling. But there were ready sales for superior articles, costing as much as 3/6d.

The Limerick Rifle Club practised firing at a chalk sketch inscribed in large letters 'Clarendon'. One marksman planted a ball on the tip of the Viceroy's nose, 'a feat which elicited much laughter', reported the *Freeman's Journal.* In Cork, six hundred Young Irelanders in regular military order marched through the streets singing the Irish 'Marseillaise'.

The Government was equally active. In Dublin, Leinster House, now the home of the Irish Parliament, was fitted up for three hundred infantry and a strong squadron of cavalry. A company of sappers and marines was quartered in the barracks of the Linen Hall and two companies of infantry in Trinity College. Even the austere members of the Royal Dublin Society decided to arm themselves with guns and accoutrements. The *Cork Constitution* reported that six hundred stands of arms, with gunpowder, balls, grenades and shot, had been landed at Monkstown Pier, to be sent to Clonmel, and five hundred stands were being sent to Fermoy, it being the intention of the Government to arm the loyal inhabitants.

THE Government now rushed through a new measure ('with the speed of an express train', Duffy wrote) to deal with the Irish threat: The Treason Felony Act. Under this Act, which was supported by Tories and Whigs alike, sedition, formerly punishable by a brief imprisonment, became treason-felony, punishable by transportation for life. It created a new offence. Any person who 'either by writing or by open and advised speaking' sought to intimidate the Queen or her Parliament, was guilty of treason-felony. Thus writing or speaking of insurrection in Ireland became a felony. Justifying the measure Sir George Grey read an inflammatory article of Mitchel's from the *United Irishman,* and quoted a speech of Duffy's about the Paris deputation.

Smith O'Brien arrived in London from Paris on the eve of the second reading, and found that his mission to France had aroused great indignation. Friends warned him of a hostile reception if he attended the debate. But he was not to be deterred from opposing the Bill. 'Disregarding these suggestions, I took my usual seat', he wrote in a personal memorandum. 'I defended myself against the imputations cast upon me, denounced the system of government and legislation adopted towards Ireland, and retorted defiance against the prosecution with which I was menaced . . .'.

The House was in constant uproar during O'Brien's speech, which was punctuated with groans and ironical cheers. A reporter compared the clamour to the howling of a menagerie. O'Brien warned Ministers that if they suppressed free speech in Ireland and denied the Irish a free

Parliament, they would encounter the risk of a Republic:

> I have been called a traitor (a tremendous burst of cheers followed this
> sentence, twice renewed before silence was restored.) I do not profess
> disloyalty to the Queen of England (ironical applause). But if it be treason to
> profess disloyalty to this House, and to the government of Ireland by the
> Parliament of Great Britain — if that be treason, I avow the treason — ('oh!'
> and great excitement). Nay, more, I say it shall be the study of my life to
> overthrow the dominion of this Parliament over Ireland — ('hear, hear', and
> cries of 'oh! oh!').

He refuted the suggestion that he had gone to France to solicit armed aid.
Had he done so, he should have come back accompanied by a 'tolerably
large legion of troops' (some laughter and 'Oh! Oh! Oh!'). But Irish
freedom must be won by Irish courage and Irish firmness. He had no
desire to impose on his country one description of servitude in the place
of another ('hear, hear'). If its redemption were won by foreign bayonets,
it could only be retained by foreign bayonets, and it was not his desire or
intention to place his country under foreign domination. And he avowed
the fact, whether it were illegal or not, that he had been instrumental in
asking his countrymen to arm:

> I conceive that under the present circumstances of all nations, it is the duty of
> every man to obtain the possession and learn the use of arms . . . and I conceive
> that it is the peculiar duty of the Irish people to obtain the possession of arms
> at a time when you tell them you are prepared to crush their expression of
> opinion, not by argument, but by brute force (loud cries of 'Oh! Oh!' and
> expressions of disapprobation.)

On 10 April, the day of the debate, the Chartists planned to assemble on
Kennington Common, in South London, and to march to the House of
Commons with a giant petition said to contain more than five million
signatures. Fearing revolution, the Government massed soldiers at
strategic points, brought four batteries of field guns into London, and
swore in tens of thousand of special constables — some put the figure at
250,000 — including Prince Louis Napoleon, then living in London. The
Chartists were not allowed to cross the Thames, and the great
demonstration was a failure, as Lord Palmerston exultantly reported to
Normanby next day: 'Yesterday was a glorious day, the Waterloo of
peace and order . . .' he wrote. 'The result will produce a good and calming
effect on this and the Sister Island'. And he added: 'Smith O'Brien
surpassed himself last night in dullness, bad taste and treason'. It was
Smith O'Brien's last appearance in the House of Commons, which he had
entered as the young member for Ennis almost exactly twenty years
before.

A week later, Palmerston wrote to Normanby: 'What we hear from
Ireland tallies with what you wrote me a few days ago, that there can be
no decided and extensive outbreak till the potato and grain harvest is in,
as men must eat and be able to fight. I trust we shall be able to keep them
quiet after all'.

Four days later, the Treason Felony Act received the Royal Assent.

The Act 'suppressed liberty of speech and liberty of the Press in controversies on the Irish question . . .' Duffy wrote. 'Had it existed in O'Connell's time, he might have been deported to Botany Bay for the Mallow defiance . . . I determined in such a crisis to reiterate, with unequivocal plainness, the ends we sought and the means we employed'.

His five-thousand word article, 'The Creed of The Nation' appeared on 29 April. 'A new era has commenced in Irish journalism — the reign of terror', it began. 'The jailer of Kilmainham is henceforth censor of the Irish press. Whoever shall adjure the young men of Ireland to *be* men, to abandon the sensual and slavish vices that degrade them, and lift up their souls to contemplate the examples of *Tone* and *Davis,* will write with the fetters of the jailer grasping for their hands'. (Unfortunately for the social historian, Duffy did not define these 'sensual and slavish vices'.) 'The law officers of the Crown, I am assured, await but this very issue of *The Nation* to make a formidable example . . . For myself, I will not yield an inch in this just quarrel with my life'.

Duffy emphatically refuted the often-repeated charges that *The Nation* was a Jacobin journal, or the Confederation an anarchical movement. Although he was a nationalist, liberty to him had never meant, and never would mean 'any barbarous community of ignorance and rapine — any right to murder or rob'. He would combat tyranny not with a new tyranny but with justice. He relied on the sword of the patriot, not the bludgeon of the assassin. And as revolution was inevitable it might be necessary to wield the sword:

> I love peace, I fear disorder — I hate anarchy; but the sudden and violent disorder of an hour, though it pain us to the quick, is better than the perpetual hopelessness of disease. If this is our only resource, let it come. But let it be understood that what the Irish people claimed, was just and eminently reasonable, and ought to be conceded without a physical contest.

Ireland could be contented with an Independent Parliament, elected by the widest possible suffrage, a responsible minister for Ireland, and a Viceroy of Irish birth. Such a Parliament would inevitably establish Tenant Right, abolish the Established Church, and endeavour to settle the claims of labour upon a solid and satisfactory basis. It would, probably, settle the church question, by providing a reasonable stipend for the Catholic, Protestant and Presbyterian clergy. But Duffy did not believe that it would go one step further in the direction of revolution. He would prefer such a settlement, made by negotiation, to a republic won by insurrection, which would plant 'deadly animosities' between Irishmen. He believed that democracy was the destiny of the world, but he did not think Ireland was in a condition to become a republic. The sudden transition from provincialism to republicanism was a doubtful experiment.

Duffy professed 'no enthusiastic loyalty' to the reigning Royal family. But

> If I could choose for my country I would prefer at this hour to see it ruled as a sovereign state by its own Senate, under the sway of the Crown. I would prefer it simply because the settled authority of an ancient Monarchy affords

the best guarantee for order and liberty, and the surest bulwark for the present against the struggles of selfish and rival ambitions.

Ireland's desperate condition during and since the famine, was attributed to British mismanagement imposed 'at the point of a bayonet'. But the Prime Minister of England, 'looking upon the awful desolation which has made our country a graveyard and lazar-house, tells us . . . that he will resist our just claims with the sword of the empire. What can we answer with but the sword of Ireland?. . .'

This, then was 'The Creed of The Nation' which Duffy believed was substantially the creed of the Irish Confederation. They do not demand Republicanism, he concluded,

> they demand the legislative independence of Ireland and will guard it jealously . . . But in a free parliament, or a free congress, the rights of private property, the just rights of every class in the state will be sacred. I proclaimed at the opening of this movement and I will practise to the end of it . . . a national amnesty; full forgiveness of the past — the quarrels of yesterday, the quarrels of 300 years.
>
> If ever the spirit of sectarian ascendancy or social disorganisation develops itself into a power in Ireland, may I perish dishonorably if I shall not be found combating it. These are my opinions. I believe they are founded on Justice and Humanity. If they are Felony by the law of England, it will be so much the worse for the law, in the end.

Smith O'Brien wrote to Duffy: 'I have read with extreme pleasure your letter . . . Without venturing to speak on behalf of the Confederation, I think it right under the present circumstances, to state I am fully prepared to hold myself responsible, both morally and legally, for the sentiments contained in that letter'.

'The Creed of the Nation' with O'Brien's letter as a postscript, was reprinted as a booklet. To the watchdog of the Castle, there was little to choose between the attitude of Duffy, as expressed in this *Creed,* and that of Mitchel. Both had obviously come within the grasp of the new Treason Felony Act.

ON 1 May, the nose-blowing Major Bryan represented the Confederation at a Chartist Convention held in London. He told the Convention that the English Government had commenced a ruthless persecution of the best and bravest of Ireland's servants and would be dealt with 'in a most cruel and bloodthirsty manner'.

With the Treason Felony Act on the Statute Book, the Government acted swiftly to apply it. Clarendon issued a proclamation forbidding the enrolment of the National Guard or the election of the Council of Three Hundred. Addressing a meeting in the Music Hall, Duffy held up a copy of the proclamation and asked were they to be paralysed at the sight of it? He was answered with cries of 'Never! Never!' and cheers. 'The answer should be simple' said Duffy 'and here it is.' He tore the proclamation into pieces, trampled on the fragments, and declared, amid cheers, that they would go on in spite of it. The cheering that followed was 'deafening and long continued'.

On 13 May, Mitchel was arrested and charged with sedition. He was imprisoned in Dublin's Newgate goal to await trial. Two days later when O'Brien came up for trial, the Clubs mustered ten thousand men to escort him, in military formation, from his residence in Ontario Terrace to the Four Courts. 'The jury was carefully packed', says Duffy, 'but this time nationality had penetrated into unexpected places'. There was a disagreement. Of the three Catholics on the jury, two were for conviction. The third, said to have been swayed by the brilliant speech of the defence counsel, Isaac Butt, refused to convict, and O'Brien was freed. Next day, Meagher was tried. Again, the jury was packed. Only one Catholic was allowed on it, but a Quaker stubbornly held out for an acquittal, and Meagher, too, was freed.

MITCHEL'S trial was the first under the Treason Felony Act. 'The failure of the prosecution against O'Brien and Meagher had enraged the Government', says Duffy. To ensure Mitchel's conviction, it packed the jury 'with a naked and cynical scorn for public opinion'. There were 3,000 Catholics on the jury-list. None were permitted to serve. The proceedings were brief, and the conclusion foregone. It was necessary only to prove that Mitchel owned and published the *United Irishman*. Mitchel's counsel, the venerable Robert Holmes, based his defence on the argument he had used in Duffy's trial for publishing the railway article. Ireland was an enslaved country, he contended, and its people were entitled to obtain liberty even by civil war. His concluding words had echoes of Robert Emmet's memorable speech from the dock:

> I speak not merely for my client. I speak for you and your children, and your children's children. I speak not for myself — my lamp of life is fluttering and must soon be extinguished; but were I now standing on the brink of the grave, and uttering the last words of expiring nature, I would say 'May Ireland be happy, May Ireland be free'.

Despite Holmes' eloquence, it took the jury less than three hours to return a verdict of guilty. Next day, as Mitchel stood in the dock, he was asked if he had anything to say before being sentenced. He replied that he had been convicted by a packed jury, arrayed by a partisan sheriff — a man who was not a sheriff but a juggler. One of the judges, Baron Lefroy, interrupted sharply to protect the sherriff, and sentenced Mitchel to fourteen years transportation. Mitchel received the savage sentence calmly: 'I have acted in this business from the first under a strong sense of duty', he said. 'I do not repent of anything I have done; and I believe that the course which I have opened is only commenced. The Roman who saw his hand burning to ashes before the tryant promised that three hundred should follow out his enterprise. Can I not promise for one, for two, for three — aye, for hundreds?' As he spoke, he pointed to his associates who thronged the galleries. They replied with cries of 'Promise for me, Mitchel, — promise for me!' There was a rush to the dock to embrace him, and a shout of execration against the judges, who hurried from the Bench in panic.

THE COMMISSION COURT.—MR. MITCHELL, AT THE BAR.

Illustrated London News, 27 May 1848

Mitchel was led from the Court heavily manacled, and escorted by a little army of dragoons. Within an hour he was on board the steam war-sloop *Shearwater,* that was awaiting him, confidently anticipating the verdict, in Dublin Bay. His destination was Spike Island, the convict depot at the Cove of Cork, and, ultimately, Van Dieman's Land, by way of Bermuda.

He still believed that an armed rebellion was inevitable, and that the Confederates would be able to rescue him. As he looked out of the prison-van that drove him from the court, he saw a great crowd, and asked hopefully where they were going. The answer was 'to a flower-show'. The Government, too, was convinced a rescue would be attempted. The possibility had been examined by the Confederates and reluctantly dismissed. There were thirty Confederates Clubs in Dublin city and country, with memberships from two to five hundred. Meagher and O'Gorman inspected them all and reported that 'the people were unprepared, unarmed, and incapable of being even roughly disciplined for such an attempt'. And despite the optimistic assumptions of Mitchel and Lalor that the trampled peasantry would rise, there was not a single Club in the agrarian districts. On the other hand, the Government had more than ten thousand regular troops in Dublin, apart from the constabulary, and controlled all strategic points.

DUFFY blamed Mitchel for the impotence of the Confederates. 'He had scoffed at the necessity of systematic preparation . . . there was no depot of arms and ammunition. He had declared that a leader would come with the necessity, and there was no officer among the Confederates who could take charge of a company . . . In truth, the insensate policy of deriding preparations had borne its natural fruit . . .' Duffy quoted approvingly the judgment of an Irish writer, John Savage, one of the contributors to the *Irish Tribune,* on his countrymen: 'The Irish are always ready for revolution, but they never make ready'. If revolution were inevitable, Duffy was determined to make them ready.

The day after Mitchel's deportation, Father Kenyon and T.B. McManus, with an unidentified 'gentleman from the North of England', called on Duffy to demand what could be done for the cause. Duffy said they should make the preparations Mitchel had derided. They should send to France for officers and arms, and to America for officers and money. (He did not say how the French Government's policy of non-intervention was to be overcome.) McManus boldly promised to seize two of the largest Irish steamers at Liverpool, and load them with arms and ammunition from an army depot at Chester Castle. A Conference of Confederates was held at which, Duffy wrote, 'for the first time, measures were taken to obtain money, arms and officers from abroad, to make a diversion in England, and procure the co-operation of the Irish residents there, and to prepare particular local men to expect the event'.

One Confederate was chosen as an agent in France, and two, for the mission to America. One of these carried a commission, signed by four persons known to the Irish in the United States. This document was smeared with gunpowder and carried in a loaded pistol, so that it could be fired off if the bearer was arrested; a refinement on the traditional method of swallowing an incriminating document. 'Two or three signal facts will enable us to gauge the hopes and fears of the hour', Duffy wrote later. The Chartists sent two representatives to Dublin, promising immediate co-operation when the rebels struck. Clarendon sent his children to England for safety, and *The Times* organised an alternative news service by way of Cork and Bristol, in case Dublin should fall to the Confederates.

The Confederates made little secret of their activities. *The Times* reported on the rapid increase in the Clubs. On 6 June, Meagher told a mass meeting in the Music Hall that 'The fate of Ireland must this year be determined'. The end was at hand, he announced, and he counselled them to 'get arms and prepare'. Dublin Castle, through spies and informers, was kept well informed of the preparations for rebellion. The police tried by bribes and threats to induce men to testify against Confederate leaders. They offered Matthew Fannin, who had been in the same Club as Duffy, up to £500 (equivalent to at least $20,000 today) for evidence against him. Mr. Fannin blandly insisted that Duffy had always preached obedience to the law, that he regarded men who preached war as 'desperadoes' and rifle clubs as mere 'fooleries'.

John O'Connell now intimated that he was ready for a conciliation with the Young Irelanders. The long-delayed conference, after seven days' debate, agreed on a compromise. The Repeal Association and the Confederation were to be replaced by a single body, known as the Irish League. The Clubs, however, were to remain, and to be increased in numbers, as the nucleus of a National Guard, armed if they so chose. But O'Connell, who had been one of the delegates to the conference, refused to join the League. It was rumoured that he was being used as a tool of Clarendon's, to keep the priests and Confederates apart. More charitably, Duffy thought he was merely influenced 'by doubt and trepidation, for his mind was as unsteady as a quagmire'.

O'Connell's defection was a great blow to the Repealers, for in Duffy's words, 'it withdrew from the cause a name which still swayed the masses, as the name of the Emperor swayed the French peasantry when he was nearly a generation in the grave'. And on the same day in June another event did even more damage to the cause. A hundred thousand Paris workers rose against the provisional government, demanding a socialist order. There was bloody fighting in the streets, and Monseigneur Affre, the Archbishop of Paris, attempting, cross in hand, to intercede between insurgents and troops, was shot dead at a barricade. He was wearing his canonical robes, and the murder shocked the clergy and alienated the middle class throughout Europe.

On the evening of Saturday 9 July, Duffy was arrested near his house in Merton, a Dublin suburb, as he was returning from a visit to D'Arcy McGee, who lived nearby. Allowed to farewell his family, he managed to whisper instructions to his wife — who was in bed convalescing — about the disposal of a tin box containing 'precious, but not dangerous' papers. He was then driven to College Street Police Office. Here he was charged with having published in *The Nation* certain specified articles the 'object and tendency of which', the informants verily believed, was

> to deprive Her Majesty of her style and royal name and dignity as Queen of these realms; and secondly, to compass to levy war against Her Majesty in that part of the United Kingdom called Ireland, in order, by force and constraint, to compel her to change her counsels and measures.

At the Police Office, he learned that *The Nation* office had been raided, and all printed copies and documents, including account books and office memoranda, seized. Duffy vainly protested against this 'plunder and pillage'. He was refused bail and led to a covered car, with D'Arcy McGee seated beside him, and an escort of three detectives. News of his arrest spread rapidly, and an angry crowd had gathered. When the police car drove off, it was followed by other cars packed with Duffy's friends, and by the greater part of the crowd, following on foot at a rapid pace. As the procession moved into Mary street, the crowd became still more numerous, and there were excited cries of 'Take him out, Take him out'. The horse of the police car was seized by the head, and the crowd, which now consisted of perhaps 1,500 persons, was about to storm the car when D'Arcy McGee whispered to Duffy, 'Do you wish to be rescued'? Duffy, facing the same problem in his own case as he recently faced with Mitchel, replied emphatically, 'Certainly not!' A rescue, he told McGee, would only be a street riot unless they could take Dublin that night, and hold it. They could do neither. They must wait for the harvest.

At the request of the detectives, Duffy persuaded the crowd to take no action.

As the police car approached the entrance to Newgate prison, the crowd completely blocked the street, and cries of 'Take him out' were repeated. Once more, the police asked Duffy to use his restraining influence. Putting his head out of the car, he said: 'My friends, I have two requests to ask of you — one is, that you go home quietly and peaceably from this place tonight; you can do no good here now. The other is, that you give one hearty cheer for Irish independence'. This was followed by vehement cheering for several minutes. The crowd, however, still refused to move, and it was more than half an hour before Duffy, McGee, Dr. Callan, and other friends, were able to persuade them to allow the car to enter Newgate. As the great iron-bound door of the prison closed behind it, Duffy's 'liveliest feeling was that blood was not shed in a bootless conflict'. He was shown to his room, which was furnished only with a bedstead and straw palliasse. He sent for his upholsterer, Mr. Dillon, of Henry Street, who fitted up a comfortable bed for him, and he was locked up for the night.

Duffy was soon joined by some of his colleagues. John Martin arrived the same day, followed on Sunday by R.D. Williams, and Kevin O'Doherty. They reported that the office of the *Tribune*, too, had been pillaged by the police. On Tuesday, Meagher was arrested in his father's house at Waterford. 'Of all the Confederates, Meagher was the darling of the multitude', says Duffy. When the news of his arrest spread, the church bells were rung, and vast crowds rushed into the streets to rescue him. Determined to occupy the town, they barricaded the long narrow wooden bridge which spanned the river Suir on the Dublin road, but Meagher would not sanction a rising without the word of command from headquarters. Standing on the top of the travelling carriage which was to take him to Dublin, he exhorted them to desist, and ordered the members of his own Club to remove the barricade. His action was unpopular, but realistic. In the river, 'within a stonethrow' were three war steamers which could have bombarded the town with impunity. The people had not a gun or a mortar.

Duffy's trial was fixed for 8 August. He remained in custody, but Meagher with D'Arcy McGee and Holywood, the silk weaver and others arrested at the same time, were released on bail. 'It was the policy of the Government to show forbearance towards political agitators to its utmost limits', says Duffy, 'so long as it could feel assured that the preservation of order was secure'.

IMMEDIATELY after Duffy's arrest, when the Irish League held its first meeting, John O'Connell found it expedient to take a holiday in Paris, having first ordered Conciliation Hall to be shut and barricaded. The League, representing both sections of the Repealers, proclaimed the policy of organisation and conciliation, on which it had been founded. But before it could meet again, the Government had taken more repressive measures. By proclamation, all persons living in four 'proclaimed' districts — Dublin, Cork, Waterford, and Drogheda — were ordered to surrender their arms and ammunition on penalty of two year's imprisonment with hard labour, and the police were empowered to search for such arms. Martin wrote an article, signed with his initials, advising the people to retain their arms. Duffy did the same. If their arms were given up, he wrote, Ireland would be beaten, though not a cartridge was burned:

> For myself if the people are robbed of their arms — if the Clubs are broken up — if all the organisation and discipline won with such toil are flung away in an hour — if the spirit of the country, so miraculously evoked, be again permitted to die out — if these things can happen after the terrible lessons we have before us, written in the blood and tears of the nation, I, for one, will not curse the packed jury that sends me far from such a spectacle.

Duffy's freedom in prison to compound with more seditious articles, the sedition for which he was awaiting trial, not surprisingly scandalised many people in England. The Government offered the mendacious explanation that the articles were written outside the prison, and not by the men whose initials they bore. But the same articles were later included in the indictments against these men.

The next blow fell on 22 July, when at Clarendon's urgent demand, a Bill suspending Habeas Corpus in Ireland, was rushed through the House of Commons, and two days later, through the Lords. What were the Confederate leaders to do? They could remain passive while their leaders were arrested and held without indictment or trial. Or they could gamble on a rising without adequate resources, without waiting for the harvest, without aid from abroad. The problems were daunting, but Dillon had no difficulty in persuading a conference of leading Confederates that 'the one honourable course' was to resist.

'None of the precautions I had consistently insisted on were effectually taken', Duffy wrote later. 'There was no central authority . . . no military leader of adequate experience . . . no treasury or store of munitions . . . But I have always been of the opinion that Dillon's decision was the only one open to a man of honour in the circumstances'.

Dillon declared they should immediately join O'Brien, who was then touring the South. If he agreed, they might seize Kilkenny, 'call the people to arms, throw up defence works, and from the old historic seat . . . proclaim the independence of Ireland'. Kilkenny was central, and stood on the border of 'the three best fighting counties in the island' — Tipperary, Wexford and Waterford. These decisions were immediately communicated to Duffy and Martin in Newgate and passed on by them, chiefly through the staff of their journals, to the leaders of the Clubs, and others who could be relied on.

On the previous day, a delegate from Glasgow had arrived with the encouraging news that the Confederates there had a considerable supply of arms and ammunition, and if a known leader were provided, four or five hundred men would volunteer for service in Ireland. They might seize a steamer on the Clyde, and sail for Sligo or Killala, to make a surprise diversion in the West. McGee undertook the mission, and sailed that evening for Scotland. Dillon and Meagher predicted that if he succeeded, he would be as famous as Paul Jones.

The same evening, Dillon, after a hasty farewell to his young wife, took the coach at Loughlinstown, and travelled all night to Wexford. When they joined O'Brien, he agreed that they must fight. Years later, Duffy paid O'Brien a generous tribute:

> It was a spectacle strangely out of harmony with the sceptical scoffing generation in which it befell. A gentleman of mature years [O'Brien was 45] of distinguished lineage and station, the descendant of a great Celtic house, the husband of a charming wife, the father of a household of happy children, a man rich in the less precious gifts of fortune called opulence, staked his life to save his race from destruction. The chance of overthrowing the British Empire by insurrection was manifestly small, but a profound sense of duty made him accept it with all its consequences rather than acquiesce dumbly in the ruin of his people.

On Sunday 23 July, O'Brien and his companions drove into Enniscorthy, County Wexford, where the local Club had no more than 150 members, and summoned a public meeting. The Vice-President, secretary, and several members of the Club were Protestants, but a young priest of great personal influence, Father Parle, took a leading part. The people were not prepared for war, he declared, but if any attempt were made to arrest O'Brien, they would resist it.

He must have known that resistance was hopeless. Though the little Club had some arms, British ships of war commanded Wexford harbour, as they did Waterford. But a large procession on foot and horse farewelled the leaders praying for their success, as they drove on to Kilkenny.

At Kilkenny, the Mayor, Dr. Cane, a prominent Young Irelander, was discouraging. No rising could be attempted in Kilkenny without considerable outside assistance, he said. The garrison had recently been strengthened, and many of the Old Irelanders were hostile. It was decided that O'Brien and the others should tour the chief towns of Tipperary, and return within a few days with as large a force as they could muster.

At Callan, the entire population welcomed them enthusiastically with a band, bonfires and green boughs. At a hasty meeting, they warned the people to be ready for a speedy summons to fight for Ireland. Many of the Royal Hussars stationed in the town attended the meeting and were said to be 'among the most delighted of the audience'. On their way to Cashel, the O'Brien contingent made a valuable recruit, a gentleman farmer named John O'Mahony, a graduate of Trinity, a noted Celtic, Greek and Latin scholar, and president of the Cashel Club, which was 'tolerably armed'. He assured them that the country between Carrick and Clonmel was ready to take the field, and advised that the insurrection should begin that night at Carrick.

They reached Carrick-on-Suir in the evening, to find the whole town wild with excitement. Meagher described the scene apocalyptically in a memoir intended for *The Nation*:

A torrent of human beings, rushing through lanes and narrow streets, whirling in dizzy circles and tossing up its dark waves with sounds of wrath, vengeance and defiance . . . eyes red with rage and desperation . . . wild, half-stifled, passionate, frantic prayers of hope, curses on the red flag; scornful, exulting, defiant of death. It was the revolution, if we had accepted it.

But in revolutions, rifles are more important than rhetoric. Though the nine Clubs in the district could muster about 3,000 men, they were mainly armed with pikes, and had no more than 300 rifles and muskets among them. Yet it was estimated that 1,200 well-equipped men — infantry, dragoons and police — with two howitzers and two field pieces, were in Carrick, or within an hour's march. Moreover, large reinforcements could be drawn from Waterford and Clonmel.

The most influential local leaders declared that an attempt to hold Carrick would be 'drowned in blood' and O'Brien agreed. He then asked that an adequately armed force, provisioned for three days, should be raised immediately — within an hour if possible — to march with him to Callan. He was confident that they would be so effectually reinforced on the route that they could successfully attack Kilkenny. This proposal, too, was rejected as impractical, and O'Brien and the other leaders were urged to conceal themselves until arrangements could be made for combined action with Waterford, Clonmel and Kilkenny. O'Brien refused to be 'hunted into concealment', and appealed to a big mass meeting. If the people were prepared to resist the aggression of the British Government, which had suspended the Constitution, he would stand by them, he said. He was promised co-operation from Carrick in whatever course they finally adopted, and the three Confederates drove on again, this time to Cashel, where there were many Confederates and few soldiers, to renew their campaigning.

After they left, a large force was seen approaching Carrick; it consisted of a contingent organised by O'Mahoney to begin action that night. They were told to disperse, and O'Mahoney went home to await further instructions. Writing with hindsight thirty-five years later, Duffy said:

> Here, and not at Waterford on the arrest of Meagher, or at Dublin on the arrest of Mitchel, the best opportunity of striking an effective blow presented itself. Had Carrick been seized, it is probable that three counties would have risen within forty-eight hours; and that preparations for a rising would have begun over three provinces.

Few modern historians would agree with him.

A confidential messenger reached Duffy in Newgate with news of O'Brien's campaign. He consulted Martin, O'Doherty and Williams, and it was agreed that they should attempt to escape to join their comrades. 'I caused a rope ladder to be immediately prepared', says Duffy, 'by which we believed that with slight assistance from outside, we could make our way out of one of the courts, which was ill-lighted, unguarded, and for the moment, unoccupied by prisoners'. The rope ladder, which, rather confusingly, he says 'was probably made of silk', was so small that it was brought into the prison concealed in a basket of laundry, and concealed in a small cloak-bag in Duffy's bedroom.

But the attempt was not made. Where were they to fly to?

> Day after day passed without any satisfactory or even any certain news from the South. The newspapers were full of contradictory rumours, but an insurrection cannot conceal itself, and the news we were expecting was plainly not forthcoming. The Post Office, the railways, and all the ordinary lines of communication were now watched by detectives; if we sent any known Confederate for information, it was certain he would not be allowed to return.

With high hopes, Smith O'Brien and his colleagues reached Cashel, once the capital of Munster, and the stronghold of Brian Boru, the ancestor of the O'Briens. They expected to find the green flag flying from the historic Rock which dominates the town, and a people busily preparing for insurrection — 'sentinels and watchfires, columns of sturdy peasants, carts laden with provisions, flaming smithies where strong men were hammering iron and steel into serviceable weapons . . .' But Cashel was like a city of the dead. The project of raising that part of the country had failed. As Cashel, like Carrick-on-Suir and Kilkenny, would not take on responsibility for striking the first blow, the Confederates decided to drive north and fall back on the rural districts. On the morning of 25 July, they reached Killenaule.

They were welcomed with bouquets and speeches. A small number of peasants, fewer than two hundred, who showed readiness to fight, were ordered to be prepared for a speedy summons. The Confederates then took the road to Mullinahone. Here, though only three members of the Club appeared, the chapel bell was rung, and there was an enthusiastic response to the call for arms and men. The smith sweated to hammer out pikes — the first made in that part of Tipperary since '98 — and before midnight about six thousand men, armed with improvised pikes, fowling-pieces, and pitchforks, were engaged in rudimentary drill. A few barricades were thrown up, but O'Brien punctiliously forbade felling of trees without permission of the owners of the land upon which they grew.

Meagher described Smith O'Brien at Mullinahone, standing with folded arms, 'looking as immutable and serene as usual'. He wore over his dress a tricolor of green, white and orange; a case of pistols hung from his belt, and he carried a large pike mounted on a long staff. His colleagues, too, were picturesquely attired. Dillon wore a large blue military cloak; O'Donohue, a thick black fur cap; and McManus, a jaunty green cap with a broad gold band, with a black glazed leather belt, supporting a cartridge box, buckled round his waist.

By morning, the little army began to melt away. There was no breakfast to be had except under their own roofs. Those who lived near enough went home, others remained the whole day in the streets without food or shelter. O'Brien, looking 'happy and dreamy, smoking a cigar', bought some food and distributed it, with the warning that in future they would have to provide for themselves as he could not do so, and would not offer violence to anyone's person or property. He was determined to conduct his rebellion with the propriety of an Irish gentleman. In the same spirit, with two companions, he visited the police barrack, surprising the sergeant and his six men, two of whom were cooking breakfast, while the others were shaving, O'Brien politely called on them to surrender and deliver up their arms. 'Oh, sir', said the sergeant, 'if we give in to three or four men we'll be disgraced for ever. Bring a force and we'll submit'. Solicitous for the honour of the constabulary, O'Brien agreed to do this, and courteously withdrew, whereupon the constabulary fled to a stronger barracks, taking their arms with them. A Carrick Confederate who witnessed the incident afterwards told Duffy it had filled him with despair. But it revealed O'Brien as a man of great courage — the courage to test his faith in the patriotism of the Irish policeman.

Next morning there was a cry of 'Up with the barricades!' as a troop of cavalry numbering at least 100 men, was seen approaching. Scores of carts of turf were seized, and hastily piled up in the streets. O'Brien, after helping with this work, was persuaded with difficulty to retire to a safe distance. When the troops, the Eighth Royal Irish Hussars, reached the first barricade, the commanding officer, Captain Longmore, asked to be allowed to pass. By this time, the rebels had collected about thirty men, armed with one rifle, two muskets, and some pikes and pitchforks. They were followed by a crowd of women and children. One of the men covered Longmore with the rifle, while Dillon, standing on top of the barricade, demanded if he had come to arrest Mr. O'Brien. Longmore gave his word of honour that he had no warrant for O'Brien, and if allowed to pass, would not molest him or anyone else. The Hussars were on their way to provide an escort for the Judge of Assizes at Nenagh. After some consideration, Dillon allowed them to pass through the barricade, one by one, and as the last man passed, the people cheered. The Hussars were Irish, and had shown sympathy with the Confederates in Callan.

Before leaving Killenaule, O'Brien reviewed his force. With a few recruits, the total number with arms of any description was about fifty. O'Brien and McManus marched to the nearby colliery district of Castlecomer. Here they were well received, but the miners were without arms, and in McManus' words, 'seemed to have had much of their physical courage starved out of them'.

The Mullinahone contingent had now dwindled to about 500 men. At its head O'Brien marched north into Ballingarry, trying, with little success, to rouse the hamlets as he passed. His efforts were for the most part frustrated by the local priests, who urged the people to put down their arms, warning that they were 'rushing on ruin'.

The cardinal question now presented itself: would the priests help the insurgents, and could they succeed without the priests? Father Kenyon gave the bitter answer. No one was more deeply committed to the fight for independence. No one was more vehement in his denunciation of English tyranny or Irish cowardice. But he received the appeal of the Confederates for his immediate participation in the struggle with 'coldness and irony'. Fight? Yes, of course, he would fight, he told them, if the people showed themselves prepared for revolution, 'but it was not becoming for a priest to begin a bootless struggle'. He firmly rejected the suggestion that he should summon his congregation by ringing the chapel bells, and march at its head to join Smith O'Brien. The Confederates were deeply disappointed. They did not know that Kenyon had given an undertaking to his Bishop not to take any action.

At Ballingarry, the Confederates were joined by Duffy's old friend Terence McManus, then a prosperous Liverpool merchant who had left England as soon as he heard of the insurrection, and O'Mahony. A large crowd had collected, and O'Brien was forced to tell them that he could not supply food. He instructed volunteers to provide themselves with at least four days' rations, suggesting 'oatmeal, bread and hard eggs'. As most of his listeners were subsisting on the Government issue of a pound of Indian meal a day, the instructions were as absurd and unrealistic as the raid on the police barrack.

On the morning of 27 July, the chapel bells of Ballingarry tolled, and O'Brien mustered all available recruits. They were hastily paraded and drilled, and by midday, the Confederates marched to Mullinahone at the head, in McManus' words, of 'about 150 slashing fellows, tolerably armed, and all in high glee'. At Mullinahone, McManus bought bread for the famished contingent. While they were eating it, the parish priest 'got among them', and induced about a third to defect. There were more desertions as the little army marched on. When they reached Killenaule, weary and hungry, after midnight, its numbers had been reduced to less than twenty.

WHILE his comrades in the South were trying to raise the green flag of insurrection, Duffy was finding it more and more difficult to bring out *The Nation* from Newgate. McGee, who had taken over the active editorship after his imprisonment, was in Scotland. Other members of the staff were campaigning with O'Brien, or in hiding. And articles, or even private letters from prisoners, could no longer be sent out from the prison. Duffy handed over the editorship to Margaret Callan, who had been a contributor since its beginning, and 'Speranza' promised to write a suitable leading article. When the police raided *The Nation* office to seize the current issue, type, proofs, and manuscripts, and to arrest the compositors and machinists, they found two articles, both unequivocal incentives to rebellion. One titled 'The Tocsin of Ireland' had been written by Duffy and smuggled out of prison. The other, titled 'Alea Jacta Est'. ('The Die is Cast') had been written by 'Speranza'. Both were afterwards included in the indictment against Duffy. 'Speranza's' piece exhibited her in her most perfervid mood:

> In the name of your trampled, insulted, degraded country; in the name of all heroic virtues, of all that makes life illustrious or death divine; in the name of your starved, your exiled, your dead; by your martyrs in prison cells and felon chains; in the name of God and man; by the listening earth and the watching Heaven, lift up your right hand to Heaven and swear by your undying soul, by your hopes of immortality, never to lay down your arms, never to cease hostilities, till you regenerate and save this fallen land.

Duffy's article was almost as febrile. He was no longer an advocate of patient preparations:

> *We fight for liberty to live.* Hundreds of thousands of Irishmen would again die in the tortures of famine; hundreds of thousands of Irishmen would again fly over the wide sea to perish of unknown horrors in the swamps of Canada and the woods of Michigan, if we bowed our necks to the Parliament of England at this hour. We fight because there is no remedy but the sword . . . There is no neutrality now. You must choose your side and choose quickly. If you love famine, stripes and dishonour . . . join the red ranks of England; if you love justice . . . your rank is beneath the green banner of Ireland.

ALARMING rumours circulated in Dublin and London. 'The whole of the south of Ireland is in rebellion', announced *The Times* on 27 July. Its report, received 'per special engine' from the *Dublin Evening Post* continued:

> The station at Thurles is on fire, the rails for several miles torn up, and the mob intend detaining the engines as they arrive.
> At Clonmel the fighting is dreadful. The people arrive in masses. The Dublin Club leaders are there. The troops were speedily overpowered; many refused to act. The military at Carrick have shown disaffection, and have been driven back and their quarters fired. At Kilkenny the contest is proceeding, and here the mob are also said to be successful.

'The Funds were considerably agitated by the news', said the *Annual Register*. But the report was without foundation. The Young Irelanders in fact were desperate. On the evening of Friday 29 July, Smith O'Brien,

Meagher and McManus held a council of war at Ballingarry. The council voted to go into hiding, and to make another attempt later. Smith O'Brien firmly refused. 'I won't be a fugitive where my forefathers reigned . . .' he declared. 'I will continue to appeal to the people, as I have been doing, until we gather enough support to enable us to take the field.'

But the hopeless insurrection was moving to its inevitable end. The position was much more serious than the Confederates knew. They had not succeeded in raising the country, and hundreds of their supporters and sympathisers were being arrested, including Fintan Lalor and Dr. Cane. The Habeas Corpus Suspension Act had arrived in Dublin on 26 July. Warrants were despatched to the South for the arrest of Smith O'Brien, Meagher and a dozen other Young Irelanders. Lord Clarendon issued a proclamation declaring the Clubs illegal, and 'strictly commanding all persons to withdraw from and abandon the same'. An immense military force was concentrated on Carrick and Waterford, and a naval force, commanded by Sir Charles Napier, patrolled the south coast. The *Rhadamanthus* was stationed at Waterford, with her guns enfilading the great thoroughfare of the town, and a fleet of armed steamers commanded Cork.

On Saturday, 30 July, just one week since Smith O'Brien had driven into Enniscorthy, McManus reviewed the insurgent force at Ballingarry. It consisted, at most, of forty-four armed men; their armament comprised about twenty-two guns — fowling pieces or pistols — with one charge of powder each, and about as many rough pikes and pitchforks. Supporting them, were about eighty men and women armed with stones. And someone had a drum.

As McManus was addressing this raggle-taggle army, a Dublin Confederate, John Kavanagh, who had left Dublin 'in search of the insurrection' galloped up, shouting breathlessly that a large body of police was advancing in a leisurely march on Ballingarry. Amid great excitement and confusion, it was decided to make a stand. A barricade of carts and timber was hastily thrown up. Smith O'Brien and a few of the men with guns took up a position in front of the barricade. The other gunmen occupied the houses commanding it. The pike and pitchfork brigade were in a hollow on the left. The stone-throwers were instructed to lie on their faces about two hundred and fifty yards ahead of the barricade, and to attack the police in the rear, after they had received the first fire. Simultaneously, the pike and pitchfork men were to charge. It was bold strategy, but the police spoiled it all by panicking. Under the extraordinary impression that they were confronted by a hostile crowd of at least three thousand persons — as their commanding officer later explained — they broke rank and fled to a large, two-storey stone house which stood in a cabbage-garden on Boulagh Common, about a mile away. The house belonged to widow McCormack, who had set out only a few moments before for Ballingarry, leaving her five young children behind.

With a yell, and without orders, the crowd dashed in pursuit of the police, sweeping Smith O'Brien along with them, while McManus, in his own words, 'very sullenly' followed. The police hastily barricaded the front windows of the house, breast-high, on both stories, indiscriminately using the widow's furniture, doors, and mantel-pieces and mattresses. They then posted men armed with carbines at all the windows, front and back. McManus, crawling on his hands and knees, reconnoitred the building and reported that it could not be taken without a piece of artillery, but Smith O'Brien, convinced that the police would surrender, was determined to attack. In that case, said McManus, the only way to succeed was to smoke them out.

Followed by about forty gun and pikemen, he broke into the stables and ordered each man to take a load of hay on his back. The men refused, afraid to expose themselves to police fire crossing the yard. McManus carried the hay himself, piled it against the back door of the house, and fired it with a rifle shot. As the hay began to smoke, widow McCormack returned in a frenzy for the safety of her children. Smith O'Brien ordered McManus to stop firing the hay. 'Here is widow McCormack', he said, 'and she has been sent round by the police to say they will make terms'. With the widow, McManus, and two or three others, he approached the front of the house. Standing on a window-sill, he thrust his arm in over the top of the barricade, and shook hands with a policeman inside, saying it was not their lives but their arms the insurgents wanted.

While the discussion was going on, a few men in the crowd began throwing stones at the house from under cover of the walls. Eight or nine struck the windows. The police immediately opened fire with about forty carbines. Two men fell beside McManus, one dead, the other badly injured. McManus and the gunmen in the front rank then, for the first time, opened fire 'on the constabulary of the Queen'. Their shots were ineffectual against the barricaded windows. The police returned the fire with a second volley, and McManus was struck in the leg by ricocheting bullets and knocked down. He joined Smith O'Brien, and advised that the attack should be called off. Ammunition was spent. The situation was hopeless. At first, Smith O'Brien, despite the exhortations of McManus and others, refused to move. 'An O'Brien never turned his back on an enemy', he declared, standing defiantly in the midst of the fire. His little force had fled in disorder, urged on by a neighbouring priest, and ultimately, Smith O'Brien was persuaded to withdraw. He mounted a captured police horse and rode away. What *The Times* derisively labelled 'The Cabbage-Garden Revolution' was over, leaving O'Brien and his colleagues fugitives, and the widow McCormack lamenting over her shattered furniture and trampled cabbages.

'This was the upshot of the insurrection', Duffy later wrote. 'A poor, feeble, unprosperous essay; a mob of disorganised peasants in frieze coats suppressed by a handful of disciplined peasants in green jackets. But it was dignified and sublimated by the unflinching courage and devotion of the men engaged in it. It was not more heroic to stake life for the common weal at Thermopylae or Bannockburn than on the Common of Boulagh . . .'

In retrospect, the 1848 rising — if it be dignified with the word — seems like an amateurish melodrama with overtones of Gilbertian farce. But it must be remembered that the principals who risked an ignominious death on the gallows were intoxicated by the heady romanticism of their times. It was only 24 years since Byron had died at

Missolonghi, a symbol of the eternal struggle for liberty, and the names of patriots such as Mazzini, Kossuth and Garibaldi were talismanic to the Young Irelanders.

Smith O'Brien made two fatal miscalculations. He expected the people to rise, not realising how greatly famine had demoralised and debilitated them. And he expected the support of the rural clergy, not realising, as a Protestant, that the Church as a body was opposed to insurrection. In this miscalculation, he was, of course, greatly influenced by the rebellious rhetoric of Father Kenyon.

At a meeting of the Privy Council held at Dublin Castle on 31 July, fifteen counties and baronies were placed under semi-martial law, and proclamations were issued offering substantial rewards:

> For the arrest of William Smith O'Brien, £500; for Francis T. Meagher, John B. Dillon, and Michael Doheny, each or either, £300; to him who shall secure and deliver into safe custody the persons aforesaid.

The charge alleged in the proclamation was 'having taken up arms against Her Majesty'.

HOW had Duffy's hopes of getting aid from abroad been realised? D'Arcy McGee succeeded in enrolling four hundred volunteers in Scotland, but the scheme of seizing a vessel had to be abandoned. It was arranged, however, for a steamer sailing from Greenock to carry the arms, disguised as merchandise, to Ireland. McGee was recognised by a former Dublin resident, and the organising committee insisted that he leave immediately to escape arrest, and make for Sligo to prepare for the projected landing. He took the train to Carlisle, sailed from Whitehaven to Belfast, and reached Sligo on 2 August. Here he learned that the barracks, guarded by fewer than one hundred men, had stores of arms, including small artillery, food, money and a printing press, 'all essential in war'.

There was no Club in Sligo. The only organised popular force was a secret society, the 'Molly Maguires'. McGee appealed to one of their leaders who told him that if they were assured the South had risen, or would certainly rise, they would enrol two thousand men within a week. On this assurance, a trusty messenger was despatched to Tipperary, while McGee took lodgings in Ben Bulben, pretending to be a Dublin student on holiday. He was still awaiting instructions from the South when he learned that the rising had failed.

He made his way to Derry where he was hidden by Dr. Maginn and some of his clergy until, dressed as a priest, with breviary in hand, he boarded a brig at the mouth of the Foyle and sailed for America. The voyage had embarrassing moments when Irish emigrants invoked his pastoral aid. One couple, perhaps with a reason for urgency, entreated him to marry them. McGee explained to all such supplicants that his 'faculties' were suspended at sea.

In America, the Irish agents formed a Directory which quickly raised the huge sum of £10,000. Two American citizens of Irish descent, one a barrister, the other in the United States diplomatic service, were sent separately to Ireland, each with a portion of the money, and the promise of more. (Every American arrival in Dublin was subject to close scrutiny, and several were in Newgate.) Both arrived too late to assist the cause, and returned with their money intact. But remittances were later sent, by devious means, to help defendants in the State Trials.

In France, General Arthur O'Connor and Colonel Byrne, who half a century before had fought with Wolfe Tone and Lord Edward Fitzgerald, received the Irish envoy with enthusiasm, and tried to procure the required assistance from General Cavignac, then Chief of the Executive, who expressed his warm sympathy with the Irish, but news of the failure of the rising reached Paris before he could give proof of it.

For a week of anguish, the prisoners in Newgate knew nothing of what was happening in Kilkenny. The Dublin papers were silent. All travellers were watched, and a messenger was unable to reach O'Brien. There was talk of escaping, but the difficulties seemed insuperable. At length came news of disaster. All was over. T.D. Reilly had returned to Dublin disguised as a groom, and was about to escape to America. Doheny and McManus, in the Galtee mountains, and Meagher and Dillon, in Tipperary and Waterford, were vainly trying to rally their followers.

O'Brien had been arrested after his hopeless stand in Ballingarry. He had been recognised on the railway station at Thurles by a guard called Hulme and had surrendered without resistance. There was satisfaction in Ireland that the informer was an Englishman who rapidly drank himself to death with the reward.

There was a bitter sequel. It was whispered in Dublin that O'Brien had deliberately betrayed the cause to make a real insurrection impossible. 'The police were probably responsible for this invention', Duffy wrote. 'But Old Ireland's prejudice welcomed it, and it was for a time successful. For the first and last time in my life, I flung myself down in despair, and declared that such an insensate multitude could not be saved'.

Dillon crossed Ireland in the habit of a religious order, and sailed from Galway to New York, disguised as an Arab fisherman. Doheny escaped as a car man, driving along highways past many police stations to Cork, where he sailed as a deck passenger to London, and thence made his way to France. O'Gorman, Jun., too, escaped to France. He was said to have been on board the steamer at Kilrush when police searched it for him. He had assumed the dress and appearance of an old lady, in which guise, it was said, he had the support of a stipendiary magistrate's arm as he boarded the ship.

DUFFY had been in Newgate about three months when he heard of plans to incite the Dublin Clubs to insurrection and to seize Clarendon and others. He immediately sent out a message 'utterly and unequivocally' denouncing any such attempt:

> It would end in a massacre of the Clubs, and afford an excuse for hanging Smith O'Brien. Whoever concurs in it will be committing a grievous crime against the country. It may be even a trap by another Dobbyn to betray the

people to the gallows. [Dobbyn was an Orangeman who acted as a spy for Dublin Castle on the Young Irelanders.] I beseech and entreat every Confederate who regards my advice to set himself against it. I would rather be hanged tomorrow than lend it the smallest countenance.

A month after his arrest Duffy wrote the usual instructions for his counsel. They were brief and explicit:

Deny nothing and retract nothing, of what I have actually written or done. But explain my motives, and defend my character from the slanders of the Government Press. They are not content to transport me; they are conspiring to bury my name under a cairn of obloquy. Let them not succeed in this at least.

DUFFY was the last of the State prisoners to be arraigned. He was brought to the bar of Green Street Court — the bar before which Robert Emmet had stood forty-five years before — on 8 August 1848. The Crown had deployed a formidable battery of forensic talent, the Attorney-General, Mr. Monahan, the Solicitor-General, Mr. Hatchell, and four eminent barristers. Duffy was defended by Isaac Butt, Sir Colman O'Loghlen and John O'Hagan. As he stood in the dock waiting for the jury to be empanelled, there was a flurry as the junior counsel for the Crown, John Perrin, son of Judge Perrin, rushed breathless into the Court, and after consulting with the Attorney-General, addressed the Bench: 'My Lord', he said: 'I shall ask to have the prisoner Gavan Duffy put back; we do not propose to go on with the trial this sitting'. Sir Colman O'Loghlen whispered the explanation to Duffy: 'Johnny Perrin', he said, 'has come to tell them that a letter of yours has been found in Smith O'Brien's portmanteau, which involves you in High Treason, and Clarendon means to send you for trial to Clonmel. We want to insist that you be tried for the lesser offence of treason-felony'. (The penalty for treason-felony was transportation for life, or any shorter period fixed by the Court. The penalty for High Treason was death.)

The contention of the Crown was upheld, and Duffy was ordered to retire. 'This ... was the first fruit of Lord Clarendon's rancour', he wrote, 'for the Lord Lieutenant regarded me with particular displeasure'. The displeasure was to be manifested in a series of vindictive trials unexampled in British legal history. Duffy wrote, 'I was sent back to prison to prepare for death. For five months my fellow-prisoners, when we met in the ghastly prison chapel on a Sunday morning, fancied the public gallows which forms its principal window was destined to open for my last exit from the edifice'.

After his arrest, Smith O'Brien had sent for his portmanteau, which had been left in Doheny's house, to get a change of linen. To the end of his life O'Brien insisted he did so on an honourable understanding with the English commander, General MacDonald, that he should receive the portmanteau unopened. Despite this, it was sent to Dublin Castle, where every fragment of paper in it, down to visiting cards, was catalogued and sent to the Crown Solicitor for scrutiny. Duffy later claimed that the incriminating letter represented 'very accurately' his position at the time. He thought that a refusal to call the country to arms, formidable as the difficulties were, would 'cover Ireland with contempt before America and Europe, but that no pains ought to be spared to make the revolution an honourable and magnanimous one. The letter read in part: 'There is no half-way house for you. You will be the head of the movement, loyally obeyed, and the revolution will be conducted with order and clemency; or the more anarchists will prevail with the people, and our revolution will be a bloody chaos . . .'

If Richmond were the best of Dublin's nine prisons, Newgate, which was reserved for prisoners awaiting trial and debtors, was un-questionably the worst. It was built in 1798, and year after year inspectors condemned its dark, airless, unheated cells. 'The actual state of Newgate . . . with its antiquated recesses, far exceeded my worst anticipations', reported Francis White, Inspector-General of Prisons in 1841. And he quoted a confidential report written two years earlier which described Newgate as 'a hotbed of the rankest vice' and 'a seminary of iniquity . . . quite incapable of improvement'.

Duffy's health, never robust, was seriously affected by conditions in Newgate, and an eminent physician, Dr. Graves, vainly urged the Executive to move him to a less mephitic prison. Duffy described the conditions:

> It is incredible what filth, foul air, darkness and horror were shut up within these walls. There are cells from which light was as effectually excluded as from the grave. It was built on the burying-ground of an ancient monastery, and reeked with odours of unknown origin. State prisoners got the best accommodation the place afforded, yet my friends reported that the walls of their bedchamber was honeycombed with the nests of spiders and cockroaches, which fell upon them in bed, and into the basins in which they were washing, and the glasses from which they were drinking.

But Newgate like Richmond was controlled by the Dublin Corporation, and at first Duffy and his colleagues enjoyed many privileges. They dined together in Duffy's room, with food from a nearby hotel, and a prison servant to wait on them. During the day, their friends visited unrestrictedly. There was a daily conference with Smith O'Brien, Dillon and others. Duffy and Martin continued to correspond with their colleagues, and to write for their respective papers, boldly dating their contributions from Newgate prison.

Thirty-four years later, Dr. Croke, then Archbishop of Cashel, recalled how he and two companions, all young priests, had visited Duffy in Newgate to offer their editorial services should any more of *The Nation* staff be arrested. (One of Croke's companions was to become Dr. Barry, Principal of St. Patrick's College, Melbourne). Duffy gratefully refused the offer, and advised Croke to resume his books and his teaching and to shun Irish politics for the present; advice which young Croke took. 'We found you sitting on a solid block of timber in a small, well-ventilated room, with lots of books and papers about you . . .' Dr. Croke wrote. 'You were thin and pale; wore your hair long; were beardless; and dressed like a cleric in black'.

Among the Newgate prisoners were two American sympathisers, and members of the Directory, a Maryland barrister, R.F. Ryan, editor of the *Irish American* and a New York shipbroker, James Bergin, who was said to look like Shakespeare, and thereafter, inexplicably, was known as 'General Shields'. Bergin had been arrested within a few days of his arrival. They were the despair of the prison authorities. Duffy wrote:

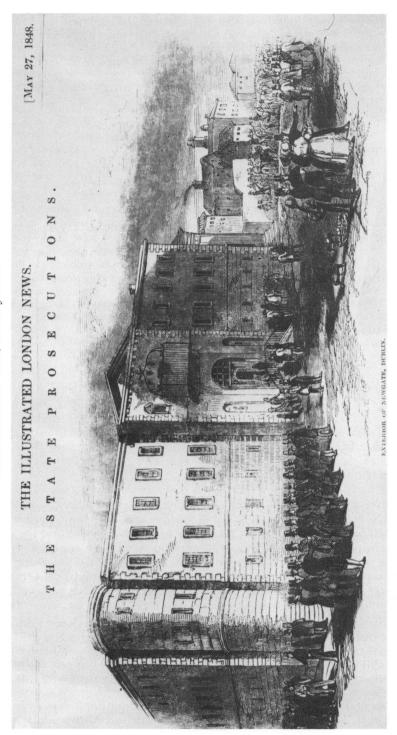

Illustrated London News, 27 May 1848

THE ILLUSTRATED LONDON NEWS.

T H E S T A T E P R O S E C U T I O N S .

[MAY 27, 1848.

EXTERIOR OF NEWGATE, DUBLIN.

Before sunset the *detenus* under the Suspension Act were mustered for exercise. Mr. Bergin, who was big and broadchested, and gifted with a voice like a trumpet, made the old walls ring one evening with the 'Star-spangled Banner'. The Deputy-Governor forbade this disedifying recreation; but the American citizen declared that unless he were gagged he would not refrain from honouring his country. From that time forth the sun never set upon Newgate without the Irish-Americans leading a chorus in which the prisoners joined *con furore:*

> Then conquer we must, for our cause is just,
> And this be our motto, 'In God is our trust';
> And the star-spangled banner in triumph will wave
> O'er the land of the free and the home of the brave.

At the end of September, the trials began at Clonmel Assizes, of Smith O'Brien, Meagher, McManus and O'Donohoe. The prisoners sustained their spirits by singing loudly a verse of Duffy's 'Watch and Wait':

> Brothers, if this day should set,
> Another yet must crown our freedom:
> That will come with roll of drum,
> And trampling files, and men to lead them
> Who can save
> Renegade or slave?
> Fortune only 'twines her garlands
> For the Brave!

O'Brien was the first to be tried. As he stood in the dock, a young girl presented him with a bouquet. O'Brien acknowledged it with an impromptu poem which began:

> Sweet girl, who gave in danger's hour
> To lift my soul, a beauteous flower
> And by thy bright yet modest eyes,
> Cheered me with softest sympathies.

O'Brien's leading counsel, Mr. Whiteside, Q.C. (afterwards Chief Justice) based the defence on the hypothesis that his client's proceedings in Tipperary were designed merely to evade or resist arrest. This might constitute an offence, but was certainly not High Treason, with which he was charged.

During the trial, the Solicitor-General produced the letter of Duffy's found in O'Brien's portmanteau and suggested that the prisoner had been pressed to his destruction by 'this diabolical tempter', Duffy. O'Brien indignantly rejected the suggestion, and protested against its obvious impropriety. Frederick Lucas in the *Tablet* described the 'gross and wanton unmanliness' of the Solicitor-General's contempt of court as 'positively shocking'. 'In England we have had nothing so bad', he wrote'. . . since Coke denounced Sir Walter Raleigh as "a damnable atheist, a spider of hell, the most vile and execrable of traitors" '.

Another incident in Smith O'Brien's trial made a great sensation. His counsel wanted to show that the Whigs who were prosecuting O'Brien had themselves considered the possibility of civil war in defence of the Reform Bill of 1832. Lord Melbourne had suggested that 'the handsomest and most heroic officer in the British army', the hero of the Peninsular War, Sir William Napier — not surprisingly an Irishman — might take command of the artisans of Birmingham if they marched on London. Napier, a patriotic Irishman, appeared in Court with a letter from Melbourne written in June 1832 which read, in part, 'Are you aware that in the event of a fight, you were to be invited to take command at Birmingham? . . . Thank God, we have been spared the trial, but, as a matter of speculation, tell me what you think would have been the result?' The Court refused to admit the letter as evidence, nor would it permit Lord Melbourne to be subpoenaed.

After a trial lasting thirteen days, O'Brien was found guilty, with a recommendation that his life be spared. He addressed the court briefly, simply and with dignity:

> My lords, it is not my intention to enter into any vindication of my conduct, however much I might have desired to avail myself of this opportunity of doing so. I am perfectly satisfied with the consciousness that I have performed my duty to my country; and that I have done only that which, in my opinion, it was the duty of every Irishman to have done; and I am prepared now to abide the consequences of having done my duty to my native land. Proceed with your sentence.

The judge went through the obscene masquerade of sentencing O'Brien to be drawn on a hurdle to the place of execution, there to be hanged by the neck, and afterwards to have his body divided into four quarters, to be disposed of as Her Majesty the Queen might think fit.

The trials of McManus, O'Donohoe and Meagher followed. The case against Meagher was the weakest of all, because he had neither erected barricades, impeded the Queen's army, or attacked police. He had left O'Brien at Mullinahone, a clear proof that he differed from O'Brien's schemes. But all the prisoners were found guilty and sentenced to be hanged, drawn and quartered. Meagher's speech from the dock maintained his reputation for rhetoric. He declared he knew that his fate would elicit sympathy and that his memory would be honoured. He had no enmity for the jury, as the Chief Justice's charge left them no option but to convict. He continued:

> I am here to regret nothing I have ever done — to retract nothing I have ever said. I am not here to crave, with lying lips, the life I consecrate to the liberty of my country. Far from it; even here — here, where the thief, the libertine, the murderer, have left their footprints in the dust; here, on this spot, the shadows of death surround me, and from which I see my early grave in an unanointed soil opened to receive me — even here, the hope which beckoned me to the perilous sea upon which I have been wrecked still consoles, animates, enraptures me. No, I do not despair of my poor old country, her peace, her liberty, her glory . . .

Lord John Russell announced that the Queen would graciously commute their sentences to transportation for life. (This, of course, would relieve her of the scandal of butchering a well-known member of the House of

Commons, and of the bother of disposing of his quarters). But under existing law, the sentence could be modified only with the prisoners' assent, which they refused to give. They preferred death in Ireland (and the halo of martyrdom) to permanent exile. Parliament resolved the dilemma by swiftly passing an Act which enabled the Queen to pardon the prisoners without their consent.

After his conviction, O'Brien, always the Irish gentleman, wrote to his solicitor: 'My dear Potter, I entertain the most sincere and anxious desire that no insult or injury should be offered to either the jury or the witnesses through whose instrumentality I have been convicted, and shall be very much obliged if you will use your utmost efforts to make known my sentiments upon this subject'. More than nine months later, on 29 July 1849, O'Brien was ignominiously paraded in chains with his fellow-prisoners through the streets of Dublin, to embark from the Pigeon House fort on *The Trident*, the vessel which was to take them to their transport, *The Swift*. O'Brien was accompanied to the fort by his wife, his brother, the Reverend H. O'Brien, and his sister. Meagher carried a volume of MacPherson's poems of Ossian to remind him, he said, of the old country he was leaving.

Mr. Stephenson Dobbyn, one of the informers against O'Brien, was paid £17 for his services to the Crown. Another informer, Mr. J.D. Balfe, one of the Confederates in the pay of the Government, was rewarded by being made an officer in Van Dieman's Land, where he watched over O'Brien and Meagher, with whom he had sat in amity on the Council of the Confederation.

THE Newgate prisoners who had thought of escaping to join Smith O'Brien still had their rope-ladder. Now that the rising had failed, why should they not use it to escape to America? 'An escape from enemies to whom we had given no parole was a feat to be proud of', Duffy wrote. 'From the flight of Red Hugh from Birmingham Tower to the evasion of Hamilton Rowan, Ireland never heard of a State prisoner breaking bounds without a thrill of joy'. O'Doherty was enthusiastic about the project, but Williams did not wish to participate. He had been advised by his father, Count Dalton, that plans had been made to ensure his aquittal.

Towards the end of October, Duffy and O'Doherty arranged with Confederates outside to hire a small vessel, and a date was given for the attempted escape, which they planned to make at midnight from a deserted court. About noon on the day fixed O'Doherty came into Duffy's room to announce 'the desperate news' that a policeman had that morning for the first time been placed on a platform overlooking the court. Duffy went out to reconnoitre, and got into conversation with the policeman:

> He told me his name was Peter Hutchinson, that he was a brother to a Confederate with whose career I was familiar and reminded me that he himself had written some trifles in *The Nation* and had consulted me repeatedly on his education and prospects. In answer to a remark on our strange juxtaposition, he used the expressive phrase that 'I would not long be a

prisoner if it depended on him'. Here seemed a man made for our purpose . . . a passionate sympathiser under the green uniform of a constable . . .
Hutchinson agreed to fly with us next night, and we undertook that the change should not damage his position but better it. More money was provided, our allies outside were warned of the change of time, and all other necessary arrangements completed.

But next morning, when Duffy was burning some papers, O'Doherty rushed into his room to announce that the Governor and Deputy-Governor, and an official from the Castle, were conversing earnestly with Hutchinson. O'Doherty was certain they had been betrayed. The rope-ladder was in a cloak-bag in Duffy's room, and he proposed to carry it out and drop it discreetly 'into the jakes'. Before he could do so, 'the gentle old Governor' and his colleagues arrived, the Governor courteously apologising for the intrusion, which he said was made under orders from the Castle. The Deputy-Governor, Mr. Bourne, ransacked Duffy's wardrobe, searched under the bed, and poked the chimney with his walking-stick, but found nothing. Duffy continues:

> After a search of some ten minutes the Governor was about ordering his party to withdraw when Bourne asked whether there was anything in a little cloak-bag which lay on a table. 'Yes', I said, unlocking it, 'there is something in it. You have not told me what you are in search of, but perhaps this is what you want?'

There lay the rope ladder. It was forty feet long and accompanied by a coil of rope of the same length. Mr. Bourne grinned with malicious joy, while the kindly old Governor muttered, 'I am very sorry, I am very sorry'.

As a result, Duffy, O'Doherty and Williams — who had no share of the business — were moved from their rooms and locked up in the same stone cell, in a more secure part of the prison, with a double guard on them. Hutchinson, who alleged he was offered a bribe to help the prisoners escape, was proved to be a police spy and *agent provocateur*. He was, however, still an active member of a Confederate Club, distinguished by the violence of his insurrectionary exhortations. As a result of these disclosures, the Government was forced to dismiss him.

FROM New York, after his escape from Ireland, D'Arcy McGee who loved Duffy 'this side of idolatory', wrote of him in the melancholy tone of an obituarist:

> All his life through he was a disciplinarian, an architect of systems. The teeming fertility of his mind was marvellous. Always and everywhere he was projecting some new move for Ireland. The large throbbing vein that descended from his forehead used to swell and blacken like an inky cord from the strain that events kept up under the power-wheels of his intellect.

When he wrote to Duffy, Carlyle offered sympathy and advice:

> If now, or henceforth at any time while I live, I could be of any honest service to you, by my resources or connections, here or otherwise, surely it would be

very welcome news to me . . . Courage, my friend: all is not yet lost! . . . By Heaven's blessing this is no *finis* in your course, but the *finis* only of a huge mistake; and the *beginning* of a much nobler course . . . Courage, I say; courage, patience, for a time, *pious silence* . . .

Duffy certainly required both courage and patience — if not pious silence. It was not till 26 October that he was again brought up to answer a charge of treason-felony. The Crown had decided against charging him with High Treason. 'How did I escape?' he later wrote. 'By the sharp practice of the illustrious Earl of Clarendon'. Up to the night before the opening of the Commission, Duffy did not know what he was to be tried for, or where. On the morning of the trial, O'Loghlen came to him in prison and asked 'Would you like to have your trial postponed again?' 'Certainly', said Duffy, 'whatever chance I have depends upon delay'. O'Loghlen explained that Clarendon, in order to get a safer jury, had transferred the trial from the City to the County. The Crown had failed to give the required ten day's notice of a change of venue. The point was debated at length, but the trial judges were compelled to rule 'with lugubrious faces' that the trial could not go on.

Before Duffy's third appearance in Court, in December, the remnants of the Dublin Clubs sent a deputation to his family offering to rescue him. How they proposed to do this was not revealed. But Duffy immediately rejected the project. 'I would not purchase my individual safety by one human life', he wrote.

He describes a second, 'more touching' incident:

Ten of my fellow prisoners, leaders of Clubs, members of Council, or American agents, came to my cell on a certain night in December, assured me that the turnkeys were drinking with the sentinels, and offered to seize on the guard and open the door. It was a project to be executed then and there; but as it meant certain ruin, either in the struggle or afterwards, to half the men engaged, and the advantage was to be mine alone, it was not a project compatible with conscience or honour.

One of the prisoners involved in this bold plan was Nicholas Rochford, who later served in the American army, and finally resided in Australia.

On 15 December, when Duffy had been five months in prison, he was again brought forward. The indictment, which occupied one hundred feet of closely printed parchment, now contained six counts, including the new one charging him with inciting Smith O'Brien to make war on the Queen.

Before the trial began astonished reporters were told that none of the proceedings were to be published. When Duffy protested that the prohibition was substantially unjust to him, Mr. Justice Perrin replied that the order was made to protect him and the Crown equally. The logic of this was lost on Duffy, and on *Freeman's Journal*, which published the court order in large type, followed by a blank column and this quotation from Lord Ashburton: 'Many causes have combined to perfect the English system of procedure: but publicity more than all the others is the essential principle and primary source of that perfection which has justly raised the English courts of judicature so high in the estimation of the civilised world'.

There was intense public indignation, shared by the press of all parties, including even *The Times*. Mr. Justice Perrin withdrew his ill-conceived order, and the trial proceeded. Duffy's ingenious counsel soon found serious flaws in the new bill of indictment. They demurred, and after a fortnight spent in debates and adjournments, the Court had to admit that four of the six counts were bad in law. The moment this decision was given, Duffy's counsel declared that he was ready for trial. They were eager to have him tried on the broken indictment, which would shut out damaging evidence. But the Crown argued there was no necessity to proceed. As Duffy had demurred, all that was now necessary was to pass sentence. Laymen will be puzzled by the complexities of this manoevure. Duffy thus attempted to explain it:

> In misdemeanour, if a prisoner demurs he admits the offence, but contends that it has not been charged according to law. If he succeeds in his legal argument, the indictment fails; if he does not succeed, he is sentenced as if he had been convicted by a jury. But in trials for High Treason a man may demur and afterwards plead, as the case involves results too serious to be risked on the whim of a judge. Treason-felony, my counsel insisted, followed the same rule, for the same reason. The Attorney-General insisted that it did not, and that I must forthwith be sentenced to transportation without trial, and on the indictment three-fourths of which had been declared bad in law. The spectators asked, in amazement, was a man to be transported because in the opinion of the Court his counsel had made a mistake in pleading?

Butt protested that in cases of High Treason, the accused could plead as well as demur, and that the same rule applied to treason-felony. Again, the courtroom echoed to the tumult of bewigged battle. After three more weeks of 'portentous ponderings' (Duffy's phrase) the Court came to the remarkable conclusion that Duffy must be tried, and even convicted, before he could be sentenced. At last, on 18 January, Duffy entered a plea of 'not guilty' and declared himself ready for trial. But the learned judges peremptorily refused to proceed. (In Duffy's words 'Gruff Perrin grunted a savage negative'.) Belatedly, they adjourned for their Christmas holidays. A series of legal skirmishes followed, in which Duffy's formidable defence team repeatedly shattered the Crown case, and it was not till 15 February 1849 that he finally appeared before a jury to enter a plea of 'not guilty'. The indictment had been reduced to two counts. Of his fellow prisoners in Newgate, one had been acquitted, two convicted, and twenty discharged unconditionally. The prisoners in Cork, Kilkenny, and Galway had also been released. O'Doherty, after three trials, had been found guilty, strongly recommended to mercy, and sentenced to ten years' transportation. Williams, as had been expected, was acquitted. Duffy was the sole political prisoner untried. This time the Government was so confident of success that the name of the steam frigate — the *Dragon* — destined to transport him, was known to confidants of the Castle.

What Duffy feared most was another packed jury. Before the trial began, he wrote to the Attorney-General, warning him that he would not consider a trial by a jury fabricated by the Castle as a fair trial, and giving a detailed account of jury-packing in other state trials. The letter was widely publicised, and Dr. Murray of Maynooth and Dr. Spratt, a Dublin friar, drew up a memorial to Clarendon against the practice of packed and partisan juries, which was signed by more than 'four hundred Catholic priests and forty prelates, deans and archbishops . . . a host of Catholic and Protestant gentlemen and upwards of seventy thousand of the people'. Lord Cloncurry, in signing it, said that to petition against jury-packing was like memorialising a Government not to commit highway robbery. A typical paragraph read: 'Let Your Excellency bear in mind that deeply at the root of the deadly hatred of English domination that festered in the hearts of the great mass of the Catholic population since that domination was first established over them, lies a feeling of utter distrust, and, in State Trials, of utter despair of an impartial administration of law'.

Clarendon politely rejected the memorial as 'elaborate and circumstantial, but absurdly fallacious'. He had no control over the Sheriff who drew up the jury panels, he explained. When the panel was announced Duffy sent the list to Macaulay, then a Cabinet Minister. In the first two volumes of his recently-published, *History of England* which Duffy had read in prison, Macaulay had vigorously denounced the practice of jury-packing under James II. (Five years before, Macaulay had sent Duffy three volumes of his essays with a friendly letter.) Duffy describes the list as an 'agreeable array of my peers and neighbours, indifferently chosen', who included:

> The jeweller to the Lord-Lieutenant, the hairdresser of the Lord-Lieutenant, his Excellency's shoemaker, the chandler to the Chief Secretary, the bootmaker to the Commander of the Forces, the engineer to the Drainage Commissioners, the cutler, grocer, and purveyor to the Castle; the saddler and seedsman of a former Lord-Lieutenant, three Government contractors, a compositor in the College Printing Office, two vicars choral of St. Patrick's Cathedral, the auctioneer to the Commissioners of Woods and Forests, and the Consul of King Ernest of Hanover.

'These exposures made it discreditable and dangerous to array another jury on which there was no Catholic', says Duffy. A complaisant Catholic had to be found who would give the appearance of impartiality, while not really sympathising with the Young Irelanders. The Sheriff picked on Martin Burke, proprietor of the Shelbourne Hotel, 'a hotel frequented by the gentry', Duffy wrote, 'and a man long accustomed to consult their wishes'. Burke was a prudent citizen, who had never taken part in Catholic agitation. Butt, knowing his reputation, wanted to challenge him, but Duffy, to the consternation of his advisers, insisted that Burke be retained. He later explained why:

> The night before the trial Mrs. Burke called on my wife . . . and admonished her not to permit her husband to be objected to. 'His daughter and myself', she said, 'will take our seats in the gallery opposite him, and if the evidence enables an honest man to find a verdict of acquittal he need not return home if he goes against Mr. Duffy'.

Mrs. and Miss Burke duly sat in the gallery, and Mr. Burke duly stood out firmly against the eleven other jurors for an acquittal. His reason, he afterwards explained, was not because Duffy was not 'technically guilty', but because in certain cases there was a justice beyond the law. He did not mention Mrs. Burke's extra-legal intervention. Jury-packing, it seemed, could be practiced on both sides.

When Duffy was sent back to Newgate to await his fifth trial, he received a generous letter from John Martin, who with O'Brien, Meagher, McManus and others, was in Richmond Bridewell, awaiting transportation. Martin praised Duffy's strategy of resisting 'the main body of the enemy's forces — his jury-packers', and regretted that he and others had not followed the same line:

> And though you know Duffy that I am so unfortunate as to differ from you on many points of policy, and upon at least one serious matter of personal opinion, I am proud to acknowledge in you, after glorious Davis, the father of Irish National Party and the chief writer of the party. But for *The Nation* which your generous boldness and your fixedness of purpose and your able pen have maintained for the last six years, as our standard and rallying point of patriotism, every one of us — even Mitchel — would have remained in dull, hopeless obscurity . . .

DUFFY did not welcome visitors to Newgate, but he was pleased to see Father Mathew. And one day William Wilde called, with Samuel Ferguson, who expressed the belief that there would be a successful middle-class Protestant movement for some sort of legislature in Ireland.

In the 'desultory and discursive' diary which Duffy kept in prison, he records a visit from a fellow-prisoner, James Fintan Lalor:

> I have seen Lalor for the first time in bed, poor fellow, with complicated maladies. Nature has been very unkind; he is almost a dwarf, near-sighted, with a face far from being winning or sympathetic. But he has a precious jewel in his head . . . H is quite confident that this country which was so recently appealed to in vain, is eager for an opportunity to fight, and may make a revolution before the end of 1850 . . . he seems totally incapable of seeing facts which contradict his theory. He is without money, and though I have little enough it is the duty of one poor patriot to help another. Imprisonment is endangering his life, and I will move any one who can help to obtain his release . . .

Lalor said he had not forgiven Mitchel 'for stealing his opinions and parading them as his own'. He had refused to write for the *United Irishman;* when he wrote for the *Felon,* it was to condemn Mitchel's 'incredible policy of inciting revolution without making any preparation for it'.

After the Clonmel trial, Duffy was allowed no visitors except his wife, and no letters or papers. But he still had his books and writing materials, and he found that, despite the defeat of his cause, time had brought tranquillity. 'I had the sense of having done my duty', he wrote, 'and the long peaceful evenings spent in thought, and lighted up with the hope of reviving the cause if I escaped conviction, have left a memory gentle and pensive, but by no means unpleasant'.

Before the next trial, Duffy was moved from Newgate to Richmond prison which was still under municipal control. State prisoners there, as before, were allowed many privileges. An invitation sent out by Meagher to one of his friends, read:

> We are having a little *soiree* here on Monday evening, and we warmly unite in requesting the pleasure of your company. We shall have something of a supper and a dance of course. The Governor has most kindly given us the use of his apartments, and desires me to intimate to all our friends his wish that they should ask at the hatch for the Governor.

Early in April, Sir Lucius O'Brien and twenty-six Irish Members presented a memorial to Lord Clarendon, urging that the prosecution be dropped. The memorial represented Duffy's long and close imprisonment, his loss of health, and ruin of property; his high character; and the political excitement all over Europe at the time he wrote the publications charged, also the inhumanity of instituting repeated prosecutions for the same offence. Lord Clarendon replied angrily that Duffy was undoubtedly guilty, and that there was no precedent for remonstrating against the trial of a person, particularly when that person had not expressed the slightest contrition for what he had done, or had offered any pledge that he would not repeat the offence. Some members of the deputation pointed out that the guilt of a person was ascertained by the verdict of a jury, and by no other way.

IN the eighth month of Duffy's imprisonment a pamphlet appeared in Dublin titled 'Vindication of Charles Gavan Duffy from the Hired Slanderers of the Government Press, consisting of Statements made by Priests and others as to Duffy's character'. It protested against the vilification of Duffy by the Government press, which variously described him as a Communist, a Socialist, a Red Republican, an Infidel, and the architect, if not the perpetrator, of horrible assorted villainies. 'Mr. Duffy's libeller', it said, 'did not imagine that with the Habeas Corpus Act suspended, a gagged press, and a paralysed people, a voice or pen could be found bold enough to vindicate the man they had crucified', and it referred to the 'singularly unique combat . . . waging now, under our eyes, between a man of frail physical constitution, the last of a scattered party . . . and the concentrated power of a triumphant Government . . .'

In an open letter to Clarendon, the 'Vindication' said:

> Look even at the English journals; *The Times* thundering against the shutting up of the Court in secret conclave by Judge Perrin; the *Standard* denouncing you for creating new precedents of barbarity in your still-beginning and never-ending prosecutions, and the *Morning Advertiser* calling on you, in the name of English humanity, to desist.

Dr. Murray did not always approve of *The Nation's* policy, but he was always Duffy's loyal friend, and he denounced the *Evening Post,* an organ of the Irish Government and a constant traducer of Duffy, in language that came strangely from the lips of a distinguished theologian:

> Three times a week these foul and fetid jaws were opened to vomit forth such abominable slanders as modest men could sometimes hardly read without a blush, and timid men without a shudder. If a convent were sacked in one place and its inmates violated; if a church were desecrated in another place; if in another a man's brains were dashed out or his throat cut ... straightway the Castle witch sent out a direful howl and stretched out her long, brown, skinny arms to protect the altars and the homes of Irishmen from the demon assaults of Duffy and Meagher and the rest.

Duffy's income had ceased with the closing of *The Nation* and after eight months of legal conflict, his funds were almost exhausted. Without consulting him, Father Mathew organised a committee which met at the Shelbourne Hotel to raise money for his defence. But Duffy would not sanction it. The management of O'Connell's Repeal Funds had so disgusted the public, that he was resolved never to accept any 'pecuniary tribute'.

The fifth trial opened on 10 April 1849, nine months and two days after Duffy's arrest. Felony cases were usually tried by a common jury. This time, the Sheriff summoned only special jurors. These, according to statute, were 'the sons of peers, baronets and knights, magistrates, ex-sheriffs, grand jurors, squires, bankers, merchants, and traders worth £5,000'.

When the panel was called, only seventy of one hundred and seventy answered their names. The list was again called, but despite a penalty of £50, only twenty more answered. By challenging man after man on various grounds, Duffy's counsel made it impossible to produce a jury that did not include a few Catholics and liberal Protestants.

The trial, which lasted three days, was enlivened by an incident which grew into a popular myth. According to the myth, which many writers have subscribed to, Margaret Callan and 'Speranza' were sitting in the gallery when the Solicitor-General attributed 'Speranza's' fiery article 'Alea Jacta Est' to Duffy, whereupon 'Speranza' leapt to her feet and claimed the authorship. In fact, it was Mrs. Callan who, roused by the Solicitor-General's wilful lying, cried: 'You know well who the author is, and you are falsifying the facts'.

It was near midnight on Good Friday when Duffy was brought from his cell beneath the courtroom to hear the verdict. He described the scene:

> The court was as crowded as a theatre on a command night, with an audience of both sexes and all ranks in the city. There was silence as in a church. The Judge despatched the Sheriff to ascertain whether the jury had agreed to their verdict. He remained away five, eight, ten minutes. 'They are writing their verdict' was the whispered opinion. The Sheriff returned, crossed the court to his own box in solemn silence, and then, after a theatrical pause, announced that the jury could not agree. A shout of triumph, that made the roof ring, burst from the audience. The jury were called into court and announced they were divided half and half. They were locked up all night. After twelve hours they returned, this time with seven voting for acquittal.

117

The jury was discharged, and Butt addressed the Court: 'Now my Lords', he said, 'I have to apply to your Lordships that Mr. Duffy also be discharged, or, if that course be not acceded to, I move, my Lords that he be admitted to bail'.

The Attorney-General said he had no objection to bail, and Duffy entered into a personal surety of £1.000 (the source of which was not disclosed) and two sureties of £500 each, provided by Mr. Grace, a Capel Street bookseller, and Mr. Dillon, a Henry Street auctioneer. 'The announcement of the Attorney-General was received with loud cheers', said the *Examiner*. 'In the course of the afternoon . . . the portals of the prison were thrown open, and the captive, after nine months' gloomy durance, was set at liberty'. A loud shout of exaltation greeted him as he was stepping into a covered car with his wife and a few friends. His appearance was pale, the *Examiner* noted.

The historic case *Regina v Duffy* had ended.

'IS Lord Clarendon satisfied now? ' asked the *Freeman's Journal:*

> Just before Mr. Duffy was put on trial a second time, His Excellency pronounced him guilty of treason-felony . . . Fortunately there is in these countries no vice-regal road to verdicts . . . Mr. Duffy leaves the jail as the conqueror of the Whigs in Ireland. To crush him they left no villainy undone. They have failed — blessed be Almighty God — disgracefully failed . . .

The London press generally expressed satisfaction with Duffy's release. The *Daily News*, for example, said:

> As we never felt a deeper interest in any trial, so we never were more gratified with the result . . . Mr. Duffy is not only a man of superior intellect, but of the purest patriotism and of spotless integrity both in the public and private relations of life. In the high character of Mr. Duffy are to be found the secret and the source of that profound sympathy which has been so universally felt in his case — and scarcely more universally felt in his own country than on this side of the Channel.

The *Illustrated London News* was less sympathetic: 'Mr. Duffy', it said, 'is more fortunate than . . . the other heroes of the Irish rebellion of 1848, though possibly quite as guilty as they, has managed to escape their fate'. And it commented philosophically, 'Trial by jury is a lottery in some parts of the world, and a farce in others'. But it urged the Crown to let the matter drop ere trial by jury was brought into 'needless and mischievous disrepute' by its failures. Mr. Duffy, it added, was very properly granted bail, 'considering that he has spent nine months in prison, and that he has lost the whole of his property in consequence of his incarceration. 'While Ireland will rejoice', it concluded, 'Great Britain will not be sorry to hear no more of Duffy'.

Nine months imprisonment had not blunted Duffy's quill. He commemorated his freedom by publishing in *The Nation* a pungent letter, of more than four thousand words addressed to Lord Clarendon. In this he recounted in detail the stratagems of the Crown in the Five

SCALPEEN.

Illustrated London News, 15 December 1849

Commissions before which he had appeared, and declared that he had escaped 'through every step of this eventful history, by the malice of George William Villiers'. He began with a summary of his long ordeal:

> There are twelve judges in Ireland, my Lord, and I have stood before ten of them in succession to answer your indictments.
> There are but six Commissions of Oyer and Terminer, and I was carried before five of them at your instance. One bill of indictment on one charge is the ordinary practice of criminal law; I answered five bills of indictment exhibiting the same charge, each in a new and aggravated form ... You called the devil to your aid, and your shots, like the fiend's bullet in 'Der Freischutz', missed their victim and struck your own purpose in the head.

The blistering indictment ended with another burst of rhetoric:

> A Christian slave led into the amphitheatre to be delivered to the wild beasts, who saw tier after tier of contemptuous faces frowning down upon him, the toga and the sword staked against him, hardly fronted a more unequal and fierce array than I the first day I was carried into Green Street. And yet the cloud of enemies have vanished away like a theatrical show, and I am still here — and free.

And Duffy quoted with pride the moral which Carlyle had elicited from the long struggle: 'Consider yourself as a brand snatched from the burning: a *providential* man, saved by Heaven, for doing a man's work yet!'

~Part 2~

Seven

A Tour of Ireland

THOUGH he seldom mentions it in his writings, Duffy was often in ill-health, and according to a writer in *The Nation*, prison life 'sowed . . . the seeds of an insidious disease, an affection of the liver, which . . . brought him more than once to the gates of death'; yet within six weeks of his release he accompanied Carlyle on a strenuous tour of the south and west of Ireland.

Carlyle had continued to brood over Ireland. He had seen little of it during his brief visit in 1846. In the spring of 1848 he contemplated a more leisurely excursion. On 17 May, he confided to his diary: 'Am thinking of a tour in Ireland: unhappily have no call or *desire* that way, or any way, but am driven out somewhither (just now) as by the point of bayonets at my back. Ireland really *is* my problem: the breaking point of the huge suppuration which all British and European society now is'. He was determined to see Ireland again, and to write about it in such a way that England might be moved into a better realisation of its obligations.

On Thursday 30 June, Carlyle sailed from near London Bridge on the steamer *Athlone* arriving in Dublin on the morning of the following Tuesday. He kept fragmentary notes of the journey which were published after his death. Off the Irish coast at Wexford, he recalled the rebellion of '98, and wrote: 'I thought of the battle of Vinegar Hill, but not with interest; with sorrow, rather, and contempt; one of the ten times ten thousand futile, fruitless battles this brawling, unreasonable people had fought . . .'

Duffy arrived at the Imperial hotel, about 10.30 pm., and sipped a glass of lemonade while Carlyle drank punch. Carlyle had 'a stock of letters, to be used or not, especially for the ruined West', and Duffy took them home with him to work out their itinerary. Carlyle 'after a silent pipe . . . tumbled into bed'. Among his letters were introductions to Dr. Stokes, President of the College of Physicians, and to Sir Alexander MacDonnell, Chief Commissioner of Education, both sons of United Irishmen, and Duffy introduced him to the barrister and Counsellor Isaac Butt, whom Carlyle described as 'a terribly black, burly son of earth; talent visible in him, but still more animalism; big bison-head, black, not *quite* unbrutal; glad when he went off 'to the Galway Circuit' or whithersoever'.

While he was in his bathing-tub next morning ('all covered with suds') he received an invitation to dine with the Viceroy, Lord Clarendon, which he declined 'handsomely' as he dried himself. After only two hours' sleep, he breakfasted with Duffy and four fellows from Trinity, including Dr. Murray, ('wild Maynooth priest'), Hancock, the Political Philosophy Professor, and Ingram, the Laureate of '98. Carlyle made a brief note of the conversation: 'Talk again England versus Ireland, a sad unreasonable humour pervading all the Irish population on this matter — England does not hate you at all, nor love you at all; merely values and will pay you according to the work you can do'.

'Oh, Goody, Goody, I am really likely to be killed with "attentions" here', Carlyle wrote to his wife from Dublin on 6 July. ('Goody' was his affectionate name for Jane.) 'I have just seen Stella's *scull* (the very cranium: it nearly made me cry) . . . and then directly to MacGregor's dinner etc. etc.'. Carlyle jotted down 'Sad reflections upon Dublin and the animosities that reign in its hungry existence':

> *Not* now the capital of Ireland, has Ireland any Capital, or *where* is its future capital to be? Perhaps Glasgow or Liverpool is its 'real' capital city just now. Here are no longer lords of any kind, not even the sham lords, with their land revenues come hither now. The place has no manufactures to speak of; except of ale or whisky, and a little poplin work . . .

After five days in Dublin, the travellers started by rail for the South and West by way of Kildare, where Carlyle recorded his first impressions of the Irish countryside:

> One of the wretchedest wild villages I ever saw, and full of ragged beggars: exotic altogether like a village in Dahomey, man and church both. Knots of worshipping people hung about the streets, and everywhere round them hovered a harpy swarm of clamorous mendicants — men, women, children; a village winged, as if a flight of harpies had alighted on it. Here for the first time was Irish beggary itself.

The itinerary planned by Duffy took them through Lismore, Waterford, Youghal, Castlemartyr, Cork, Killarney, Limerick, Clare, Lough Derg on the Shannon, Galway, and Castlebar to Westport. They drove the seventy miles from Cork to Killarney on the roof of the coach, 'a rapid wild journey', Carlyle wrote to Jane, 'thro' some of the saddest miles I have seen; land drearier almost all than most Scotch moors, and filled with the horridest scenes of human beggary':

> We met once a heap of human males and females, huddled into carts, escorted by green Police, criminals going to Cork for trial. Another time we passed thro' two long rows of tattered wretches, sitting under the screen of the hedges waiting for 'outdoor relief'. In every village were hordes of beggars, scrambling, sometimes fighting for the coppers, or even for the hope of them.

At Westport Carlyle inspected the workhouse, 'the wonder of the universe at present', which had a Government grant of £1,100 a week. 'Human swinery here has reached its acme, happily', he wrote. (Thirty thousand paupers in this union, population supposed to be about 60,000. . . Abomination of desolation, what can you make of it'. Three or four hundred 'big hulks of fellows' were engaged in 'Out door quasi-work', pretending to be shovelling earth. In each shovel there was an ounce or two of mould. It was 'all make-believe'. So was the work of five or six hundred boys pretending to be breaking stone. 'Can it be a charity to keep men alive on these terms?' Carlyle asked himself. And he offered a simple solution: 'In the face of all the twaddle on the earth, shoot a man rather than train him (with heavy expense to his neighbours) to be a deceptive human being'.

In a workshop in Kilkenny, described as one of the best-conducted in Ireland, they found a crowd of infant children crowded into a tiny room, 'the mephitic atmosphere of which would poison a grown man'.

Carlyle's bitterness increased as they journeyed on. At Sligo he wrote:

> Beggars, beggars, only industry *really* followed by the Irish people. 'For the love of God, yer hanar!' etc. etc. 'Wouldn't it be worth your consideration, whether you hadn't better drown yourself, or hang yourself, than live a dog's life in this way?' They withdrew from me in horror, did at least withdraw!

But the picture had another side. The travellers were shown the residence of a baronet who lived in London on a rental of £30,000 a year extracted from his Irish tenants. Within a few months he had evicted 320 of them, and he was in arrears with his poor-rate.

Carlyle had much else to grumble at in this troubled land of beauty and beggary. He found all its religious 'too irreligious . . . really in sad truth doing mischief to the people instead of good'. And, persuaded to try Killiney's popular drink, a mixture of whisky and goat's milk, he pronounced it, not surprisingly, a 'greasy abomination'. But he had pleasant memories of Irish hospitality.

At Killaloe, he was entertained by the sixty-eight-year-old Sir Richard Bourke, a former Governor of New South Wales, who had bought the estate on his return from Australia. Carlyle described him as 'a fine soldier' with 'a lean clean face hacked with sabre scars and bullet scars', who still rose at 6 o'clock every morning. In Galway, Carlyle's genial host was an editor Edward Butler, later to become Attorney-General of New South Wales.

To Carlyle's family at Scotsbrig, Ireland was a wild and terrifying place. He was able to reassure them. He wrote to his brother John: 'Tell my dear mother that the Papists have not hurt me in the least; on the contrary, they were abundantly kind and hospitable to me . . .'

'Owing to the magic companionship of Mr. Duffy', wrote Froude, 'Carlyle met and talked freely with priests and patriots'. Carlyle noted how people were 'most reverent to Duffy'. He was 'the idol, and sacred martyr of all the repeal population, which I think means all the mere-Irish population taken together . . .' Wherever they went, crowds gathered to honour him. In Dungarvan, the entire population turned out to gaze at him, and in Castlebar, a young woman shyly thrust a bouquet into his hands, accompanied by a welcoming verse.

Carlyle was, in his own words 'in sad health and sad humour', but Duffy found him always a gracious and appreciative companion. 'We travelled for six weeks on a stretch, nearly always tete-a-tete' Duffy wrote. 'During those weeks of close and constant intercourse, there was not one word or act of his to the young man who was his travelling companion, unworthy of an indulgent father. Of arrogance or impatience not a shade'.

Sometimes, Duffy recalled, they broached 'dangerously explosive topics', as when Carlyle, in his own words, 'argued with Duffy about Smith O'Brien, I infinitely vilipending, he hotly eulogising the said Smith'. They were on safer ground when they discussed writers. Carlyle was uncompromising in his verdicts. Wordsworth was 'essentially a cold, hard, silent man', with 'an immense head and great jaws like a crocodile'; Coleridge, 'a poor, greedy, sensual creature who could not keep from the laudanum bottle though he knew it would kill him'; Shelley was 'a poor shrieking creature who had said or sung nothing worth a serious man being at the trouble of remembering)'. Carlyle's association gave Duffy invaluable moral support. Half a century later, Duffy told Carlyle's biographer David Alec Wilson, with pride and gratitude:

> It was a rare good thing for him to go about with me as he did, and what nobody else who counted so much would ever have dreamed of doing. The Castle resented it. He showed me a letter of private remonstrance he received from the Lord-Lieutenant, Clarendon. It made no difference at all — he stood by me steadily, and merely by doing so, did me immense good.

Through Bundoran and Ballyshannon the travellers drove to Donegal, and saw little life in the 'dingy desolate' country. From Donegal, they travelled over high dark moors, with 'here and there a speck reclaimed into bright green — and the poorest cottier oftenest gone'. Carlyle's journey ended at Derry, where he was to board a steamer for Scotland. He had been more than five weeks in Ireland. In a later diary entry, Carlyle summed up his Irish tour: 'Ugly spectacle . . . a thing unjoyful to look back upon. The whole country figures in mind like a ragged coat: one huge beggar's gaberdine, not patchable any longer; far from a joyful or beautiful spectacle'.

Duffy, too, made a resume in his diary. It was rather more sympathetic:

> We travelled slowly from Limerick to Sligo, and we found everywhere the features of a recently conquered country. Clare was almost a wilderness from Kilrush to Coforin. The desolate shores of Lough Corrib would have resembled a desert, but that the stumps of ruined houses showed that not Nature, but Man, had been the desolater. Between Killala Bay and Sligo, during an entire day's travel, we estimated that every second dwelling was pulled down; and not cabins alone, but stone houses for the residence of a substantial yeomanry.
> The degradation which had fallen on the generous and spirited Celtic race was a sight such as I had nowhere seen or read of. The famine and the landlords have actually created a *new race* in Ireland. We saw on the streets of Galway crowds of creatures more debased than the Yahoos of Swift — creatures having only a distant and hideous resemblance to human beings. Grey-headed old men, whose idiotic faces had hardened into a settled leer of mendicancy, and women filthier and more frightful than the harpies, who at the jingle of a coin on the pavement swarmed in myriads from unseen places; struggling, screaming, *shrieking* for their prey, like some monstrous and unclean animals.

In Westport the sight of the priest on the street gathered an entire pauper population, thick as a village market, swarming round him for relief. Beggar children, beggar adults, beggars in white hairs, girls with faces grey and shrivelled; women with the more touching and tragic aspect of lingering shame and self-respect not yet effaced; and among these terrible realities, impostures shaking in pretended fits to add the last touch of horrible grotesqueness to the picture! I saw these accursed sights, and they are burned into my memory for ever . . .

'PEOPLE say the Queen is coming to look at Ireland, foolish creature', Carlyle had written to Duffy in June 1849. No British monarch had crossed the Irish sea since the visit of His Corpulent Majesty, George IV, in 1821. When Lord Bessborough, then Lord Lieutenant of Ireland, had suggested a visit by Victoria in 1846, she had written to Lord John Russell: 'It is a journey which must one day or other be undertaken, and which the Queen would be glad to have accomplished, because it must be disagreeable to her that people should speculate whether she *dare* visit one part of her dominions. Much will depend on the proper moment . . .'. And Her Majesty added cautiously that the visit should be a 'National thing . . . a State act . . . done handsomely', and not paid out of the Civil List, which would not be able to bear it. The omens for a visit in 1849 were not propitious. Ireland was still agonised by famine, destitution and evictions. To these unexampled miseries were now added epidemics of cholera, dysentery and opthalmia. But Clarendon believed a visit by the thirty-year-old Queen, who retained much of her youthful charm, might help Ireland forget her troubles, and perhaps stimulate trade.

In a letter addressed to the Corporation of London, in the middle of July, Clarendon said he was convinced Ireland's evils were entirely social in their origin. 'The whole social system', he wrote, 'has been based on the potato, and the failure of that root has consequently entailed universal distress'.

> Hence so many landed proprietors are now unable to pay the interest on their mortgages. Tenants can no longer pay their rent; and the peasants, for want of employment, are driven upon the rates, of which the collection daily becomes more difficult. Such a state of things . . . must go from bad to worse, for the means of improvement are altogether wanting, and the national resources are gradually wasting. Even if the potato were to revive (and to that all classes are now clinging with desperate hope) it would only bring back the evils under which the country has long been labouring. It is manifest that a complete change of system as regards agriculture, the tenure of land, and the social habits of the people, has become indispensible and that change can only be affected by the introduction of English capital, enterprise and skill.

The *Illustrated London News* agreed. The Corporation of London had all these requirements, and there need be no fear that the Irish peasant would not work when he was fairly treated. The cultivation of the land on the principle of a fair return for capital and labour would wean him from 'the root of idleness and mischief, the potato' and supersede the old system of 'a reckless rental, a small potato patch, a multitudinous family, and a pig'.

How would the Irish people react to a Royal Tour? Two years before — in October 1847 — Clarendon had noted two apparently contradictory attitudes in Ireland. In the same letter, he had written: 'Distress, discontent, hatred of English are increasing everywhere', and 'whatever may be the political feelings or animosities of the Irish, their devotion to the Queen is unquestionable and whenever Her Majesty shall think proper to come to Ireland I am convinced she would be received with enthusiastic loyalty'. It seemed that the Irish, even the Repealers, could dissociate the Monarchy from the Ministry. Daniel O'Connell had waded into the waters of Kingstown Harbour to welcome George IV, and when the Young Irelanders held one of their biggest meetings in Dublin on 15 April 1848, Victoria's health, as Queen of Ireland, was proposed and drunk (in tea, of course) with gusto, while an Irish harpist played 'God Save the Queen'. But at first the Dublin press was not entirely enthusiastic about the forthcoming visit. *The Freeman's Journal* thought that the Queen would see a better picture of Ireland in an unroofed hut in Connaught, with the 'miserable, emaciated inhabitants . . . perishing on the dung-heap beside it', than in the beauties of Killarney. To which the *Illustrated London News* replied:

> The Queen, it has been alleged, will not see the dark side of Ireland. She will not behold with her own eyes the wretchedness of the peasantry, the fertile acres lying uncultivated for want of capital and of skill — the roofless cabins of myriads of homeless people . . . she is not ignorant of these matters . . . She knows them, she deplores them, and she will do her best to relieve them. She does not proceed to Ireland on a holiday trip.

One Dublin paper — the Tory *Daily Mail* — had a practical suggestion to save Her Majesty from unpleasant sights. Dilapidated, windowless houses in the streets through which she would pass should be 'patched up', and furnished 'as well as possible with window curtains, muslin blinds and flower pots'. In the second issue of the *Irish Felon* (1 July 1848) Meagher wrote an article headed 'The Queen Will Visit Ireland this summer'. 'Why not?' he asked. 'Her Gracious Majesty had been to the Chateau d'Eu, to the Highlands, to Brussels, and up the Rhine. Ireland, too is worth seeing, and might furnish an interesting sketch or two for the Royal Scrapbook':

> Besides, the people here have been fretting about a famine — which killed a few thousand last year in the quietest possible manner — and, of late, their discontent has been intemperate. They are a forgiving people, however, and a Royal visit — the nod of a crowned head, the salute of a white and jewelled hand — will reconcile them at once more, and for ever, to their garrets, their rags, and their crusts.
> The enthusiasm will be unbounded; the cheers — deafening! triumphal marches — magnificent! crowds delirious with joy! It will be a brilliant picture, on the whole. Gold lace and ostrich plumes — balconies full of dimples — and silks, and bouquets — sandwiches and sunshades — fealty and fashion — pauperism in Sunday clothes — the entire Government stock shown off to the best advantage.
> And then — all along the quays — the bridges — clinging to lampposts —

127

looking out from chimney pots and parapets — the loyal and gallant people of Ireland. How rapturously they fling their tattered hats in the air — how vehemently they wave their felon flags in token of loyalty and repentence. How madly they shout 'Long Live the Queen!'

'Is it thus', he concluded, 'with a bit of polished court-plaster, that this wild and wounded nation will be cured and tamed? Have we not learned as yet to set the proper price on golden fripperies — flimsy fireworks which whiz and sparkle, but which neither heat the soil nor purify the sky'. However, the smiling Victoria charmed the people she encountered, especially when she appeared in an evening dress of green Irish poplin, elaborately embroidered with gold shamrocks, and enjoyed a drive in a jaunting car.

With the traditional trappings of a Royal Tour — arches, decorations, flags, illuminations, bands, processions, receptions, banquets and balls — Dublin had a brief reminder of its pre-Union splendour. The Queen wrote to her uncle Leopold, King of the Belgians:

> Our entrance into Dublin was really a magnificent thing. We drove out yesterday afternoon and were followed by jaunting cars and riders and people running and screaming, which would have amused you. In the evening we had a dinner party and so we have tonight . . . You see more ragged and wretched people here than I ever saw anywhere else. *En revanche*, the women are really very handsome — quite in the lowest class — as well at Cork as here: such beautiful black eyes and hair and such fine colours and teeth.

There was an awkward moment when Mr. James Nugent, one of the Guardians of the North Union Workhouse, approached the Royal barouche which was moving slowly along Parkgate street, with its four horses, postillions and outriders. He cried: 'Mighty monarch, pardon Smith O'Brien'. Before the fellow was vouschafed a reply, Lord Clarendon rode up and 'put him aside'.

Another nationalistic and discordant note was struck by the Catholic clergy and inhabitants of Balingarry, who presented the Queen with an address that read, in part:

> If the bones of those who perished of want and misery in this land for the last 18 months were disinterred and strewed at moderate intervals, they would form an appropriate footway for the ministers from Cork to Dublin. . . Let us assure thee, that the bones of young mothers, who perished for want of sustenance . . . would alone fill the largest suite of apartments in the proud castle of Windsor up to the ceilings . . . The £42,000 lately voted for the British Museum, to furnish nick-nacks for the amusement of what is termed the British Public, would have saved thirty thousand lives in Ireland. The Admiralty expenses attendant on the Royal visit to our shore, would have saved the lives of five hundred young mothers; and when that hour of death will come, which must come to all, and late may it come on thy Majesty, the recollection of those five hundred young Irishwomen saved, and of their grateful tears and blessings, would afford thy Majesty more consolation than all the cannonnadings, triumphal arches and honeyed speeches that ever graced the progress of a monarch . . . Picture to

thyself, thy royal children reduced by some such catastrophe . . . imagine them inhabiting some cold and damp hovel, without fire, almost without clothing, without a blanket to cover them in the long winter night. Imagine them obliged to subsist on two unsavoury meals of four ounces each through the inclement days of a long and dreary winter. Imagine thy Royal husband sharing the same sad lot . . . Imagine him obliged to work on such diet for eight hours, and to walk daily six miles without shoes, and half naked, to fulfill his thankless and wageless task; and then, Madam, thou wilt have realized some notion of what is called in Ireland, outdoor relief.

One assumes Her Majesty was not amused.

While the Queen was admiring the beautiful black eyes of the Irish women, the correspondent of the *Illustrated London News* was reporting on the horrors of the Irish countryside. In one despatch, he described a visit to Killarney, where a whole street of cabins had lately been demolished:

> The wretched inhabitants were unable to pay rent or rates and refused to go out unless evicted . . . they now swarm in the lanes and alleys of the town, along with hundreds of the peasantry who have been evicted . . . for the same reason and in the same fashion . . . roofless walls remain to show the number and the extent of the wretched but doubtless well-beloved home, that are homes no more for these poverty-stricken Irishmen.
> The Irish peasant lives in a wigwam and shares it with a pig. The smoke of his peat fire escapes by the low door or by the narrow unglazed aperture that serves for a window. His children swarm half-naked about him. The atmosphere he breathes is thick with peat smoke and foul exhalations . . . These are generally the cabins from which the inmates are evicted. Their miserable inhabitants if they do not die by the roadside — a not infrequent case — swarm into the already overcrowded towns or villages, or take refuge in the Union.

A few months later, he was at Kilkee where the scene 'baffled description':

> Adults who appeared idiotic; children wrinkled with care . . . men more helpless than children with scarcely a rag to cover them. The habitations were mere kennels. I was heartsick and said 'Surely there cannot be so much suffering and neglect in any other spot on the face of the earth!'

He compared the mortality at the overcrowded Kilrush Union workhouse with that of the black hole of Calcutta. Most of the occupants had been evicted from their 'wigwams':

> Sixteen thousand and odd persons unhoused in the Union of Kilrush before . . . June in the present year; 71,000 on 130 holdings, done away in Ireland, and nearly as many houses destroyed in 1848; 254,000 holdings of more than one acre and less than five acres, put an end to between 1841 and 1848; six-tenths in fact, of the lowest class of tenantry driven from their now roofless or annihilated cabins and houses . . . The ruin is great and complete . . .

Even destitution had its class distinctions. The correspondent described two types of hovels he saw in Kilrush. The 'scalp' was a hole dug in the earth, two or three feet deep, roofed over with sticks and turf laid in the shape of an inverted saucer. 'It resembled one of the anthills of the African forest though it was not quite so large', he wrote. A 'scalpeen', too, was a hole but the roof was 'rather loftier' and 'grander', and it was altogether superior to the scalp.

> The mud cabins and turf huts that the peasantry lived in before 1846 were denounced by every traveller as the scandal of civilized Europe; it was supposed that worse habitations were not on the earth; but the Irish have proved . . . there is still a lower deep — that a scalpeen is worse than a mud hut and a scalp worse than a scalpeen . . . What hope, then, can be entertained to elevating the Irish . . . even to the dignity of mud cabins and plenty of potatoes? They may die out or may be killed off; but when the heart of the whole live on 6d a week, and are thankful for being allowed to burrow in scalps, there must be more hope of the savages in New South Wales or the Brazils . . . The present condition of the Irish, we have no hesitation in saying, has been mainly brought on by ignorance and vicious legislation . . .

DUFFY returned from his tour with Carlyle to find Dublin 'in a flutter of factitious enthusiasm' welcoming the Queen. The day after his arrival, 'a young Dublin priest (who afterwards died a martyr to his duty)' but whom Duffy does not identify, came to him in a fever of excitement to announce that the Secret Societies (also unidentified) were about to seize the Queen, and hold her as a hostage for the State prisoners:

> 'Hold her!' I said; 'have they got a Gibraltar for the purpose?' 'They'll carry her to the Dublin Mountains' he replied, 'and secrete her where "General Holt" so long baffled all the efforts of the British troops'. 'Folly, my friend', I rejoined: 'If we assume (and it is a preposterous assumption) that they succeeded in snatching the Queen from ten thousand British troops in Dublin and carrying her to the mountains, there is not a dell or glade in Kippure which would not be as well-trodden as Sackville Street before twenty-four hours'.

In spite of Duffy's warning, the attempt was still contemplated. On the night of 8 August when the Queen attended a private concert at the Royal Lodge in Phoenix Park, a band of volunteers were summoned to assemble at nine o'clock on the banks of the Grand Canal. About two hundred answered the call, armed with pistols and daggers. They decided they had no chance of defeating the garrison and dispersed.

The Queen did not forget her Irish subjects. After her next visit to Ireland in 1853, she and Prince Albert offered to subscribe £300 towards improving the housing of Dublin families if a public subscription, with a fair promise of success were opened. Her Majesty also intimated that some attempt should be made to 'improve the feeling of the lower classes with regard to their clothing as that they may be induced to keep them in a decent state of repair'.

Eight

'It was a glorious licking you gave that "Baptised Spaniel" . . .'

ACCORDING to all accounts Duffy had been bankrupted by his battle with the Crown. It is not clear what he and his family lived on when he set about reconstructing his life, but he did not lack advice from friends. Some urged him to seek tranquillity in the practice of law, and not to revive a struggle 'which had proved so barren and disastrous'. A few on the other hand suggested he resume it at the point it had reached before the suspension of Habeas Corpus. Some, notably Fintan Lalor, thought he should conspire for a speedy revival of insurrection.

John Dillon wanted him to transfer *The Nation* to London and to make it, not only the organ of Irish nationalism, but of philosophical radicalism throughout the Empire. Ireland, he thought, was not in a condition to maintain an outspoken, independent journal. 'Suppose' Dillon wrote to his wife, 'he (Duffy) were called upon to express his opinion on the relation of the Pope to his subjects, and suppose him to state his opinion truly (which he would not fail to do) would have the whole Irish Church upon his back . . .'

D'Arcy McGee agreed with Dillon, but he considered *The Nation* might with advantage be transferred to New York. He had started a *Nation* in New York, where he had decided to stay. 'I will not go back to Ireland', he wrote to Duffy, on 8 May 1849, congratulating him on his release. 'I have thrown myself on the race in America. I aspire to be the Duffy of our emigrants . . . They have sustained me handsomely. Seven months ago, I entered this city with £11 in my purse, since then I have received £5,000; all of which has been sunk . . . in their *Nation* at the same time my heart longs and strains itself after Ireland and you . . .' He offered to share his resources with Duffy, and to be his second in an American publication, but he admitted it was unlikely that Duffy would leave Ireland.

To Dillon, Duffy replied that the motive power of his life was not Radicalism or Republicanism, 'but the desire to put a sceptre into the hand of Ireland'. He would rely, not upon Irish landlords, but on the people. Dillon's pleasant dream of 'a fraternal union of the imperial democracy' did not appeal to him. To McGee, Duffy said that New York was impossible. A country must be regenerated from within, not from without. He was the last of a party deeply pledged to nationality, and he could not lay it aside without dishonour.

Duffy was exaggerating when he described himself as the last of a Nationalist party. Within a few weeks, he was able to summon a conference of 'the most experienced Nationalists left in Dublin, a very impressive show'. They unanimously advised him to revive *The Nation* and after a time, political agitation. Duffy told them that little then could be done for nationality but to keep alive its traditions. The 'ghastly clamour of unreal threats and promises' was odious to him. A large design must be patiently worked out, month by month, year by year. Meanwhile, Ireland lay in ruins and needed to be rebuilt. This was to be the policy of a revived *Nation*. Duffy corresponded with a number of men who could effectually help such a policy. He visited London and persuaded Frederick Lucas to transfer the *Tablet* to Ireland, so that they could win the support of the Catholic clergy whom Conciliation Hall had alienated.

For the first months after his release, the Government took a flattering interest in Duffy's movements. Whenever he left the house a covered car emerged conspicuously from a nearby alley and followed him.

The Habeas Corpus Suspension Act expired on 31 August 1849, and next day *The Nation* reappeared. Its format was unchanged, but Duffy's first editorial — which occupied six columns and was continued the following week — was written in what *The Times* approvingly described as 'penitent language'. The editorial, headed 'Wanted, a few Workmen', defined a new programme for the regeneration of Ireland. It began rhetorically:

> An Irish 'Rebel' for whom the transport ship floated in Dublin harbour but four months ago; who has since seen his dearest friends and comrades carried away into penal exile; who sees the wrong they rose up to redress at peril of their heads, daily widening and aggravated since their fall; and who knows that the country they hope to save, is sinking deeper into an ignominious lethargy, is called upon today to show cause, if there be any for still believing in the deliverance of Ireland.

How, then, was Ireland to be renewed? Unhesitatingly, Duffy answered, not by returning to the struggle of 1848, with its 'bluster and bravado'. Ireland could not win her rights at a blow, she must win them in detail. The first practical effort should be to give the people security of land tenure. And Ireland urgently needed workmen, able and willing to work. There was plenty of 'spouting, speeching' and 'writing sonorous and swelling sentences'. O'Connell had made a guerilla of 'ruthless speechifiers', and Young Ireland must plead guilty to having created 'a mob of gentlemen' who wrote with ease; but there was no country in Europe with so little 'practical genius, practical skill, or fruitful practical knowledge' as Ireland.

In Australia, 'where the kangaroo and the cannibal shared the silent shores a few years ago', cities had grown up, which already vied in riches and even in social organization with many of the fountainheads of civilisation in Europe. 'It is true that these countries have wide territories, and are not pressed upon by old domineering institutions — but the essential difference does not lie here — but in the hopefulness and irrepressible energy with which men work in these new growing countries . . .' If the young men of Ireland preferred sloth and apathy, great results, of course, were impossible. If they preferred inane noise and nonsense, they were more hopelessly impossible . . .

'Capital article, dear Duffy', wrote Carlyle 'in great haste', saying 'Amen' to every word of it:

> I call this the best article I ever read on Ireland; a noble 'eloquence' in this, the eloquence of sorrow, indignation and belief. Cart is not put before horse in these utterances of yours — the first time I have ever seen that condition observed (that I can remember) by any patriotic Irish writer or speaker whatsoever. Steady, steady! Hold on that course, which will spread out wide as the world for you: and you will do immense good.
> *Tet fiat!*

From the lofty uplands of Printing House Square, *The Times* complimented Duffy for describing 'with the pen of a master' the folly of endeavouring by agitation to make 'a miserable, a degraded, and it must be added, a repressed people, at once a great nation!' Addressing himself to the Ireland of 1849, he had declared that revolution had failed, and that independence was no longer the sole springhead of all that would enrich the country. And Samuel Smiles, congratulating Duffy on *The Nation's* rebirth, wrote: 'All true forces of progress in England wish you well; and bid you God speed! . . . You have made a great beginning in the education of the people to self-reliance and self-help. This must be the foundation of all true progress in a nation'.

Many volunteers answered Duffy's call for 'workmen', among them three gifted journalists, Edward Butler, Cashel Hoey, and Edward Whitty. The latter was a young London journalist of Irish descent, born and reared in England, and a passionate champion of the Irish cause. He was one of the writers on *The Leader,* a weekly started in 1849 with a staff headed by George Henry Lewes, that included his mistress, Marian Evans ('George Eliot'), Herbert Spencer and the traveller and historian William Kinglake. Whitty contributed pungent articles to *The Leader* on the 'Governing Classes' and wrote a notable but forgotten social-political novel, *The Friends of Bohemia.*

DUFFY had two approaches to the land problem. One was to establish, under the recent Encumbered Estates Act, a new 'plantation' in Ireland — a plantation not of strangers, but of native Irishmen. The other was to unite with the Ulster tenantry to bring about a reform of the Land Code by means of a Tenant League.

Whatever the landlords had done before, in 1849 as many as one-third were said to be practically bankrupt — a condition which Duffy, rightly or wrongly, attributed to 'a long career of extravagance and sloth'. The Encumbered Estates Act established a court authorised to sell compulsorily the estates of insolvent landowners. Under this Act great numbers of estates passed into new hands. This did not benefit the tenantry. The new proprietors, some of them English and Scottish, were often greedier and more relentless than landlords 'of the ould stock'. The price of land fell disastrously and new owners often evicted tenants simply to increase the market value of their properties.

Duffy's proposal was to buy the land at prevailing low prices, and resell it to farmers at the wholesale price, enabling tenants-at-will to achieve independence. To this end, he planned a Freehold Land Society, modelled on successful Societies in England. The idea was widely approved, even by Carlyle, who wrote of the prospectus: 'I almost feel a kind of desire to invest money in the scheme myself — if I had any money worth investing'. Among others whom Duffy consulted about the feasibility of the scheme were John Stuart Mill who commended it 'very favourably', and John Bright, who wrote: 'There is no country in the world where such a Society is more needed, and therefore, none in which more beneficial results may be looked for'.

For nearly a year, Duffy was largely occupied with this project. It failed because he innocently got involved with John Sadleir, M.P. not knowing he was dealing with a master-swindler. When Sadleir joined the management committee, and sought to have the Society's funds transferred from the Bank of Ireland to his own Tipperary Bank, and to sell the Society some of the derelict properties he had already acquired, Duffy resigned. The movement then in his own words, 'wasted away'.

Ireland, as Duffy had said, was in ruins. The horrors which he and Carlye had witnessed were not confined to the West. In County Kilkenny, for example, the Earl of Desart, who owned a great part of Callan, had evicted some 500 people since the beginning of the famine. It was said of his property that 'the ordinary fences along the road and through the fields consisted too often of bedsteads and broken furniture'.

Two Callan priests, Father Tom O'Shea and Father Mathew Keefe, in October 1849, established the Callan Tenant Protection Society, the first of its kind. Membership cards bore as a motto Thomas Davis's famous saying: 'Property has its duties as well as its rights'. Similar societies sprang up quickly throughout the south and east, and early in 1850, in Ulster. Their general aims were fair rents, tenant rights and employment. The next need was for a central authority to unify the policies of these scattered bodies, and on 6 August 1850, a remarkable conference was held in Dublin, attended by Protestants and Catholics, landlords and farmers, priests and journalists, magistrates and politicians. The conference was called by the Protestant journalist, John Gray; the Catholic journalist Frederick Lucas, and the Presbyterian barrister, Mr. Greer. The chair was taken by Sharman Crawford, a benevolent landlord with a rental of £8,000 a year, who represented the English borough of Rochdale in the House of Commons. No such spectacle had been seen since the days when Irishmen of all creeds and parties met together to condemn the Act of Union. Duffy, an active participant in the conference, described it with understandable enthusiasm:

Reserved stern Covenanters from the north, ministers and their elders for the most part, with a group of brighter recruits from a new generation, who came afterwards to be known as Young Ulster, sat beside priests who had lived through the horrors of the famine which left their churches empty and their graveyards overflowing; flanked by farmers who survived that evil time like the veterans of a hard campaign; while citizens, professional men, the popular journalists from the four provinces, and the founders and officers of the Tenant Protection Societies completed the assembly.

There was not a dissenting voice when an old Belfast friend of Duffy's Dr. James McKnight, editor of the *Banner of Ulster*, the official organ of the Presbyterian Church, at Duffy's invitation, accepted the presidency. After three days of harmonious discussion, the conference agreed to campaign through deputations, publications and contested elections, for fair rents, fixed valuations, security of tenure, a tenant's right to dispose of his lease, and relief for arrears of rent accrued during the famine; principles which at the time seemed wildly utopian. The conference concluded by setting up an Irish Tenant-Right League, and appointing a general council of the four provinces.

In the columns of the *Fermanagh Mail*, a rigidly Protestant journal, jubilation burgeoned into flowery prose:

> It was a grand, an ennobling sight to see the children of the Covenant from the far North, the Elizabethan settlers from the Ards of Ulster, the Cromwellians of the centre, the Normans of Pale, the Milesians of Connaught, the Danes of Kerry, the sons of Ith from Corea's southern villages, the followers of Strongbow from Waterford and Wexford, and the Williamites from Fermanagh and Meathall, all united in harmonious concert for this dear old land.

And one of *The Nation's* young songbirds contributed a poem, a couplet of which passed from mouth to mouth:
> *The news was blazed from every hill, and rung from every steeple;*
> *And all the land, with gladness filled, were one united people.*

Duffy, many years later, recalled with pride some of the men who sat on the governing Council of the League:

> Of seven or eight who reside in the Australian colonies three have risen to be Ministers of State, three are now administering justice as Australian judges, and one has just laid down a permanent legal office to enter the Parliament of New South Wales in vindication of opinions which he cherishes.

The League was opposed by the Government and by the Irish Members of Parliament, but throughout the country, it aroused great enthusiasm. County meetings organised by a sub-committee of which Duffy was chairman, drew tremendous crowds. Thousands of farmers often travelled for miles to attend. Speakers were greeted by processions, bands, banners and messages of welcome from prominent Protestants and Catholics. In Kilkenny, Dr. McKnight, urging Irishmen of different faiths to abandon aimless party distinctions, grasped the hand of Father O'Shea, a gesture which 'roused the popular enthusiasm to a tempest'. Father O'Shea replied by telling the gathering that they held in their hands a weapon sheathed for three hundred years, a weapon never yet tried against England, the weapon of the union of all Irishmen. The landlord's slogan was 'Divide and conquer'. The Irish people had raised the holier cry of 'Unite and conquer'.

Duffy pointed out the unparalleled success of the League in winning the adherence of the country:

> In the south, gifted young Presbyterian ministers from Ulster addressed meetings of Catholic farmers, and were as cordially received as their own clergy; while Catholic barristers and journalists from Dublin expounded the principles of the League in Belfast, Derry, and Ballabay, to meetings where resolutions were moved by masters of Orange lodges and tylers of Orange lodges helped to keep order. It is only Irishmen who will comprehend the entire significance of these facts.

Later historians point out that Duffy was too optimistic. Thus Dr. Leon O'Broin, in his perceptive monograph on Duffy, writes that Duffy was exaggerating considerably in suggesting that the League had united North and South. The League, says Dr. O'Broin, 'was never more than a Southern movement with a few Northern allies, and had to face considerable opposition. McKnight and his Northern colleagues were assailed by the landlord press in Ulster; and in the South, John O'Connell announced once a week that Duffy, who had proved such a dangerous leader in 1848, would be sure to tempt the people into illegal courses'.

Yet the organisers of the League appeared to have good reason for congratulating themselves on its success. Local societies were started in nineteen counties. Money, the touchstone of a political movement, 'came in on a golden tide'. In more than thirty constituencies, members pledged themselves to elect to Parliament only men who supported the League's principles. And some landlords had already abated rents and conceded the practice of public valuation.

'On this sunny prospect broke a sudden storm', Duffy wrote. The storm was caused by the English Catholic bishops assuming, contrary to statute law, the titles of their dioceses. Lord John Russell, who had gained office in 1846 with the aid of the Irish Catholic vote, raised the clamant and infectious cry of 'No Popery' in a famous — or infamous — letter to the Anglican bishop of Durham. It shattered for the time the possibility of any political alliance between protestant and catholic.

In November 1850, when Cardinal Wiseman arrived in England to become Archbishop of Westminster, there was a tremendous upsurge of sectarian hysteria. All over England at tumultuous demonstrations, the cry of 'No Popery' resounded. On Guy Fawkes Day, effigies of Pius IX and of Wiseman replaced the traditional 'Guy', and fed the flames of bonfires. Duffy 'confidently counted on seeing Carlyle vehement against the insensate outcry of ignorance and bigotry, but the old Covenanter, who lay beneath his latter-day philosophy awoke'.

'Our poor old friend the Pope has committed a sad blunder in sending his pasteboard Cardinals with their Bull thunder over to us just now', Carlyle wrote to Duffy in December. 'All men think it an impertinence and futile infatuation on the part of the old gentleman'. But Carlyle still had kind words for *The Nation*': In point of real talent (bating perhaps a little worldly wisdom and *savoir faire*') it seems to be the cleverest weekly paper I read . . . Go on and prosper!'

EARLY in 1851, Russell introduced his Ecclesiastical Titles Bill, which forbad the Roman Catholic hierarchy to assume territorial titles within the United Kingdom, under penalty of a fine, and declared void, bequests or donations made to persons under such titles. It was, as Bright said, 'a paltry miserable measure', and in Rochdale, which had many Irish immigrant workers, there were serious riots, in which some were killed and many injured. The dissent in England eventually died down, but in Ireland it was fatal to the League.

Among some forty politicians in the League were men of shining honesty, such as George Henry Moore, a charming, cultivated, nimble-minded Irish Liberal. But there were also two very dubious characters, both lawyers. John Sadleir, a man of remarkable ability, the Catholic Liberal member for Carlow, who since his election to the House of Commons had become a banker and speculator, and was reputed to be enormously rich. William Keogh was the Catholic Liberal member for Athlone, a seat bought for him by a Birmingham banker. These two, with the equally unsavoury James Sadleir, John's brother, and Edmund O'Flaherty, were the most conspicuous members of the Tenant-Right party in the House of Commons. John Sadleir, says Justin McCarthy, 'was not merely a political adventurer . . . he was a swindler of no ordinary unscruplousness, and no ordinary address. He got about him a gang of rascals like himself, no less unscrupulous, only a little less gifted in deceit and fraud'.

The operations of this 'Sanhedrim of scoundrels' (popularly known as 'the Brass Band') were multiform. They owned the Tipperary bank, one of the most popular in Ireland, and controlled many companies. Like most eminent swindlers they spent money lavishly, orated convincingly, and traded on people's genuine grievances to enrich themselves. They were also demonstratively Catholic. Many people believed in them as, in later years, many people were gulled by such a plausible rogue and demagogue as Horatio Bottomley. John Sadleir and Keogh fought the Ecclesiastical Titles Bill tenaciously, and were acclaimed as popular heroes. Their spirited opposition to the Bill won them the proud title of 'The Irish Brigade'.

They played a prominent part, too, in a great protest meeting held in the Rotunda on 22 August 1851. The chair was occupied by the Archbishop of Armagh and Apostolic Delegate, Dr. Paul Cullen, soon to become Archbishop of Dublin. Keogh roused the gathering to wild enthusiasm by giving Cullen his territorial title, and by promising that he and his colleagues would have the Act repealed if the people of Ireland would send them a few more Parliamentary allies. Resoundingly, he declared: 'We will make no terms with any Minister, no matter who he may be, until he repeals that Act'. He repeated this solemn assurance at a public banquet in his own constituency in October, and again in Cork a few months later, when he piously called upon God to help him have the Act repealed.

Dr. Cullen, formerly Rector of the Irish College at Rome, was in Duffy's eyes, wholly unsuited to his new and important mission. He had spent a cloistered life in Rome, 'knew nothing of men, had an inordinate belief in maxims of policy designed for other regions, and a rooted reliance of his own judgment'. Duffy conceded that he was a devoted and steadfast churchman, but found him 'awkward, unimpressive . . . clumsy, slow of speech, intellectually narrow and ill-informed'. He had a simple idea of government; Ireland should be ruled, as was Rome, by ecclesiastics. The only function of laymen was to provide a 'sympathetic and deferential audience'. Ireland's foreign policy was to echo the foreign policy of the Vatican. He knew nothing of the 'lively, joyous loud-speaking Celt, with his strong sense of individuality', says Duffy, and, though subscribing to the Tenant League, was suspicious of its 'rash councils and temerarious projects' of which he believed Duffy was 'a focus'. He was essentially a foreigner, 'zealous for religion and indifferent to everything else'.

Cullen formed a Catholic Defence Association, and chose as two of his lieutenants John Sadleir and William Keogh, who seized the opportunity to exploit the religious struggles for their own advantage. They needed an influential political base, and the Catholic Defence Association provided it.

Lucas, as a devout Catholic journalist, joined the Association. Duffy refused to do so, for he considered himself committed to work 'of far higher importance, failing which another million of the Irish people would be shovelled into pauper graves'. He denounced the 'knaves and hypocrites' who, ranting as devoted Catholics, were trying to destroy a popular movement that threatened their speculative enterprises. 'We shall not serve the Church', Duffy said, 'but we shall lose the land'. Duffy was prepared to defer to the hierarchy in matters of religious discipline, 'but in politics', he said, 'I must follow my own judgment and conscience'. He was not interested in theology. His unwavering concern was self-government for Ireland.

Conflict between himself and Cullen, who equated Irish Nationalism with Italian Nationalism, was inevitable. *The Nation* had once praised the Carbonari, giving Cullen some excuse for regarding Duffy as an Irish Mazzini, tainted by continental liberalism. When they met, Cullen permitted himself an engaging smile, but friendly clergy warned Duffy of his real opinion, and Lucas told him that Cullen had urged him to end his dangerous association with Duffy.

Cullen not only disliked Duffy intensely: he disliked the whole Young Ireland movement, particularly its attempts to reconcile Catholic and Protestant. He distrusted Protestants, and thought that O'Connell had been betrayed by politically active Protestants, including Thomas Davis, Smith O'Brien and Mitchel. When the Catholic University was established by Dr. Newman in 1854 he coldly disapproved of Young Irelanders being appointed to its staff. Dr. O'Broin suggests that he may have kept Duffy out of the chair of Modern History, which, the doctor thinks, would explain much of Duffy's antipathy to Cullen.

Material now available from church archives shows that Duffy's interpretation of Cullen's actions was not always accurate. Dr. O'Broin points out that Cullen was not consciously trying to hand over the Government of Ireland to the Bishops, nor to make himself, as was often said, the leader of the Irish Whigs. 'Neither was he in any sense a Castle bishop, although that was widely alleged against him', says Dr. O'Broin. 'He never attended Castle functions, and refused to serve on Government Commissions. He wanted to be a political neutral'. But Duffy was convinced that he shared with Sadleir and Keogh responsibility for the collapse of the Tenant Right League.

Despite the dissent over the Ecclesiastical Titles Bill, Duffy, in the columns of *The Nation,* tried to keep the Tenant League afloat, and for a time seemed to succeed. But old antagonisms soon revived. In Limerick, a League candidate for a parliamentary seat was beaten because of the opposition of the local Catholic bishop. In Longford, a landlord, a former colleague of Lord John Russell, and a corrupt party hack, was elected as the candidate of the League's County Club largely made up of the priests of the diocese. *The Nation* scornfully denounced this act of treachery and published the names of the offending priests.

While the Tenant League was rocked by these betrayals, the Catholic Defence Association flourished, supported enthusiastically by most of the English and Irish bishops, and of course the Sadleir 'Sanhedrim'. It started its own newspaper in 1852, the *Catholic Telegraph,* in opposition to the *Tablet,* and at half the price. This was aimed at Lucas, who had become disillusioned with the Association. And Keogh achieved a brilliant coup by inducing Sharman Crawford to join forces with him in presenting a Land Bill to Parliament. Duffy was appalled that a man of Crawford's integrity and intelligence could join the gang of shameless jobbers that Keogh represented. Crawford justified his action on the grounds that the Tenant League then had not a single representative in the House of Commons, and that 'the Irish Brigade' was backed by many eminent churchmen.

IN February 1852, Lord John Russell's Government was defeated by eleven votes on a militia bill. The elections that followed were accompanied by serious riots in many parts of the United Kingdom, particularly in Ireland, where party passions were highly inflamed: mainly about the Tenant Right, but also about the Ecclesiastical Titles Bill. The Tenant League was not well equipped to fight an election. It lacked funds, and it was difficult in a poor country like Ireland to find fifty or sixty dedicated men with the necessary property qualifications (a legal estate of £300 a year) who were prepared to live in London for half the year at their own expense, championing an unpopular cause. But the Council of the League decided to make the attempt.

In *The Nation* Duffy defined a policy which he believed might crown the cause with the success; the policy of Independent Opposition. In an almost evenly divided House, Irish members would hold the balance of power. Duffy was invited by the Council of the League to present himself as one of three candidates for consideration by the local election committee in New Ross, Wexford. The most influential member of the Committee was Father Doyle, the senior curate of the town, who told him frankly that he had no chance of success. During a sleepless night, Duffy decided to make that day a cardinal one in his life, 'signal and decisive'. He told the committee, which had mustered eighteen or twenty persons, that he knew of their prejudice against him, but they had probably heard only one side of the case, and should now hear the other: 'If after hearing my defence of the conduct of the Young Irelanders, and my aims in entering Parliament, they declared that I was not a fit candidate for New Ross, I would abandon my candidature, resign my seat on the Council of the League, discontinue *The Nation* and retire from Irish affairs for ever . . .'

His ultimatum took about an hour to deliver. When it was finished Father Doyle, though suffering acutely from influenza, promised Duffy unequivocal support, made a passionate appeal for fair play, and moved the audience to a salvo of thrilling cheers. Duffy won the nomination, and found himself opposed by an old opponent — Sir Thomas Redington, Under-Secretary to Lord Clarendon during Duffy's long conflict with the Castle; and by Henry Lambert, a former representative for County Wexford, who had been elected as a Repealer in 1832, but had deserted O'Connell in the House of Commons.

When the *Freeman's Journal* announced that the Reform Club in London was backing Duffy's rivals, a fund was opened in Dublin, London and New York, to meet his election expenses. Justifying this, with that faint whiff of priggishness that sometimes creeps into his memoirs, he declared, 'I have many times before and since refused to accept tribute or testimonial for public services to the Irish people, but to relieve a man from the necessity of buying a seat which he does not intend to sell is a wise national policy and a good public investment'.

Among the Irish contributors were Father Mathew and Dr. Croke. Duffy's name, Croke wrote, fell like a household word upon Irish ears. His heroic devotion to the cause of nationality was his best security for future services. The official organ of the Castle assailed Duffy in every issue. One writer said it was preposterous and presumptuous to compare him with Sir Thomas Redington, and described him as an adventurer 'with no stake or fortune in his country'. Duffy replied with gusto:

Well, be it so. I have no more stake in the country than Henry Grattan had when he entered the Irish Parliament. I am not much richer than Andrew Marvell when he sat in the English Commons. But let it be noted that whatever I have, great or small, was honestly earned. Not a penny of it was won, Sir Thomas, by denying the country or the creed of my fathers. There is no blood-money in it, Mr. Under-Secretary. Dublin Castle stood open for me also if I could walk in the miry footsteps of a Monahan or a Redington . . . I am 'an adventurer!' 'Thank Heaven I am independent', Robert Burns wrote, 'for I have learned to hold a plough'. If I might venture to echo so noble a sentiment, I would say, 'Thank Heaven, I am independent, for I have learned to held a pen!'

Redington campaigned spectacularly with a troop of dragoons, a company of infantry, three detachments of police, and a hired retinue of disreputable tenants. But Duffy discounted this pomp by recalling sombre episodes in Redington's career: he was a minister in Russell's government which armed Orangemen against the Repealers in 1848; he had packed juries against political prisoners; he had helped pass the Ecclesiastical Titles Act; he had evicted one hundred and eighty persons from his Galway estate since the Famine.

In the end, the harassed Redington withdrew, leaving Lambert to fight a hopeless contest. Duffy won resoundingly by a majority of more than two to one. That night the town was illuminated, and from neighbouring hills bonfires celebrated his victory; a victory which he attributed to the leadership Father Doyle and the young priests had given. From across the Atlantic Meagher wrote: 'It was a glorious licking you gave that "baptised spaniel" and all the curs, of high and low degree, that hunted with him ...'

On 8 September 1852, the League summoned a conference in Dublin of the friends of Tenant Right, to which all the members of Parliament pledged to support Sharman Crawford's Land Bill, were invited. Crawford presided, and more than forty members of Parliament, which included nearly all the League's main principals, two hundred Catholic and Protestant clergy, gentlemen farmers, traders, and professional men from all parts of the country, attended. Among the members were Keogh and John Sadleir. The Conference resolved unanimously that members returned on Tenant Right principles should oppose any Government whose policy did not embody the principles of Crawford's Bill.

Duffy announced in *The Nation* that the principle of Independent Opposition was at last triumphant. 'The Irish members will keep themselves apart as an independent party', he wrote. 'They will vote for every measure of benefit to Ireland ... They will vote against ministers opposed to the Irish measures, *not* ... on every question, but on any question (not involving the serious interests of Ireland) on which they can be turned out of office ...' Duffy's happiness was complete when Frederick Lucas, despite the opposition of the Catholic Defence Association, supported by the local bishop, was elected for Meath by a majority of four to one.

On 7 November, the day before he left Ireland, Duffy wrote to Smith O'Brien. 'I am going tomorrow to take my seat in the British Parliament, and I cannot leave Ireland without writing to you'. One of the objects which he rejoiced in thinking he might accomplish in Westminster was to secure O'Brien's liberation. Meanwhile, he counselled O'Brien to fill the long hours with some regular work, perhaps farming. 'The heart preys on itself when the mind and hands have no task'. But as there was no evil without its compensation, O'Brien had escaped much in Ireland which would have wounded him deeply.

> The bigotry which seemed dead is revived again, upon both sides. The destruction of the people goes on ... and the very memory of our National hopes has died out of all but a few hearts ... Many a time since you left Ireland in a prison ship I have wished that I had gone too, rather than live among the sights that remained. My election was the only compensating circumstance *personally* ... but it is a weary and disheartening task to go to the English Parliament with doubtful allies, and relentless enemies. I will make the experiment, however ...

Duffy added that he had gathered material for a history of the Confederation but opinion was greatly divided as to the policy of publishing it while O'Brien was in the hands of the enemies. And he finished more optimistically: 'A new Young Ireland party has grown up, young men whom you never saw, but who are jealous of your name and honour, as sons of your own house. Ireland has often been weak cowardly, mean spirited, but she seldom forgets those who were martyrs for her sake'.

T*he Illustrated London News,* in a lengthy 'Parliamentary Portrait' of Duffy, drew a moral from the fact that the man '. . . who was, not five years ago, tried as a rebel — as the chief organiser of the partial outbreak of that period', had now become a member of Parliament. 'Could a better evidence be referred to of the thorough "freedom" of the English Constitution?' it said.

It recounted Duffy's creation of *The Nation,* a journal which had reformed the newspaper press of Ireland, created a new Irish literature, and electrified Dublin's political and literary circles by the 'unreserve and originality of its tone and topics'. In five years, he had created a public opinion, collected a party; and the contest with O'Connell and the artifically forced 'rebellion' of 1848 were the results . . . 'Indirectly, it cannot be said that Mr. Duffy failed. He had destroyed the huge imposture of O'Connellism in Ireland, and he had evoked a manlier spirit in public affairs and insisted upon a higher standard for public men'.

Nine

Quitting Parliament and Ireland for Australia

MORE than fifty Irish Liberals, including the ambiguous members of the Catholic Defence Association who had made common cause with the Tenant Leaguers, assembled in Westminster on 11 November 1852 to hear the Queen announce, in her speech from the Throne, that her advisers contemplated a liberal and generous policy towards Ireland. Soon after, four Bills dealing with the Land Question were submitted to the House of Commons by the Irish Attorney-General Joseph Napier. Clearly, the Irish party was worth conciliating.

Parliament to Duffy was 'a focus of new emotions'. The most striking figure was Benjamin Disraeli, then holding office for the first time as Chancellor of the Exchequer. To Duffy, he was aloof, insouciant, and conspicuously un-English with his goatee beard and plum-coloured vest, 'a sight as perplexing to true propriety as Roland's shoe-ties in the Court of Louis XVI'. Disraeli could not tell the time without his glasses, and had recently hailed a police-van in mistake for an omnibus. Lord John Russell was a figure 'diminutive and insignificant to deformity, ill-dressed, ill-posed, with unsympathetic, melancholy face, timid gestures, and feeble gait, he seemed an intruder on the scene'. Duffy was convinced that were he not the son and brother of a duke, 'he should not have distinguished himself in a parish vestry'. Gladstone was 'as smooth as silk', but 'habitually grave and . . . spoke as if he uttered oracles'. Palmerston's 'gay *debonair*' appearance found much favour in the House which relished his persiflage, but to Duffy, he gave the impression of 'a play actor cast in the part of a patriot statesman'. And Duffy noted in his diary: 'Carlyle says he is a fitting leader for an age without sincerity'.

The Derby administration was short-lived. When the session was proceeding, Sergeant William Shee, a distinguished and impressive lawyer, introduced the League Bill, demanding that it and the Government Bills be given a second reading before the Christmas recess. After much discussion, and to the fury of *The Times*, the Tory press and the landlords, the Government reluctantly agreed to read all the Bills a second time, and to send them to a Select Committee, chosen fairly from the landlord and tenant parties.

Two ermined landlords counter-attacked with private Bills; one giving them greater powers of eviction, the other, inflicting severe penalties on tenants who cut crops after sundown, thus imperilling the landlord's claims on the entire cereal harvest.

Duffy was a member of the Select Committee of twenty-nine. Half were landlords or their friends, among them Irish-born Palmerston, who had a vast estate in Sligo. Others, supposedly neutral, included James Sadleir and some of his cronies. Duffy was supported by Lucas, Bright and Sergeant Shee. The Committee met at noon each day and sat till after midnight. Between parliamentary duties and his work for *The Nation* — he was Westminster correspondent as well as an active editor — Duffy had little time to relax. 'I breakfasted on Blue Books', he wrote, 'and lunched on Irish correspondence, and I never had leisure to go to a theatre or exhibition . . .' but 'when a bore of vigorous lungs was on his feet', he sometimes escaped to Westminster Abbey for an hour, or the National Gallery.

There were also a few social occasions. He dined with Cobden, and John Bright. He also met the forgotten — and forgettable — dramatist, Sheridan Knowles, who had taught rhetoric in Belfast twenty years before, and in London, had been a close friend of Hazlitt, one of Duffy's 'earliest masters in literature'. They discussed Hazlitt's unhappy fate — slandered by 'the Blackwood gang', patronised by his inferiors, and scarcely recognised, except by Charles Lamb; Duffy recalled that Horne had told him how he visited the house where Hazlitt lay dead, to find his body lying on a piano, covered with a sheet, and not a human being in attendance on a man 'who had done more for popular liberty and personal freedom . . . than any of the Broughams or Jeffreys'.

Every Sunday, Duffy spent a couple of hours talking with Carlyle in Hyde Park or Battersea Park, or on the lawn behind his house, where Carlyle puffed at his long clay pipe, and pontificated. Here Duffy encountered him in a new aspect. Among friends, despite his ineluctable prejudices, he was always simple and genial. But pursued by hordes of inquisitive Americans, he submitted them to long, soporific, pre-packaged harangues. 'When he delivered himself of one of these set speeches', says Duffy, 'his conversational manner disappeared',

> and his language came forth like a douche-bath, in a strong, unbroken stream, while, like the Ancient Mariner, he fixed the spectator with his glittering eye. This foaming torrent was as unlike the ripple of his familiar talk as Niagara to a trout stream. To arrest it was nearly impossible, and he was impatient of interruption, even by way of assent, much more of dissent.

Duffy took notes of his personal conversations with Carlyle, and used them in a book published more than thirty years later. Carlyle often reveals himself in a far from attractive light. One day, discussing the fall of the Derby administration, Duffy said that though he had voted against it, he had a certain sympathy with Disraeli 'for the indomitable pluck with which he had faced his enemies at the head of a party which distrusted him only a little less than the honourable gentlemen opposite'. Though the Peelites hated him with 'a preternatural animosity', Duffy had never heard that Disraeli had ever done anything cruel or cowardly against them, or anyone else. 'He was a political gladiator, no doubt as Bolingbroke or Canning had been before him, but it was idle to complain that he struck deft blows at his opponents; that was his vocation'.

> A base vocation, Carlyle exclaimed. The case was not a perplexing one. A cunning Jew got a parcel of people to believe in him ... he was an imposter ... A man from whom no good need be expected, a typical Jew, ostentatious, intrinsicably servile, but stiffnecked in his designs.

Duffy sprang to Disraeli's defence, saying he had exhibited a generous courage on behalf of his race, in the face of fierce hostility from his own party. Duffy had a personal satisfaction in seeing a race who were persecuted for a crime committed centuries and centuries before they were born, reassert themselves. (In February 1853, Duffy had voted for a Bill to free Jews from all civil disabilities, as Roman Catholics had been freed since 1829. Jewish Emancipation Bills were repeatedly passed in the Commons and rejected by the Lords. That was the fate of the 1853 Bill.) Carlyle replied in terms that would have won warm approval from the late Dr. Goebbels. Jews were paying for their own sins, as well as of their ancestors. They were an impotent race who had never distinguished themselves in their entire history by an estimable quality ... there was always an odour of old clo' about them. They made great quantities of money and glorified the speculator who made most, as the most venerable of mortals. Their vices of character were intractable ...

Carlyle took Duffy to see Thackeray, both of whom seemed to have forgotten Thackeray's puerile gibes at the Young Irelanders in the pages of *Punch*. Duffy found him 'a large, robust, fresh-looking man', with hair turning grey. 'The expression of his face disappointed me, the damaged nose and the teeth mar its otherwise benign effect, and were imperfectly relieved by a smile which was warm but hardly genial'. They discussed the unsuccessful uprising of 1848, and Thackeray said he never doubted Ireland's right to rebel, if there were any possibility of success. But in the name of commonsense, he denied the legitimacy of unsuccessful rebellion. Duffy replied that in an insurrection as in a game of roulette you had to take chances. He spoke of the famine, the exportation of food, the hopeless fatuity and feebleness of the Russell Government, the horrors of Skull and Skibereen, and asked Thackeray to tell him, were he an Irishman, what he would have done under the circumstances? Thackeray paused a moment and replied, 'I would perhaps have done as you did'. They walked out amicably towards Hyde Park.

About this time, Duffy had his one quarrel with Carlyle. Inevitably, it was about Ireland. Commenting on some current issue, Duffy spoke indignantly of England's treatment of Ireland. Carlyle replied that Ireland had brought all her misfortunes on herself. She had committed a great sin in rejecting the Reformation, and was punished accordingly. Duffy became very angry, and declared that Carlyle himself did not believe in a tittle of the thirty-nine Articles, yet he justified Ireland being plundered and trampled upon for rejecting them. Elizabeth or her father would have made as short work of him as they did of the Popish recusants. Carlyle criticised the Irish for being ignorant, but did not trouble to consider that for three generations to seek education in Ireland was an offence sternly published by law. The Irish people were lazy,

Carlyle said, taking no account that the fruits of their labour were plundered by landlords without mercy.

The argument raged, with Duffy becoming more and more emphatic, in defence of his faith, and his country, and Jane Carlyle and John Forster looking at each other in consternation, as if a catastrophe were imminent. Finally Duffy, much heated, took himself off. That evening, he and Carlyle met at Forster's, and had a pleasant talk. 'Neither then, nor at any future time', says Duffy, 'did he resent my brusque criticism by the slightest sign of displeasure'.

Disraeli was about to present his first Budget. A Cabinet Minister, Spencer Walpole, secretly conferred with Duffy, Lucas and Shee, to solicit the essential support of the Irish party. They replied in writing that, according to their pledge, they would vote for the Government only if it accepted the leading principles of Crawford's Bill — 'a moderate measure framed by a great landowner, and introduced into Parliament by a great lawyer'. If the Government agreed, they would muster at least twenty members to support the Budget.

News of the negotiations leaked out, and Derby was asked in the House of Lords whether the Government was prepared to adopt the principles of Crawford's Bill if the Select Committee approved of them. Derby reassured his friends that the Government certainly would not adopt them — and so pronounced its death sentence. At 4 o'clock in the morning of 17 December, Parliament divided on the Budget. Only the Tories supported the Government. A combination of Whigs, Peelites, Radicals, and "the Irish Brigade", defeated it by nineteen votes — 305 to 286.

The Irish party had cut its teeth — and shown them. But its high hopes were swiftly extinguished. When Lord Aberdeen formed his coalition Government of Whigs and Peelites, two appointments, in Duffy's restrained words, 'excited a pause of amazement, and then a storm of indignation'. Mr. John Sadleir had become Lord of the Treasury, and Mr. William Keogh, Solicitor-General for Ireland! Both had categorically, emphatically and up to the last minute, pledged themselves never to support, much less take office from any Government that would not repeal the Ecclesiastical Titles Act, abolish the Church Establishment, and support Sharman Crawford's Land Bill. Now they had joined a Government ineluctably opposed to all these measures. It was their reward for voting against the Tories in the crucial division.

'The Leaguers. were not surprised at a perfidy which they had predicted', says Duffy, 'but they were outraged by its audacious cynicism, and alarmed at its evil example. No one could tell how far the treason would spread'. Its spread became apparent when Parliament reassembled. Of 38 Irish members who attended a conference, only twenty-one declared their continued support for Independent Opposition. 'It was plain that the Government had bought more than a brace of deserters', says Duffy. 'They had driven a wedge through the Independent party, dividing it into two sections . . .' The deserters were vociferously denounced in the Nationalist press, and from public platforms. George Henry Moore accused Keogh of a breach of morality, but Dr. Cullen, now Archbishop of Dublin, remained silent. Duffy saw him as the head of a conspiracy of bishops.

'In politics', the nimble Sir Harold Wilson has reminded us, 'a week is a long time'. On this basis, a hundred years is an eternity, and the peripheral political conflicts of the 1850s make dreary reading. The disintegration of the League need not be analysed at length. The Leaders, as Duffy puts it, knew that the high tide of success was ebbing fast. 'We failed', he declared 'because we were betrayed by prelates in whom the people had a blind confidence . . . The leaders of the League knew that they had now opposed to them three great social forces — the Executive, the bulk of the Catholic bishops, and the entire landed gentry'.

Charges and counter-charges accelerated the disintegration. Dr. McKnight acclaimed Keogh and charged Lucas with treachery, warning Duffy against him as ardently as Cullen had warned Lucas against Duffy. Sharman Crawford deserted his own Bill and defended both Keogh and Sadleir in the ingenuous belief that they would use their ministerial positions for the public good. The League struggled on for a time, but ceased to function as an active organization. The dissension which destroyed it also affected the circulation and influence of *The Nation*.

DUFFY'S maiden speech was made when Parliament reassembled in February 1853. The House was debating a Bill to discontinue State grants to Maynooth College. One speaker supporting the Bill had referred to a book, *A Fortnight in Ireland,* by Sir Francis Head, a former Governor of Upper Canada, in which he quoted a number of fiery speeches allegedly made by Irish Priests. Was a system to be tolerated, he asked, which produced such firebrands? Duffy pointed out urbanely that all the speeches except one had been made, not by priests, but by Presbyterian ministers. The exception, in which the speaker had said: 'I am a descendant of farmers and the time is coming, I trust, when it will be as hard for an exterminating landlord to get into Parliament as a camel to go through the eye of a needle', had been made by Duffy himself!

Duffy went on to ask whether the purpose of the Bill was to prevent the teaching of the Catholic religion in Ireland? If so, it behoved the House to look at the facts. When it was martyrdom for a Catholic priest not only to teach but to appear at all in Ireland, there was no lack of priests to do their duty. He was glad to see that Parliament had at last learned to consult the wishes of the people for whom it was to legislate. This had been shown by their policy towards the Cape of Good Hope, and more recently, towards Van Dieman's Land, and Canada. Why not give Ireland the benefit of that experience?

The Bill was defeated by 262 votes to 68.

Duffy awaited his opportunity to denounce the Sadleir-Keogh defection. It came in May, when the new Chancellor of the Exchequer, William Gladstone, proposed, for the first time, to impose income-tax on Ireland; a measure which Disraeli had considered and abandoned, and which the Whigs, when they were soliciting the Irish vote, promised never to take. (Income-tax in England was then seven pence in the pound on incomes over £150 a year.) The proposal aroused a storm of protest in Ireland, and Gladstone aggravated the Whig breach of faith by also increasing the Irish duty on spirits. At the same time, he reduced the duty on a variety of luxury goods.

The Budget was opposed by the Tories and could not be carried without the support of the Irish members; this the Government counted upon with Keogh and his confederates in the Treasury. At the second reading of the Bill, seventy-two Irish members voted against it, but thirty-two went into the Government lobby. When the Budget reached the Committee stage Duffy rose to denounce the Irish renegades. His speech began quietly, with a sardonic reference to the reduction of duty on a variety of goods. 'It is cheerful news, certainly', he said, 'for the struggling traders and professional classes in Ireland, whom the famine had reduced to half their income, that turtle and anchovies, brocade, jewels, ostrich feathers, and *eau de cologne,* might be had at reduced prices'. Or perhaps they were to find increased comfort in the fact that every Irish trade with any vitality in it was exposed to new competition. 'Linens, whisky, ham, eggs, butter — almost everything that Ireland exported — must at the same time meet the double exigency of producing less money and paying more'.

MR. CHARLES GAVAN DUFFY, M P. FOR NEW ROSS.——FROM A PHOTOGRAPH BY BEARD.

Illustrated London News, 7 May 1853

148

Duffy then discussed the attitude of the Irish members towards the Budget. Seventy-two of them had voted against it, men representing all kinds of political opinions. 'I do not know how so many Irish members have been persuaded to vote in favour of it', he continued. 'Some few of them, I am sure, voted from conscientious motives; but, short as my experience of Parliament has been, I don't think in the worst days of Walpole and the Pelhams more scandalous corruption existed than I have seen with my own eyes practised upon Irish members'.

Uproar followed. There were loud cries of 'Name! name!' during which Duffy made several attempts to continue. At length, he said: 'If the Chairman tells me, on the part of the House, that it is their wish I should name the persons to whom I alluded, I shall do so'.

> Mr. Vincent Scully: Sir, I rise to order, and ask you, as Chairman, whether such language as that which has been used by the hon. Member for New Ross is to be tolerated in this House?
> Mr. J. Ball: Sir, I move that the words used by the hon. Member for New Ross be taken down. ('Hear, hear!' 'Oh, oh!' 'Name, name!' and general confusion)
> Mr. Gavan Duffy again essayed to speak, but was met with loud cries of 'Name, name!' The hon. Gentleman then repeated what he had before said. 'If the Chairman calls upon me to do so, I will name'. (Cries of 'Order, order!' 'Chair, chair!' and great confusion.)

It was moved that the Clerk of the House be instructed to take down Duffy's words. A spirited debate, continuing late into the night, took place on the motion. There was some doubt about the exact words Duffy had used and considerable doubt about what they implied. Disraeli could not find any imputation of corrupt motives in them. He found, however, a 'much more important thing, namely, a distinct allegation of corrupt conduct'. A Member was not guilty of acting disorderly because he accused a Minister of improper conduct. If he could substantiate the charge, he was exercising the highest duty of which a member of the House was capable.

Palmerston agreed with Disraeli on this point, but challenged the member for New Ross to prove his charge against Her Majesty's Government. The charge against the Irish members, however, stood upon a different footing. It implied an imputation upon their honour and conduct, and he put it to the hon. Member ('he is a young Member of this House, and will excuse me, who has been a member longer than he has') that it would redound to his credit if he said that he regretted 'fairly, handsomely and candidly', that in the warmth of debate he had cast reflections which he had no good grounds for maintaining. Duffy rose again, and announced:

> I do not mean to alter a single word of what I said. I am, as several hon. Members have stated, not an old Member of this House. I am therefore, unacquainted with its forms, and I may consequently have got into a position of some difficulty through my ignorance of these forms. But there is one position which I shall never get into — I will never unsay anything I have said, believing it to be true. When the Chairman said I was disorderly, a distinguished Member of the House said in his opinion I was not so. How was I to decide which was right or wrong?'

If the Committee wished to be informed of the fact which had led him to the conclusion he had expressed, he would give them that information. 'If, on the contrary, it be the wish of the Committee that I should declare what I said was untrue, or explain away its force, then whatever may be the consequences, I decline to do so, and await them without fear. (Renewed cries of 'Name!' and 'No!' and confusion.)

Mr. Bright, in a generous spirit of conciliation, pointed out that many Irish Members, though from the west, took an Oriental latitude in the language they used. It was often a very figurative description. He was inclined to think that the expressions complained of might be fairly classified under that category. After all, the hon. Gentleman did not say that any of the Irish Members had succumbed to the temptation. He only spoke of their being operated upon, and they all knew that operations were not necessarily successful (Great Laughter).

Mr. H. Herbert, as an Irish Member, said indignantly that Duffy was a person deserving the name of — 'I hesitate to use the word'. Unfortunately, the *Hansard* reporter also hesitated to record it. Duffy, however, protested against Herbert's 'gross language', adding that he did not mean to alter a single word of what he had said. He repeated his conviction that the present Government had operated on certain Irish members in the same way as Walpole and the Pelhams had corrupted Parliament.

The offending words were taken down, and Duffy was ordered to appear before the House the following day. 'The House of Commons was crowded last night in every part to witness the sequel to the Duffy affair, personality always being more attractive than business', reported the *Spectator* on 7 May:

> The speaker formally, but kindly called on Mr. Duffy to explain or retract his words. Mr. Duffy said that he should have explained on the previous night, but that he was interrupted, first by Mr. Disraeli's declaration that it is not disorderly to bring a charge of corrupt practices against Ministers, and next by Lord John Russell, who challenged him to the proof of what he said. What he meant to say was, that in the time of Sir Robert Walpole and the Duke of Newcastle men had been induced to abandon solemn and circumstantial pledges, in order to accept place; he charged certain Irish Members with doing so, and that he called political corruption. If he had broken the rules of the House, he regretted it. Lord John Russell observed that this was a very different description of the charge from that implied . . . It was not a charge of corruption by money, and therefore it was different from the corruption of Sir Robert Walpole's time. It was a matter of opinion; he did not think that the Irish Members in question or the Ministers need fear any amount of discussion on the subject. He did not think the House need proceed any further.

Duffy's own account of the incident, written forty-five years later, differs materially from *Hansard*, and presents him in a much more defiant role:

> I was assured I should be sent to prison, perhaps expelled, if I did not make a humble submission. My course was different. I declined to withdraw my words, but I undertook, if a Committee of Inquiry were granted, to prove that

the career of Messrs. Keogh, Sadleir and some of their associates justified all I had said. But this was an inquiry which did not suit the Government. The Leader of the House objected to the investigation, on the ground that his colleagues had not been corrupted, but only converted to better opinions, and the deserters sat dull and gloomy amidst the jeers of the Opposition ... As the Government proposed to let the matter drop without more ado, it was recognised that we had scored a decisive success, and the infamy of the transaction . . . was made known to the English people for the first time.

The vote of the Irish members on the Budget reassured the Government that it had nothing to fear from them. Palmerston, who had gone to the Home Office, told the Select Committee, that he saw no necessity for the Land Bills. Next day, Crawford's Bills were set aside by nineteen votes to nine, and Napier's Bills were carefully pruned. Soon after, half-a-dozen by-elections took place in Ireland. Despite Cullen's support, the electors of Carlow were persuaded to reject Sadleir, but he won a seat at Sligo with the support of the bishop of the diocese, many local priests, and Cullen's uncle and confidant, Father Maher.

IN 1854, long days in Committee, late sessions in the House, anxiety and frustration, brought Duffy's never robust health to the point of collapse, and he was advised to take a long holiday. He had read a pamphlet of Bulwer (later Lord) Lytton's *Confessions of a Water Patient*, which gave an extravagant account of the wonders of Malvern water as a remedy for exhaustion. Duffy found the early hours, simple meals, and enforced rest, 'balsamic', and he enjoyed the conversation of other patients — Indian officers, Oxford professors, Californian diggers, and London men and women of letters — but he had no faith in the water cure. 'We were told how patients were carried into the establishment, and after a few weeks, walked out', he wrote, 'but nothing was said of the cases where the patients walked in, and were carried out in an oak box'. He discovered that Carlyle had taken the waters, on Lytton's assurance that they would cure his dyspepsia. They did not.

From Malvern, Duffy and his wife took a holiday in Belgium, where he interested himself in the farming of peasant proprietors in the most thickly populated district in Europe. He revelled in the grand Gothic architecture, and in 'the exquisite domestic art' of the Flemings, contrasting it with the Italian art with which he was best acquainted; it was the difference, he thought, between the realistic story of Robinson Crusoe and the vision of Dante. A run to Paris followed, and after two months of pleasant idling, back to Dublin to face a crisis in the League.

Exacerbating his difficulties, Duffy now had to face an extraordinary attack by John Mitchel, who had escaped from Van Dieman's Land as 'Mr. Wright' on a Sydney-bound passenger brig, the *Emma*. The escape had been organized by Irishmen in America.

In New York, Mitchel established a paper, *The Citizen*. In it, he urged patriotic Irishmen to repudiate the Tenant League, and to revert to insurrection, backed by an Irish Expedition from the United States. He had learned nothing and forgotten everything. What he himself described accurately as his 'holy hatred of English rule' had become so obsessive that he turned on Duffy with pathological malignity. In his prolix but absorbing 'Jail Journal', originally published as a serial in *The Citizen* (January — August 1854), he blamed Duffy for having encouraged O'Brien upon his 'Tipperary war'. He accused Duffy also of subsequently damaging the National cause, when on trial, by producing witnesses to his character, and by allowing a memorial to be presented to the Government, cravenly petitioning for mercy. And he derisively labelled him 'Mr. Give-in Duffy'.

Duffy published every line of the 'Jail Journal' in *The Nation* week by week, before he permitted himself a reply. This was issued in pamphlet form as a supplement to the paper. He described Mitchel as an 'unhappy man' who had carried 'the hell of envy and rancour' to the Antipodes and back. He was easily able to refute Mitchel's wild charges. He was not responsible for 'O'Brien's ill-starred expedition, but at least it had more to commend it than Mitchel's theory of revolution which was reducible to two maxims worthy of Bedlam — that whatever was meditated against the English Government should be proclaimed beforehand, and that officers or preparations were superfluous. 'You neglected every precaution . . . You had no agent in France, no agent in America, no agent among the discontented Chartists of England. When you were arrested you had not a barrel of gunpowder, or a case of muskets. You did not know where to lay your hand upon pickaxes or crowbars to make the first barricade. Your resources literally began and ended with the ink-bottle . .'

Duffy accused Mitchel of stealing Lalor's ideas, and of hating Duffy because he was aware of this. 'Your opinions are a fragment of Davis's, which you misunderstood, and a bundle of Lalor's, which you have appropriated', he wrote. But his most serious charge against Mitchel, the most galling he could have made, was that, in escaping from Van Dieman's Land, Mitchel had broken 'the word of an Irish gentleman' by a 'disgraceful' breach of his parole. Whether or not Mitchel was guilty of this, is still a matter of controversy. Smith O'Brien argued that he was not, since the parole 'was extorted not in order to confer advantage on us, but as a "security" to the Government'. This, surely, is casuistry. Writing of Mitchel thirty-three years later, Justin McCarthy commented: 'It is certain that he effected his escape while he was a prisoner on parole . . . It may be urged . . . that it is not necessary to keep faith with a hostile Government. To such an argument it is impossible to agree. It is the duty of a patriot to keep his faith and word unsullied'.

The miserable controversy dragged on. Duffy emerges from it in a much more favourable light than Mitchel. He published not only Mitchel's savage attacks, but Mitchel's elaborate reply to Duffy's pamphlet. Mitchel did not publish a line of Duffy's defence. 'The verdict of any gentleman upon that proceeding will, I think, be decisive', wrote Duffy. So is the verdict of the historian, gentleman or not.

VICTORIA had separated from New South Wales in November 1850, but neither Colony had self-government. Late in the session of 1855, the Victorian and New South Wales Constitution Bills were introduced into the House of Commons, and some Irishmen in Melbourne and Sydney asked the Irish Members to give the Bills their 'benevolent attention'. Duffy conferred with Robert Lowe, (later Viscount Sherbrooke) as the Member best-informed on Australian politics.

Lowe who had the white hair and pink eyes of an albino, was one of the most remarkable men in the House. Though not popular, and like Burke, a poor rhetorician, he was always listened to attentively. An Oxford graduate and member of the London Bar, he had spent nearly eight years in Sydney (1842-1850) as a practising lawyer, sometime member of the Legislative Council, and journalist. He took a notable part in the agitation to end transportation, and for land reform. When he returned to London, he worked on *The Times* before his election in 1852 to the House of Commons. 'We fought the interests of the colonies with persistency and some success', says Duffy rather complacently. Neither the fight nor the success was conspicuously notable.

Lowe suggested that the Victorian Bill should not be opposed, but amended in Committee. The New South Wales Bill, however, which provided for a nominee Upper House, should be opposed at every stage. Duffy agreed. Speaking on the Victorian Bill in June 1855, he described it as 'a wise and liberal measure' except for some points that could most properly be dealt with in Committee. One, the provision that related to the qualification of Members of the two Houses, was open to very serious objection:

> The qualification for Members of the Upper House was £5,000 worth of freehold property, and for the lower House £2,000 worth of freehold property, or freehold property of the annual value of £200, situated in Victoria. The result of this provision would be to throw the whole Government of the colony into the hands of a small class, against whom there was a violent popular prejudice.

The Bill, Duffy continued, would make it easier to become a representative for Liverpool or London, than 'for a village or a sheep-walk in Australia'. If it were passed as it stood, the future Government of Victoria would be committed to a handful of persons, the landlord proprietors. It was scarcely probable that a practising barrister or doctor in Victoria, who might be a very fit person to sit in the legislature, would possess £2,000 worth of freehold property. The population of the colony were strong and resolute, Duffy warned the House, and were 'by no means disinclined to take the law into their own hands'. Under the present system, the 'diggers' were offered one representative in the Legislature, but under the proposed new constitution, they would not have even one. 'These "diggers" created the wealth, and paid the taxes and, to a great extent, constituted the strength of the colony — to shut them out from political action in its government was madness'.

Duffy proposed moving an amendment upon these grounds, when the Bill came into Committee. And if the noble Lord [Lord John Russell] would not consent to abolish the property qualification, Duffy suggested a medium course. The qualification for a voter of the Upper House included the learned professors and retired officers of the military or naval services. These classes might be allowed to sit in the Assembly. And surely chattel property as well as freehold property, ought to be a qualification, as it was in England? Lowe, too, criticised the limitations imposed on membership of the two Victorian chambers, but the objections of both men were brushed aside, and the constitution was approved, very much in the form in which it had been submitted.

'I did my best to have your nominee Upper House abolished', Duffy wrote to Edward Butler . . . 'Lowe, Alderly, Lord Lyttleton, Walpole, myself and others had a consultation on the best course to be taken, but the obstinacy of Lord John rendered all our operations useless . . .'

Disciplinary action against three of Duffy's clerical supporters convinced him that Cullen was continuing to campaign against the League. Father Doyle was removed to an inferior parish because he had so ardently supported Duffy in the general election — admittedly to the point of publicly insulting his parish priest — and the Callan curates, Father O'Shea and Father Keefe, were instructed to take no further part in politics. Duffy and Lucas decided to appeal to the Vatican and announced that they would resign their seats in Parliament if the Pope did not restrain Cullen and his bishops 'from destroying the cause of the Irish farmers by illegitimate methods'. Lucas, though in poor health, undertook the delicate mission. The Pope in private audience received him graciously, and suggested a conference with Cullen, then in Rome for the Vatican Council. At the conference, Cullen violently denounced Duffy for his conduct in 1848; conduct so wicked, he said, that it was impossible to act with him until he had fasted fifty years on bread and water. (At the end of this penance, Duffy would have been eighty-nine.) When Lucas defended Duffy as a peace-loving and pious Christian, Cullen became even more vehement. Duffy, he said, had been responsible for people being massacred; he was not a pious man, and it was discreditable for Lucas to defend him or act with him.

The immediate cause of this immoderate and un-Christian outburst was, apparently, some vigorous articles in *The Nation*. Duffy claimed that these, though plain and direct, were not disrespectful. They were certainly direct. In one, Duffy had written that if some of Ireland's best priests had been sent to rot in bogs and morasses, if a Catholic bishop shared a platform with a man of the character of William Keogh, if political profligacy had lost much of its horror in the eyes of the people, the chief cause was the alliance between Cullen and the Catholic agents of Dublin Castle. Whether or not this statement was disrespectful, it certainly was not true in alleging complicity between Cullen and the Castle.

Lucas' health rapidly deteriorated under the strain of his mission and the heat of a Rome summer. When he returned to London, his appearance had so changed that the doorkeeper of the House of Commons did not recognise him. After he had recuperated a little, Duffy, for the first time in six months, was able to have a confidential talk with him. Duffy argued that Lucas and he should both resign from Parliament and dissolve the Tenant League. Only by such action would the Irish people be made to recognise who were responsible for the calamity that had destroyed their cause. Lucas did not agree. The Pope, he said, had requested him not to quit Parliament, and so leave Catholics without an adequate spokesman. He was determined to follow the Holy Father's advice. Duffy reminded him of their joint pledge to retire if the appeal to Rome failed, and it had failed 'egregiously'. An entry in Duffy's diary summarised the discussion:

> I said . . . he was bound to resign his seat in compliance with a promise of a most specific kind he and I had made . . . He said his constituents did not wish him to resign. Very likely, I replied . . . nor did mine, but the object with which I had consented to make such a promise in concert with him was to teach the Irish people the difference between Irish members who had abounded in promises which came to nothing, and men who meant what they said . . . I am determined to retire, and Lucas is determined to hold on.

'The Pledge which Mr. Duffy made . . . to retire from Parliament if the Irish Cause was hopelessly deserted by those who ought to guide and bless it is one he will not shrink from fulfilling', *The Nation* had written when Duffy was elected. He now fulfilled it. He decided not only to quit Parliament, but to quit Ireland also. 'I could no longer promise the suffering people relief', he afterwards wrote, 'and to witness injustice without curb and wrong without remedy would render life too painful. An Ireland where Mr. Keogh typified patriotism and Dr. Cullen the Church, was an Ireland in which I could not live . . .'

DUFFY had decided to leave Ireland, but where to go? The 'considerable part', as he assessed it, he had taken in framing the constitutions of New South Wales and Victoria, turned his thoughts to Australia, to which he assigned 'a provisional preference' while, with characteristic thoroughness, he made searching inquiries about conditions there. In December 1854, he consulted O'Brien, still a prisoner in Van Dieman's Land, despite the fact that O'Brien had no knowledge of life on the Australian mainland, and had spent most of his time in penal settlements: 'I have laboured till my health broke down [Duffy wrote]. I have neglected my family and lived only for the Irish cause, and at every point I have found myself thwarted . . . After twelve years of fruitless struggle my heart is weary and longs for tranquillity . . .' But what of *society* in Australia?: Were there men 'of intellect and cultivation in such a number and of such a class, as to give a man friends and associates with whom he can live contentedly'? O'Brien's answer is not on record.

Duffy now systematically sought advice from people who knew Australia; Charles Joseph La Trobe, Victoria's first Governor, a gifted and cultivated man, an amateur, in the eighteenth century tradition, of diverse interests and accomplishments, then living in retirement in London; Robert Lowe, Thomas Woolner, the pre-Raphaelite poet and sculptor, a prolific manufacturer of frock-coated celebrities (and nonentities), frozen in marble, who had spent two years in Australia (1852-54) unsuccessfully gold-digging, and more successfully, making portrait medallions; and the no-less-prolific writing team, Mary and William Howitt, who had followed the golden trail to Australia on the same ship as 'Orion' Horne in 1852. William had just published a two-volume account of his experiences, titled *Two Years in Victoria*, and Duffy gave the book a long and adulatory review — more than a page — in *The*

Nation, drawing a moral from the rapid progress the colony had made, 'ruled by its own laws and its own people. Australia will now become a home', he prophesised. 'Hitherto, it has been looked upon much as the rich booty of an enemy in time of war'.

> Men made a foray to the gold fields — they prepared for a campaign of two or three years, and were mightly wroth and disappointed if they did not find the dreams of their nursery days realized in 'streets paved with gold'. Lawyers abandoned their briefless chambers, doctors their apocryphal practices, clerks their steel-pens, and shopmen their yard measure to rush to the diggings. Armed with pick-axe and shovel they sought the El Dorado, and because in a district, where, two years before a human foot had not trod, they did not find macadamized roads, decent inns, fair charges, and honest company, they clamoured frantically against the country when it was their previous training, and habits, which totally unfitted them for hardships, that were in fault . . . Every unsuccessful digger was naturally soured; and too many took out their revenge by slandering the colony, its social condition, above all, its climate. Some writers represent Australia . . . as a Garden of Eden; others as a sort of 'Inferno', in which a broiling sun and a plague of insects serve as brimstone.

Howitt certainly did not gloss over the vigour and virulence of the insect population, particularly the 'millions of flies . . . At your meals, in a moment myriads come swooping down, cover the dish and the meat on your plates till they are one black moving mass; dash headlong into your tea, or whatever you are drinking, and fight you to the last moment for the last morsel. Every meal is a pitched and hard-fought battle too'. There were many other unpleasant, singular and curious insects: venomous ants, an inch long; red spiders, whose bite was said to be deadly; centipedes and scorpions. Howitt said the heat of the summer was greater than any accounts had led him to expect. It varied, of course, in different parts of the continent, but on the whole, he found the climate fine and genial.

Duffy called on the Howitts in their modest but charming London house, and Mary Howitt reassured him not to be too much alarmed by her husband's opinions of the Australian climate. Woolner, too, was reassuring. He declared that the climate was delightful, the air exhilarating, the flies counted for nothing, and there were some men of brains and culture in Melbourne. Duffy pertinently asked him why then had he quit this 'terrestial Paradise?' Woolner replied, 'Well, I am an artist, and art won't be born there for a generation or two, and meantime I must live, if possible'.

Next, Duffy spoke to Lowe and his wife. She was enthusiastic about Australia. Yes, the climate was delightful, and the trouble from dust, of which Duffy had also heard, was not worth mentioning. Insects were probably a trouble in newly occupied districts, but she suffered no more inconvenience from them in a Sydney drawing-room than she did in London. They lived four or five miles out of town, and Lowe said how much he enjoyed riding in daily. But he criticised the practice of building Australian houses after unsuitable English models. There were in Sydney 'wealthy and cultivated families in the second generation who enjoyed many of the comforts of Europe in their houses and habits of life.

Books were as easily had in Sydney or Melbourne as in London, only a few months later, and a few shillings dearer'. As for friends, Lowe added with a little cynical smile, 'if you insist on that luxury you must import it'. La Trobe confirmed these favourable reports and Duffy was convinced.

In March 1855, a telegram from Trieste reached Dublin, announcing an Australian Declaration of Independence. 'The news was premature, and on the whole, we are rejoiced it was', Duffy wrote in *The Nation*. And he offered some speculations on Australia's future, and some reflections on its past. Australia would inevitably become independent, he wrote, 'but let the new State be a man come to the years of discretion, not a blustering boy impatient for the *toga virilis'*.

He predicted that Victoria, which then had no more inhabitants than the city and county of Dublin, would have a population of a million within a few years. [It reached a million in the 'nineties'].

> And a million men and women of more than ordinary courage and vigour . . . By that time the fever of gold hunting will have been mitigated by success; a large section of the people will have won an independence and exchanged their gold dust for the broad acres of *Australia Felix*, and the country will possess the moral as well as the material elements of a nation. At present, the rage of private gain is too intense, and the interest in public affairs too slight, to afford a security for the healthy development of that noble country into the great empire which it is destined to become.

Like many of his contemporaries, Duffy overestimated the rewards of gold mining. 'Despite the immense production . . . the producers were too numerous for many to gain a worthwhile share', writes a distinguished historian of the period, Geoffrey Serle. 'No precise estimates of the earnings of miners are possible', says Serle. 'But it is probable that . . . eight out of ten made no more than the equivalent of reasonable wages...'

DUFFY performed the traditional antic of applying for the Stewardship of the Chiltern Hundreds, the acceptance of a paid office under the Crown being the only way a Member of the House of Commons can relinquish his seat.

After the escape of Mitchel and Meagher, the British Government allowed Smith O'Brien and his associates to return to Europe on the condition that they did not visit any part of the United Kingdom. Before leaving Parliament, Duffy drew up a Memorial to Palmerston requesting the withdrawal of this restriction. He had little difficulty in getting more than 140 members of Parliament to sign it; including a former Solicitor-General, Sir Fitzroy Kelly, Lord Goderich, Cobden and Bright. Duffy mentioned the Memorial to Disraeli in the House, and was invited to talk it over privately in Disraeli's Park Lane residence. He received Duffy in his library, and began the conversation by telling Duffy he was impatient in leaving the House of Commons. He likened human life to a wheel; it was constantly turning round, he said, and what was the bottom today would some other day be at the top. Duffy replied that the wheel was

157

worked with a strong pulley by the party whips, and the Irish nationalists never came to the top.

Duffy brought the talk round to the Memorial, and Disraeli agreed to support it. He spoke frankly of the Irish question, and Duffy told him that the Conservatives, by a generous policy, might make themselves more acceptable to Ireland than the Whigs, whom Lord John Russell's conduct had made detestable. Disraeli said he had taken great pains to induce Cabinet to accept Napier's land reforms, and he meditated other concessions.

The conversation drifted from politics to novels — Disraeli's novels. Duffy said that though the public preferred *Coningsby*, he considered several of the earlier novels much better: '*The Wondrous Tale of Alroy*, as it used to be called, was the most entrancing romance since *Ivanhoe*. *Contarini Fleming* . . . was *sui generis*, an insight into the desires and dreams of a youth of genius; and *Ixion in Heaven* was of the *genre* of *Candide* and worthy to be set on the same shelf'.

And Duffy compared the first time he read *Vivian Grey* to the first time he drank champagne. It intoxicated him with 'an altogether new and mysterious enjoyment'. As he said this, he noticed a flush rise to Disraeli's cheeks, 'for under the mask of abstruse political profundity . . . he was always at heart a man of letters, and the only one among his contemporaries'. Duffy again brought up the subject of reforms in Ireland which a Conservative statesman might make without violating his party's principles. Disraeli listened graciously and they parted with a warm handshake.

The Memorial failed. Palmerston waited till the session ended before replying, through Sir Denham Norreys, that he and Sir George Grey could not at present 'with propriety recommend to Her Majesty', O'Brien's free pardon, but that the 'door of hope' was not shut. Duffy would have the satisfaction, wrote Norreys, of knowing that because of Duffy's 'untiring energy' O'Brien stood in a far more favourable position than he did at the commencement of the session.

Duffy spent a few days with O'Brien in Brussels, and they discussed the events of 1848. Duffy said he believed Ireland was just to O'Brien's character, 'and unjust to his policy'. His own class would not be persuaded that he was morally justified in attempting a revolution; the middle class thought that French or American officers should have been put in charge of the operation and 'the new secret societies' believed that a grand opportunity should not have been sacrificed to sentimental humanity; he should have burned Widow MacCormack's house, and her family, if necessary. O'Brien replied 'with great feeling' that he would not be guilty of such a murder for any political success whatever.

Released from public duties, Duffy found time to see more of London, 'the wonderful city', and to enjoy a busy social life. The National Gallery, the Abbey, and the British Museum occupied much of his leisure. He rode on Rotten Row, dined at Richmond's 'Star and Garter', accompanied Whitty behind the scenes at the opera, breakfasted with the *Punch* artist Richard Doyle (who drew its famous cover) and with Godley, the founder of the Canterbury Settlement in New Zealand. He met the dwarfish French socialist, Louis Blanc, and spoke of Ledru-Rollin's vehement promises of help to Ireland in 1844 and how little the Provisional Government had done in 1848. Blanc said the good intentions of his colleagues had been paralysed by Lamartine.

In a lengthy and emotional editorial in *The Nation* of 15 August 1855, Duffy explained his decision to leave Ireland:

> The Irish Party is reduced to a handful, the popular organisation is deserted by those who created it, prelates of the Irish Church throng the ranks of our opponents, priest is arrayed against priest, and parish against parish — shameless political profligacy is openly defended and applauded, the special opportunity sent by Heaven for our deliverance is bartered away to an English faction, and the ultimate aim for which alone I laboured — to give back to Ireland her national existence — is forgotten or disdained.
> Till all this be changed, there seems to be no more hope for the Irish Cause than for a corpse on the dissecting table.
> I have done my best to change it. For the last twelve months I have spared no pains, in public or private, to rally the national party. But in vain . . .

He continued that in quitting public life in Ireland, he would also be quitting his native country altogether. 'I cannot look on in dumb inaction on her ruin. I cannot sit down under the regime of corruption and terrorism . . .' He intended to make Australia his home, if the climate promised him better health: 'At worst', he wrote, 'I will see a country full of new and curious interest to me as the home of a multitude of our own race'. Duffy's property, *The Nation,* he announced, would pass into the hands of two young Irishmen, 'bred up in its doctrines', A.M. Sullivan, a brilliant and accomplished orator, and Michael Clery. As editor, they would retain Cashel Hoey who had been part-owner and associate-editor of the paper since its revival in 1849.

For weeks, *The Nation* published pages of extracts from English and Irish papers, commenting on Duffy's valedictory address. The Dublin correspondent of *The Times* considered it, on the whole, a calm and temperate document which might be perused with some advantage by 'enthusiasts' who had yet actually embarked on 'the stormy sea of Irish politics'. The editor of *The Times*, John Thaddeus Delane, was less charitable. He paid Duffy the ambiguous compliment of devoting his main editorial — more than two thousands words — to a sardonic commentary on the address. *The Times* was not sure whether Mr. Duffy had been tempted by the offer of a stipendiary magistracy, or a nice colonial place. If not, it suggested 'the Attorney-Generalship of the Cannibal Islands, whenever a hungry client has made a vacancy in the office'.

Many English and Scottish papers rebuked *The Times* for its editorial. The *Standard* said Duffy's valedictory address was written in a style which must command respect from all but the 'insolent' Thersites of *The Times*. 'Habitual truculence is one of the great and enduring characteristics of *The Times*'. said the *Hull Advertiser*. 'Its heaviest blows are always aimed at men that are down'. The *Glasgow Commonwealth*, while disagreeing with Duffy politically, thought his farewell was manly, touching, genuine and deserving of sympathy. The *Edinburgh News* said: '*The Times* pursued Mr. Duffy with stinging scorn and heartless derision; nevertheless, we would far rather be in the position of the warm-hearted, sorrow-saddened emigrant, than the scribe of *The Times,* who tries to pierce him with the shafts he aims from his secrecy. . .'

Who was this anonymous, shaft-launching scribe? Whitty wrote to Duffy that in journalistic circles it was generally believed to be Thackeray. Certainly, the style was not dissimilar from that in some of Thackeray's unsigned contributions to *Punch.* Duffy, 'amazed and wounded at such an unexpected hypothesis', wrote to Thackeray, with whom he was then quite friendly, and asked if it were true. He received a prompt denial;

> My Dear Mr. Duffy, — There is not one word of truth in your correspondent's information. I have not written one line in *The Times.* Ye Gods! when will well-informed correspondents leave off swallowing *mouches* and telling fibs? I wish you a happy voyage and prosperity wherever you are; and don't think I should be the man to hiss the boat that carried you away from the shore. . . .
>
> Yours very sincerely,
> W.M. Thackeray.

The *Morning Post,* Palmerston's own paper, observed that Duffy, 'a notorious demagogue', was wise in his generation because 'only a few years ago', he had a chance of being compelled to repair to Australia 'under auspices infinitely less propitious'; and the *Globe,* another Whig organ, noted that Duffy was 'a living examplar of the difference between the English and Russian treatment of traitors':

> Were he the editor of *St. Petersburg Nation* — if such a thing were possible — he would long since have been consigned to some more useful employment in Siberia . . . and instead of being sent by government, Mr. Duffy is going as a volunteer, to Australia, once our Siberia, but now one of the most flourishing, independent, and comfortable communities within the British dominions.

The Conservative press, for the most part, wrote generously of Duffy as a person, but was highly critical of the interference of the Vatican in Irish affairs.

AFTER saying good-bye to his 'oldest and dearest friends' at a levee in *The Nation* office, Duffy made a hasty visit to London to farewell the Carlyles, the Forsters, the Howitts, and many others. John Stuart Mill called with a dinner invitation, spoke with indignation of *The Times* editorial, and deplored Duffy leaving Parliament. (Mill had not yet written his famous treatise *On Liberty* but his radical *Principles of Political Economy,* which influenced more than a generation, had appeared in 1848.) They discussed Australia and Mill said there was no political economy objection to a duty on gold.

Duffy received many farewell letters. From the Vicarage at Eversley, the troubled Rev. Charles Kingsley, whose most successful novel *Westward Ho* had recently appeared, wrote: 'Let me say good-bye to a man whom (deeply differing from him on many points) I have long admired for his talent and fearlessness, even when I thought those great powers misapplied'. Thomas Woolner wrote, thanking Duffy for the trouble he had taken in arranging for Carlyle to sit for a bust, and hoping that he would find Australia as pleasant a place as Woolner had.

These sympathisers were all Liberals. Duffy was keenly touched to receive a letter from a Conservative, Sir James Emerson Tennent, the traveller and author who had held subordinate office in the 1852 Ministry, and been a contributor to the *Press*, the weekly journal founded by Disraeli in 1853. Tennent wrote to Duffy: 'And here let me say that I think in the management of *The Nation* you have done more than any living man, Moore only excepted, to elevate the national feeling of Irishmen . . .' Father Thomas O'Shea wrote 'I can't bear the idea of you leaving us. Alas! for poor Ireland . . . In all her struggles since you arrived at manhood, you can say with truth *liberavi animam meam*. And for the part you have so ably taken in the present contest for the unfettered civil and political liberty of the Irish Catholic priesthood, I feel grateful beyond all power of expression. . . .'.

DUFFY'S intention in going to Australia was to practice law. All his friends predicted a political career for him, Lowe for example, suggested he would be 'member for Sydney' within six months. Before he sailed, Duffy tried to use his influence on a Select Committee investigating Maynooth College, to defer a feared move by Dr. Cullen to bring the College under his personal control. In Duffy's words, Cullen would seek 'to denationalise it, to Italianise it, and crush the professors who cherished some spirit of independence!'

It was an era of prodigious gourmandising, accompanied by prodigious speechifying. 'In these realms what event is too sombre or disheartening to be celebrated by a public dinner?' Duffy asks, and such celebrations were projected in his honour; one in London, organised by John Stuart Mill, the other in Dublin, by the professors of Newman's new university. Among the many churchmen who accepted the Dublin invitation was the Very Reverend Jeremiah Vaughan, P.P., Ruan and Dysart. But he wrote: 'I cannot understand how a festive gathering . . . can be suitable to so mournful an occasion. I think the wild Banshee wail would be more fitting on the departure of one of the purest, most inflexible men that ever struggled for Ireland'. The wail of the Banshee was not heard because Duffy insisted on the banquet being cancelled. Lucas was dying, and Duffy wrote to the organisers: 'Our friend and colleague, the foremost man among us, lies on a bed from which he will rise no more. Surely it is not fit, or permissible, to hold a public festival at such a moment?' He also cancelled the London banquet.

However, he was persuaded to receive an enormously long farewell Address from the Irish Provident Society in London. The Address, which moved many to tears, compared Duffy to Moses, who 'preferred to dwell in the wilderness with a suffering and enslaved people, rather than enjoy the luxuries . . . of the Royal Court of the Egyptian oppressor'. Duffy, replying in an eloquent speech of even greater length, said that though he hoped in Australia to earn a competency for his family (cheers), he would never put away from his mind those interests of his country and his race which were entwined around every feeling of his heart (great cheering.)

Colonel French, a well-known habitué of the Reform Club proposed a Gavan Duffy Testimonial Fund, and offered a contribution of £20 to launch it; Duffy graciously repudiated the proposal, saying he had never put the people's money in his pocket. But he accepted a loan from Thomas (later Lord) O'Hagan to clear his debts, and another from Arthur Geoghan, a young Protestant Nationalist in the Excise Department.

'Beside the little oratory at Brompton . . . all that is mortal of Frederick Lucas was committed to the grave last Saturday' said an editorial in *The Nation* on 3 November 1855. 'Amid the masts of the Mersey, there is one that will wend its way far South, towards tropic skies, and grander stars, on Monday next, carrying Charles Gavan Duffy . . . What more melancholy commentary on the conditions of Ireland can be conceived that to these two men, honest and useful public life had become impossible'.

Ten

Life and politics in Colonial Victoria and New South Wales

ON 5 November 1855, the thirty-nine-year-old Duffy with his twenty-nine-year-old wife, Susan, and three of their children; Susan Anne, seven, Frank Edward, four, and Charles Gavan, four months, sailed from Liverpool on the Black Ball line clipper *Ocean Chief*, 1092 tons register, Captain Tobin master. John, his eldest boy, and the only surviving child by his first wife, had been left at Stonyhurst to be educated at grandfather McLaughlin's expense. In his memoirs, Duffy says there was no mail service to Australia in 1855, but the Black Ball line contracted under penalty to carry Her Majesty's mails to Australia, in sixty-five days. (The average time for the voyage for ships of one hundred tons or more was just over ninety days, but mails went overland to Brindisi.) Black Ball ships provided 'full bands of music', as well as chess, draughts, and backgammon sets for entertainment. The *Ocean Chief* also carried a cow, and baths 'for all classes of passengers'.

Accompanying Duffy was Moses Wilson Gray, the lawyer who had given up a career at the American bar to help his brother, Dr. Gray, conduct the *Freeman's Journal*. He had been a contemporary of Davis and Dillon at Trinity College, and was one of the great contingent of Irish barristers, at least forty-five, who migrated to Victoria between 1840 and 1860. Many became distinguished judges or advocates in Australia.

(Duffy's party was small compared with that of another Trinity law graduate, William Foster Stawell, who sailed for Melbourne in 1842, together with his future wife, her father, mother and six brothers, their governess, butler, head groom, second groom, gardener, herd, useful boy, laundress, man cook, housemaid, nurse, carpenter and the carpenter's family — a total of more than twenty-three. The Stawell entourage was augmented by two bulls, a Durham cow, two thoroughbred horses, a hunter and a mare. All travelled on the *Sarah*, five hundred tons register, together with a good library, which included most of the standard works, and a fine edition of the *Encyclopaedia Britannica*.

Despite the amenities of books, backgammon and baths, a voyage to Australia in the 1850s was inevitably hard, even for the few privileged cabin passengers. The fast, fully rigged ship of the time has been described as perhaps the most dangerous and uncomfortable vehicle ever invented. Captains in their zest for speed took terrifying risks. The notorious 'Bully Forbes' of the *Marco Polo* was proud of his slogan 'Hell or

Melbourne!'. He once made the run in seventy-four days. A writer in Dickens' *Household Words* described a typical shipboard scene in rough weather, 'everybody ill, everybody groaning, all the women whimpering, all the children crying'. And in a storm, chaos reigned, with men struggling waist-high in water amid a confusion of ruined deck-houses, panic-stricken passengers and terrified live-stock. Nor was the captain, on whose calm judgment the survival of the ship depended, always sober. Captain Tobin, a frank and friendly Nova Scotian of Irish descent, told Duffy of a skipper he knew who had entered in his log-book: 'I regret to state that during the greater part of this entire day the first mate has been intoxicated and disorderly'. Some days later, the first mate made his entry in the log. 'I am rejoiced to be able to state that during this entire day the captain has been sober, and his instructions for sailing the brig were quite intelligible'.

'On my first Sunday at sea, I may be said to have begun my Australian career', wrote Duffy:

> The bell was rung for ten o'clock in the morning and the captain read passages from the Book of Common Prayer to the bulk of the cabin passengers. When he finished I . . . asked him if there was an Established Church on board the *Ocean Chief*. 'Certainly not', he said. 'Well, have the goodness to have the bell rung again and I will read prayers for some hundred Irish Catholics in the second class and steerage . . .' I got through the business fairly well and continued the practice till the end of the voyage.

For the first fortnight, the *Ocean Chief* was never beyond a day's sail from Ireland. A head wind bedevilled her in the North Atlantic, followed by an extraordinary calm. But when she crossed the Equator favourable winds filled the sails for the next eight thousand miles, almost unceasingly. The passengers amused themselves in traditional fashion, with sweepstakes, deck billiards, loo, concerts, amateur theatricals, and a mysterious game called 'spoil five'. Duffy does not record what part he played in these madcap diversions, but he had plenty of time to discuss the land question with Wilson Gray, who had studied the American system, and thought that prosperity derived from small farms. He tended to regard grazing as 'intensely evil'.

EIGHTY days' sail from Liverpool, the *Ocean Chief* was in sight of the Australian coast, and on 28 January 1856, she sailed through the Heads, into what Duffy described as 'the noble land-locked harbour of Port Phillip', on which Melbourne is situated. A health officer who came on board handed him a letter requesting him not to land till he had received a welcoming deputation. 'The deputation', reported the *Argus* next day, 'was very numerous, consisting of about eighty persons, including Englishmen, Scotchmen and Irishmen, the latter naturally being in the largest proportion'. It was led by John ('Big Jack' or 'Long John') O'Shanassy, an intelligent, dogged, genial, self-educated Tipperary Irishman who had migrated in 1839, prospered as a draper, became the spokesman of Victoria's Irish Catholics, and was then the second member for Melbourne, and the Leader of the Opposition in the Legislative Council.

The Irish population in Australia had increased greatly with the gold rush. During the famine years, of the two millions who left Ireland permanently, more than three-quarters went to the United States and the remainder to Canada. Australia's share of the emigration from 1847 to 1852 was only two per cent. But in 1855 when sixteen thousand Irish came to Australia, it represented roughly twenty per cent. Among the emigrants who came out the following year were Margaret Callan, Duffy's cousin and sister-in-law, with her doctor husband, and some of her five children, one of whom, another Margaret, later married Duffy's eldest son.

The Melbourne where Duffy was to start his new life was, in his own words, 'a thriving village', less than twenty years old. Its population, swollen by the gold rush, was about one hundred thousand. Stumps of trees remained in some streets, and huge chasms separated others. Streets were ill-lit and ill-paved. After rain, great pools of slush made many impassable. Citizens were stifled with dust when the sun was high and spattered with mud when the rain fell. Many of them lived in unhealthy squalid, over-crowded hovels, and drunkenness was widespread. Wild and drunken fellows 'galloped furiously through the town, and the streets at night were infested by the felons of Van Dieman's Land and their dissolute associates', Duffy wrote. Of 282 inquests held in a year, death from drunkenness accounted for 78.

Duffy recalled the progress of some government building:

> The Government offices were a two-storey villa, the law offices occupied a vacant corn store, the Public Works Department was housed in a wooden shanty; but some progress had been made with an ambitious Customs house, and the young community had built a creditable Public Library and Museum, and the foundations and class rooms of a University. The Legislative Council met in a small brick building known as St. Patrick's Hall, hired from the St. Patrick's Irish Society.

And despite its crudity and its remoteness, Melbourne was not entirely divorced from the culture of the Old World. The Melbourne Philharmonic Society founded in 1853, gave regular concerts, including performances of the *Messiah*, the *Creation* and *Israel in Egypt*. In 1855, the Irish *prima donna*, Catherine Hayes, appeared in a four-week season of Italian opera, and the same year the great Irish Shakespearean actor, Gustavus Brooke, began an Australian tour in Melbourne that lasted six years. In that golden year, too, Melbourne's Theatre Royal, seating three thousand, was built at a cost of £95,000. And if Duffy had wandered into Robertson's Circulating Library soon after his arrival he would have found such recent London publications as Thackaray's *Newcomes*, Tennyson's *Maud*, Professor Wilson's *Noctes Ambrosianae*, Mrs. Gaskell's *North and South*, and W.H. Russell's *Letters from the Crimean War*. Dickens' *Little Dorrit* which was appearing in monthly parts in London, was being serialised in the *Leader*, a Melbourne weekly, published by the *Age*, which also carried a page of digests from French, German and Italian journals and original articles in French.

The fever of the gold rush had abated, but Duffy was entertained with lively stories of its virulent days. Some, no doubt were apocryphal. Many have passed into folklore. One suspects at times that veterans of three febrile years were not averse from pulling the legs of newcomers. 'I have heard from eye-witnesses', sayd Duffy, 'stories of diggers ordering the entire stock of champagne to be decanted into a washing-tub, and stopping every passer-by with an invitation to swill'. He had also heard from eye-witnesses

> of one frantic toper . . . insisting upon having the bar-counters washed with claret . . . of pier glasses smashed with a stockwhip . . . of diggers throwing down nuggets to pay for a dram, and declining to accept change; of pipes lighted with a cheque; of sandwiches lined with banknotes.

A favourite recreation of the digger on the spree was to get married — temporarily. Duffy describes the process with circumspection: 'A bride was not difficult to discover, who permitted herself . . . to be adorned with showy silks and driven in an equipage as conspicuous as the circumstances permitted to a bridal which, in many cases, bound them together, only during good pleasure'.

AMONG the Duffy papers is an undated fragment, apparently written soon after his arrival, in which he has scribbled his impressions of colonial life:

> There is little jealousy of men rising by their ability, except among new chums, who murmured 'this was decidedly not the way things were done at home. . .'

> The most vigorous and intelligent men in Australia have selected small towns for their home; and prove that a fortune was to be made there more safely than in the capital. The life of the shepherd, solitary and melancholy; if he be a married man his children never see the schoolmaster or a clergyman, and are reared up like wild creatures who fly at the sight of a stranger. His enjoyment is commonly comprised of a weekly carouse upon poisonous gin at the nearest bush public house.

> *Cobbs Coaches:* Light coaches built of hickory wood, iron and leather, horsed by four blood mares, and driven by an American citizen who speaks of the principal men of the country as if they were his private intimates, and dines at the table with his passengers, but to do him justice, gets over the road in a style not known before his advent . . . But the weary immigrant landing on these new shores will pass by railways and telegraphs, courts and parliaments, familiar trifles, and long to reach the great country behind, over hundreds of miles of unbroken pasture. It is impossible to enjoy a more exhilarating pleasure than such an excursion in the Australian spring, while the grass is still emerald green and the delicious fragrance of the mimosa fills the air. The country is said to be deficient in natural scenery, but in whatever direction the traveller turns he will find scenes of striking beauty within easy ride of Melbourne. He may make acquaintance with the rich tranquil waters of the Moonee Ponds, the beautiful Pentland Hills, the charming end reaches of the Yarra, and Dandenong and Heidelberg, which look upon a landscape as varied and pleasant as one sees from Richmond Hill.

> The Australian cattle is often underfed, overdriven, badly butchered and abominably cooked. The beef is often not fit to eat, but it is better than French

or Italian beef. Overstocking has caused great deterioration in sheep and cattle.

Someone ought to make a dialogue in the Australian dialect:
'I say mate, are there many of you here?'
'A good few'.
'Come, I'll shout for the lot'.
'Don't be so bounceable'.
'Have you a *down* upon me?'

ONE of the ninety-five leading Melbourne citizens who signed an Address of Welcome to Duffy was Ebenezer Syme. A Scottish evangelist and a graduate of St. Andrews, he had been assistant editor of the radical *Westminster Review*, had migrated in 1852, and now, with his brother, David, owned the Melbourne *Age*. For many years, the *Age*, backed by Melbourne's nonconformist merchants, and inspired by Ebenezer Syme's idealism, was the voice of a nascent Victorian democracy — a powerful foe of privilege, injustice and corruption.

The rival Melbourne morning paper with the biggest circulation, was the *Argus*, owned by Edward Wilson. Duffy described him as 'one of the most remarkable men in Victoria . . . large, sombre, silent . . . a striking figure'. The son of a prosperous London linen-merchant, Wilson had drifted into journalism after failing as a calico-printer. He was a polemicist in the Cobbett tradition. At the time of Eureka, he had supported the miners and advocated republicanism. His friend Henry Parkes called him 'a Radical of the Radicals'. His enemies called him 'Edward the Black Prince' — a reference to his swarthy complexion.

Though an invalid when he arrived in Melbourne, Duffy could not escape a whirl of social engagements. At a welcoming banquet at Hockins' Hotel, he confessed that he had no hand-pikes in his portmanteau; the most destructive weapon he had brought with him was Chitty's *Practice of the Law*. In such a land as Australia, he said, where there was fair play for all, he could be what nature intended him to be, had national injustice not turned his blood into gall. Essentially he was 'a man who lent a cheerful obedience to the laws . . . and who desired no more than to be permitted to live in peace under their protection'. Then came a passage that was long remembered. Amid cheers, he declared:

> Let me not be misunderstood. I am not here to repudiate or apologize for any part of my past life. I am still an Irish rebel to the backbone and the spinal marrow, a rebel for the same reason that John Hampden and Algernon Sidney, George Washington and Charles Carrol of Carroltown, were rebels — because tyranny had supplanted the law.

He still thought his country's liberty was worth fighting and dying for. But he was a Radical reformer, and 'no more a Red Republican than a Red Indian'. Then rising to apocalyptic heights — or sinking to bathetic depths — he told his rapt audience that he was happy to be laying the foundations of an Empire 'which will some day claim as its inheritance the thousand teeming islands of the Pacific, which will carry our Christian civilization into the swarming hives of China, and in the fullness of time, grasp the sceptre of India itself'.

About six hundred people attended the banquet. Among them were O'Shanassy, who occupied the chair, Wilson Gray, Peter Lalor, Ebenezer Syme, and the American consul. It was a boisterous affair. 'Vehement applause greeted nearly every sentence that fell from the lips of the guest of the evening', says a contemporary report. But Syme, proposing the toast of 'Self-government — the right of a free people', and several other speakers, could not get a hearing.

Duffy was regaled with heady draughts of adulation. 'The accession of talent like his is more important than the discovery of a goldmine' said O'Shanassy. 'If the presence of the great Napoleon in the French army was deemed equivalent to forty thousand troops; the presence of such a master mind in an Australian Parliament . . . will be still more influential and still more effective', wrote Dr. Dunmore Lang, the head of the Presbyterian Church in New South Wales, and a Member of its Legislative Council. Giving the toast 'Erin go Bragh and Charles Gavan Duffy' at another banquet, the Melbourne historian, Edmund Finn ('Garryowen') said:

> By pen and tongue he soothed the sectarian animosities which long estranged the Catholic, Protestant and Presbyterian countrymen . . . to speak figuratively, he drew the Giant's Causeway to the Rock of Cashel, and sprinkled the old treaty stone of Limerick with the waters of the Boyne (cheers). Like the seven cities of old which claimed to be the birthplace of a dead poet, so the two greatest cities of the southern hemisphere were contending for the possession of the living patriot.

FEB. 21, 1856.]   MELBOURNE PUNCH

A PUBLIC DINNER IN MELBOURNE;
OR,
A FEAST OF REASON AND A FLOW OF SOUL.

'Orion' Horne, who had been a gold digger, commander of a gold escort, and a gold Commissioner, was now clerking in the office of Melbourne's leading advocate, Archibald Michie. He made Duffy welcome with a poem composed in his honour, a copy of Horne's *Life of Napoleon,* and a letter which read, in part:

> Welcome to Australia! . . . How many associations with Dublin — all pleasing and full of energy — are at once conjured up with your name in my memory . . . We don't think ourselves so barbarous here. What do you say to a publisher having brought out an Australian *Orion* a twelvemonth ago, and found people to purchase?
> Well, you have come to a vast new field. You can make a fortune, if you choose, but may also do something much better . . .'

Always conscious of his literary associations in London, Horne had appointed himself a sort of unofficial cultural attache to the raw colony. The last distinguished visitor whom he had welcomed was the sensational dancer Lola Montez, who had impressed him with her intensely dark blue eyes.

DUFFY took chambers in Temple Court, the Melbourne lawyers' quarters, and began to practice his profession. But the men who had welcomed him on his arrival insisted that he should stand at the forthcoming elections, the first under the new constitution. This required a property qualification of £5,000 for the Legislative Assembly, and £1,000 for the Upper House, the Legislative Council. A fund was quickly organised with committees throughout Victoria and New South Wales, to raise the required sum, and New South Wales gave striking earnest of its regard for Duffy by subscribing £2,000.

A typical tribute to him was paid by Daniel Deniehy, secretary of the Goulburn appeal. Deniehy, a brilliant, ill-starred young lawyer and journalist of Irish descent, said that Duffy was the most eminent Irishman then living, and assuredly the greatest man who had ever visited Australia.

> Ireland is under greater obligations to Charles Gavan Duffy than to any man living, and it may be laid down as an axiom that if a man has really and truly benefited his country, he has more or less directly or indirectly, benefited the whole human race. The great lesson of Mr. Duffy's teachings and example to the Irish people is — to be a free man you must be a true man and an enlightened man. And what a lesson to a dispirited and scantily educated people, whose cause for years has been turned into matter for whining melodies for the pianoforte, and ranting speeches, and declamatory promises, impossible of performance!

Goulburn, a straggling township 130 miles from Sydney, with a population of about three thousand, contributed £74.15.8 to the fund. Victoria raised £3,000.10.6. Most of the money was spent in buying Duffy a house in Burwood road, Hawthorn, a pretty Melbourne suburb, only a few miles from Parliament House. The balance he invested in bank shares. The generous New South Wales contribution was accompanied by a no less generous illuminated address. This was signed by William Bede Dalley, an urbane and accomplished Sydney-born lawyer, and the unofficial spokesman for its Catholic community; by the Speaker of the Legislative Assembly, Daniel Cooper; by the Mayor of Sydney, George Thornton, and by fourteen Members of Parliament, and other distinguished citizens.

In the address, they expressed regret that Duffy had chosen to live in Melbourne, denying New South Wales 'the advantage of his eminent talents and tried public integrity'. Duffy replied: 'It gives me inexpressible comfort to know that in beginning a new career in Australia, I may count on the sympathy of so large a body of men'. Residence in Melbourne would for the present limit his opportunities of communicating with his New South Wales friends. But it was his business to prepare for the time when Sydney and Melbourne would be as easy for mutual access as Liverpool and Southampton, or New York and Boston. The time could not be far away when the Parliament of a Federated Australia would sit in each of the great cities in succession. In Duffy's opinion it was then that the true history of Australia would begin.

The title deeds of the house were presented to Duffy at yet another public dinner at Hockins' Hotel, where Duffy and his family were staying. 'Your generous gift, gentlemen, has, I believe no parallel for munificence in the history of this country', said Duffy. 'But its weight in gold is not its true value. The immense constituency which it represents makes it a political demonstration of peculiar interest and significance . . . I accept it as a noble retaining fee to serve the interest of Australia. . .'

Duffy spoke of the precious opportunity the colonists enjoyed in a new social experiment of adopting whatever was best in the habits of kindred nations, 'till a national Australian character grows'. But in adopting whatever was best from the Old Country, they should be careful not to revive 'its parliamentary system steeped in corruption, its government by one favoured class, and its bigotry which teaches men to hate their neighbours and love themselves. . .' He elaborated on the theme of bigotry. He could not see what any man could hope to gain by setting Protestant against Catholic and Catholic against Protestant. No one would pretend that Catholics were aiming at some undue and unreasonable power. In fact, they had not one solitary representative in the government or on the bench.

It had been argued, he continued, that Catholics ought to be deprived of political power, because political and religious liberty were denied in Catholic countries. But was this true? 'It is as true as that witches ride on broomsticks, that one Englishman can beat five Frenchmen, or any of the hundred other fables of ignorance and prejudice'.

Belgium was a Catholic country, yet it had selected a Protestant as its king. Hungary was a Catholic country, yet it placed a Protestant, Kossuth, in the highest office of State. France, a Catholic country, had set an example of religious equality to the world. Poland, a Catholic country, was the first to emancipate the Jews, an example which England had not yet followed. There were Catholic countries, of course, ruled by old despotic systems, which did refuse civil and religious liberty. But there were also Protestant countries which refused them. America dealt in Negro slaves and plundered the Mormons for their religious opinions. Catholics were as ill-treated in Protestant Sweden as Protestants in Catholic Naples. In Prussia a Catholic was as uncomfortable as a Protestant was in Austria. Swiss Protestants had shown themselves as great tyrants as Spanish Catholics. In the reign of Queen Mary, English Protestants had found refuge in Catholic Dublin:

> Look at the example England herself has set down to this generation. Thirty years ago no Protestant Dissenter could sit in Parliament; it is but two years since he was admitted to the Universities (I had myself the pleasure of voting for the measure); he has still to pay church-rates for the support of the Establishment; and it is not a very long time since carting Quakers, and burning the houses of Unitarians, have ceased to be a popular pastime. These facts might teach us that there has been bigotry and cruelty wherever uncontrolled power existed, no matter to what creed it belonged.

Duffy continued 'I hate Catholic ascendancy and Protestant ascendancy alike and while I breathe, I will resist one and the other. . .'

Over the chimney-piece of his new home, Duffy hung portraits of Thomas Davis and John Dillon.

DUFFY was urged by the politician and newspaper proprietor Henry Parkes and Edward Butler, who was practising law, to visit Sydney; here an equally enthusiastic welcome awaited him. As his ship — the intercolonial steamer *Telegraph* — entered Sydney Harbour, it was met by the steamer *Illalong*, decorated with Irish and Australian colours, and carrying a welcoming group of ladies and gentlemen. When the two ships reached the quay, many thousands had gathered: 'Irishmen, Englishmen, Scotchmen, and Australians of every sect and creed', reported Henry Parkes' paper, the *Empire*, 'to honour the patriot of Ireland'.

His admirers had spent weeks organising a magnificent banquet. This was held in the Prince of Wales Theatre, transformed for the occasion into a lush bower of eucalyptus, ferns, cabbage-tree palms, flowers and flags: British, French, Sardinian and Turkish. More than two thousand guests attended, including several hundred ladies, demurely occupying the upper circle and boxes. Music was provided by a Hungarian band in national costume, and the repast, according to the *Empire* reporter, was 'of a very delectable and substantial character'. Wealthy capitalists, such as Thomas Mort and Robert Tooth, rubbed shoulders with well-known radicals, such as Parkes and William Pennington, who was in the chair.

Duffy said that with all its faults, he believed the New South Wales constitution was one of the most liberal in the world. This was his deliberate belief, demonstrated by the fact that he was there. With all the world before him, he had chosen Australia. As for the nominee Upper House, he entirely favoured the elective principle. 'I supported your wishes in this respect in the House of Commons', he said, 'and have no doubt that you will, at no distance, elect both your Houses'. He went on to urge the federation of the Australian colonies in words remarkably ahead of their time:

If you want speedy communication with Europe, if you want the uniform administration of justice — if you want cheap and registered postage, you must have some assembly competent to act for all of Australia, and I would trust to see such an assembly undertake another duty, to name anew some or all of these colonies. How ludicrously unsuitable a name, for example, is New South Wales, for a country so extensive and rich as this (laughter) names after the half of a little principality, scarcely equal to a squatter's station (laughter). You might as well call a Hercules after Tom Thumb. And South Australia, which is not the southern country of this continent, and Victoria which already shares its name with ten or twelve other Victorias in all latitudes of the world. I am sure there are natives of this soil who love their country as profoundly as any men on the face of the earth, but I think they are hardly treated. You sir, (turning to the chairman) call yourself an Englishman (loud cheers) and are proud of the name. I call myself an Irishman (loud cheers) — and rejoice to be so called; but how can any man venture to call himself a New South Welshman? He may be proud indeed of the name of Australian which I trust, will be a memorable name in history, but you are not Australians till there is some federal connection between the separate members of Australia. Some Sydney friends . . . have asked me where I meant to live, and I have answered that I meant to live in Australia . . . (loud cheering) What matters on which side of the imaginary line which separates you from the neighbouring colony? . . . I believe your interests are identical and that all Australia will rise or fall together (loud cheers) . . .

A notable and regretful absentee from the banquet was the Irish Catholic Premier, John Hubert Plunkett. The Governor of New South Wales was Sir William Denison, who had governed Van Dieman's Land when Smith O'Brien, Meagher, and their comrades were prisoners there. His malevolent treatment of them had earned him the nickname of 'the black snake', and Duffy positively refused to attend any function where his health was honoured. As the organising committee conceded this point, Plunkett, without breaching etiquette, could not attend.

New South Wales gave many other manifestations of the esteem in which Duffy was held. One admirer registered a rent charge in his name, to qualify him for election to any constituency in the colony. Henry Parkes made him the flattering offer of £800 a year to join the staff of the *Empire*. Duffy refused this, but agreed to contribute occasionally. Perhaps even more flattering than Parkes' astonishing offer was the fact that, within a month, two Sydney hotels and an omnibus were named 'Gavan Duffy'. But nothing gratified Duffy more than a tribute in the *Sydney Morning Herald*, then, as still, the prosperous organ of Conservatives. The Reverend Mr. West, the historian of Van Dieman's land wrote:

Mr. Duffy left this city yesterday, attended by the best wishes of thousands... He had been invited to several of the principal towns of the interior. To have gratified all his admirers would have consumed time which no man worthy of such an honour could spare. In Mr. Duffy we have recognised a representative man — one who presents a view of a great section of our population. We have found him in personal contact a pleasant, earnest, and practical man . . . accustomed to deal with great questions of government where rodomontade and sham cannot gain a second hearing. We shall always look back upon our share in the reception of Mr. Duffy as a public recognition of the natural and religious equality of all subjects of the Crown.

In 1852, West, under the pen-name of 'John Adams', had contributed a series of articles in the *Sydney Morning Herald*, arguing the case for a union of the Australian colonies. He edited the paper from 1852 till 1871.

DUFFY had been tempted to stay in Sydney, which had a much larger Irish population than Melbourne. 'The fact that most impressed me in New South Wales', he wrote, 'was that a second generation, with . . . more cultivated tastes and more settled opinions, now occupied the public stage . . .'; and he wrote to Smith O'Brien that he found Sydney, 'in civilisation and society . . . a hundred years in advance of Melbourne'. (It had been founded forty-nine years earlier.) But there were far better prospects for radical politics in Victoria, and he looked forward to working with O'Shanassy, 'a man of massive good sense, and a fine heart'.

After his return to Melbourne, he received a letter from Parkes so fulsome that one wonders whether it was written tongue in cheek, or glass in hand — or simply whether Parkes, who had literary aspirations, was attempting a trial ascent of Parnassus. 'Your decisive words leave no hope of your leaving Victoria', it began, and continued at great length:

> The wish you have so frankly and affectionately expressed — that we may work together to the end of life — will remain a perfect light of gratitude within my troubled existence. If it could have been, I should have felt it a glorious privilege to have had a spirit like yours, mourning, rejoicing, admonishing, and encouraging in the trials and wrestlings of daily life, and I think I might have grown almost great in the gentler strength of a high-principled brotherhood such as I can now only dream of . . . Now I cannot help teasing you with a faint picture of some of the good things you have missed. Here you might have been at once the popular leader and the highest Minister of State, with a fairy nook on the romantic shores of our noble haven for your home and the most cultivated men in the community as your admiring friends . . . here you would have had a direct and definitely-ordered mission which there is no one else to enter upon.

Duffy's enduring friendship with Parkes was, in its way, even more remarkable than his friendship with Carlyle. Parkes, who was then forty-one was to be prominent, if not dominant, in the political life of New South Wales for more than forty years. A native of Warwickshire, he had been put to work in a rope-factory at the age of eight. Later, he was apprenticed to an ivory-turner. He had come to Sydney, an assisted migrant, with Chartist associations, in 1839, and worked as an agricultural labourer, before opening a shop in Sydney where he sold, among many other things, ivory by the tusk or pound, cricket and boxing gloves, bugle-horns for omnibuses and mail coaches, musical instruments, toys, Bohemian glass and mahogany writing-desks. In 1850, he established the *Empire* newspaper, and in 1854 was elected to the Legislative Council, beginning his long and ambiguous political career.

Another incongruous friendship developed between Duffy and Dr. Dunmore Lang, a fiery, uncompromising radical and democrat. Lang had been a pioneer of the Victorian separatist movement and looked forward confidently to the day when Australia would become a republic. He wrote to Duffy congratulating him on his arrival and apologising for not being among those 'other Liberal Members' of the late Legislative Council of New South Wales who had sent him an address of welcome from Sydney on his arrival in Melbourne. The reason, Lang explained, was that he was in prison, convicted of criminal libel 'before a packed jury'. (The expression was not unfamiliar to Duffy!)

Lang expounded to Duffy his views on Australian independence, visualising 'a great federation of sovereign and independent republics', eventually comprehending 'the great Islands of New Guinea and New Zealand'. He saw in Duffy a natural ally, but Duffy was convinced that 'it would be better policy to leave the question . . . in abeyance for the present . . .' Lang considered a Federal union utterly useless, unless accompanied by 'entire political freedom and national independence'. Duffy argued that separation from England was impracticable', especially with the prospect before us of war and rumours of war, which are sure to recur in Europe after the present patched-up and discreditable peace'. The peace, which ended the Crimean war, had been signed at the Congress of Paris on 30 March 1856.

Four years later, another distinguished Irish editor-politician, George Higinbotham, expressed similar views: 'In the present state of the world . . .' he wrote, 'a people that would be independent must be able to defend themselves. If they cannot defend themselves, they must attach themselves to some superior state'.

The electorate selected for Duffy to contest was Villiers and Heytesbury, in a sparsely populated part of south-western Victoria. Villiers was rich farming country, and Heytesbury, a squatting district. Duffy employed no agent, and did no personal canvassing, except when he visited a village called Killarney, which he had been told was inhabited by evicted Irish tenants who had prospered greatly in their new home. The first house he entered had 'all the evidence of rude careless plenty':

> A bottle of Martell's brandy was immediately placed on the table, flanked by a huge decanter full as it seemed of sparkling transparent water. I had slight experience in drinking raw spirits, but it was impossible to refuse pledging the prosperity of an Irish village. I poured a spoonful of brandy into a tumbler, and after drowning it . . . put it to my lips. The brandy, I concluded, must be of abnormal strength . . . and I had recourse to the decanter for a second time, and filled my tumbler to the brim. 'Is this water bewitched?' I cried, 'The brandy does not grow weaker but stronger, the more I pour upon it'. The farmer and his good woman burst into a merry laugh; the transparent fluid . . . was gin. There was a similar plenty in all the houses, and a similar hospitality.

Some 'screech owls' in Melbourne tried to stir up sectarian animosity against Duffy, but in the constitutency he was supported by Irish of all creeds. 'I have just returned from my election where they fought for me like lions in the name of the poor old country', he wrote to William Carleton, 'and to do them justice, Protestants as well as Catholics. We have bigots here, but the love of country is a stronger passion than bigotry in the heart of the exile'.

During the campaign Duffy was asked at a Warnambool meeting

whether he would accept a Government appointment. Ambiguously, perhaps indiscreetly, he replied: 'The best answer I consider such a question requires is that I might have come out to Australia as its Governor if I had chosen to traffic in situations'. He was probably referring to the venality of the Sadleir gang who had certainly trafficked in situations. But the answer was interpreted by Duffy's enemies — and still is by some historians — as a manifestation of arrogance and vanity. It gave his opponents something to laugh at. One of them, Captain Charles Pasley, a Conservative candidate, wrote: 'He fancies himself a whale among minnows'. Whale or minnow, Duffy had an easy victory. Edward Wilson congratulated him on 'the flattering circumstances' of his return, and sent him twenty-six suggestions for reform. In an accompanying letter, he wrote:

> The colonists are inclined to give you a fair trial, combined with a slight shade of suspicion, and anything which may be construed into an over-eager grasping at office would be permanently injurious to you. This colony strikes me as being a singularly favourable field for the trying of enlightened experiments . . . Do not you, then, imagine that because you are exiled from your favourite Ireland, you are therefore in no position to benefit Ireland. You may benefit her by proving to the British public that they may venture freely into reforms . . . Never mourn then over 'exile' but turn it to the best possible account. That is the part of the true patriot.

Many of Wilson's proposed reforms — some of which he agreed might seem 'wild and Utopian' — were not to be adopted for years. The included:

1. Justice to the Aborigines. This should be one of the first acts of our free Parliament. . . Hitherto we have behaved to them like cowards, tyrants and swindlers. . . We should now give them food, shelter, protection, clothing, and medical attendance, while any of them remain.
2. Agriculture ought to be made a department of the State . . . placing it upon the most enlightened footing.
3. A properly appointed Board of Audit of Accounts, securing good value for moneys expended . . .
4. Establishment of a mint.
5. Introduction of the ballot into municipal elections.
6. Leasing Crown Lands for cultivation; the tenants to have the right of ultimate purchase. . .

Wilson also recommended amendment of the Criminal Law, improvement in the magistracy, and better regulation of public houses, among other social reforms.

Parliament opened with appropriate ceremony on 25 November 1856. The historic day was proclaimed a holiday. Bands, flags and banners enlivened the streets. Judges wore their robes, the Mayor his regalia, Town Councillors their uniforms, and foreign consuls, their ribbons and medals. The day was oppressively hot, and fire-plugs with hoses attached were opened to cool the air and lay the dust. The streets were speedily awash, and the energetic wielders of the hoses deluged the closely-packed crowds. Escorted by volunteer cavalry, the Acting Governor, Sir

Edward Macarthur, a popular veteran of the Napoleonic wars, now Commander-in-Chief of Australian forces, arrived at a Chamber crowded with gaily dressed ladies. One small breach of protocol occurred. The Chief Secretary William Clarke Haines, announced that the Governor, when he reached the Council, would 'command' the attendance of the lower House. The Speaker, Dr. Murphy, sent Duffy a scrap of paper on which he had written 'Are we to be commanded?' Duffy punctiliously consulted O'Shanassy and a conscientious lawyer colleague, Henry Samuel Chapman. They agreed that the phraseology was unacceptable. After some negotiation, the Governor 'requested' their attendance. The two legislative chambers were not quite ready, and the top hats of some members collided with the scaffolding. With no mock modesty, Duffy writes in his autobiography: 'The making of Victoria now commenced, and I need not hesitate to say that for a quarter of a century I took as large a share as any man . . . in that reproductive work'.

Just before Christmas, the Governor, Sir Henry Barkly, arrived. He was a tall, cultivated and experienced administrator, the son of a West Indian planter, a former Peelite M.P., who had successively and successfully governed British Guiana and Jamaica.

In the New Year, he held his first levee. Duffy found the incongruities of costume amusing, 'from the silk stockings, buckled shoes, and unexceptional toilet of the Speaker', to the boiled white trousers, vest and archaic cocked hat of a venerable, unnamed member of the Council.

'I thought my position in this country would be a long one of retirement from public affairs, but it has proved otherwise', Duffy wrote to Father Doyle. 'I have been drawn back to them, by the reception of such generous and exuberant confidence that has left me no choice. If a man can find a second home on the earth I have found it here. . . A great future undoubtedly waits this country'. There was 'a certain competence, and even opulence', in it for every industrious and sober man. However, nothing compensated for 'the tender and mystical ties' which bound Irishmen to their mother country, and Duffy would not counsel any man to leave Ireland who was able and content to live there.

JOHN Pascoe Fawkner, a cantankerous, abusive, but honest and well-meaning son of a convict, in Van Dieman's Land had been in turn a baker, timber-merchant, bookseller, publican and newspaper-proprietor. He feared the Papacy, disapproved of Anglican ascendancy, and had the dual honour of being, with John Batman, the co-founder of Melbourne, and the proprietor of its first public house. Fawkner now turned his vituperative pen upon Duffy, in fiery letters to the *Argus*. He recalled Duffy's conduct in Ireland, and asked: 'Pray, Sir, have you ventured into Victoria to form a party? Or have you been invited here by the "active genius" who pulls the puppet wires of his church in this colony? Have you been invited here by or through the chief mover of your church in this colony as an appanage of the Roman See?' And he announced that O'Shanassy was not only a squatter's man, but a lay brother of the Jesuits. 'I see that waspish little creature . . . has been attacking you in the press', Lang wrote. 'I have had a similar honour myself'.

When Duffy was facing the preposterous 'No Popery' attacks of Fawkner, and other bigots, he received a letter from George Moore telling him that Monsignor Barnabo, writing from Rome, had forbidden some Meath priests from attending Tenant League meetings without Dr. Cullen's express permission. 'If the country bears in silence that most scandalous aggression of Barnabo's . . . I will not believe there is any hope'. Duffy wrote back to Moore:

> The Lord God be thanked I am living among Irish Catholics who would go to the stake rather than deny their faith, but who would fling that insolent missive into the Yarra Yarra. It makes my blood boil to think of a peasant in a mitre, a shallow, conceited dogmatist, a dense mass of prejudice and ignorance, squatting down upon the Irish cause and smothering it. What is the use, my friend, of motions in Parliament and meetings in Dublin if this stupid tyranny is to remain triumphant and unquestioned?

It was indeed ironic that while Duffy was denouncing the domination of the Vatican in Ireland, he was being denounced as its alleged emissary in Victoria. As he wrote at the time to Bishop Moriarty of Kerry, he was being 'bowled at in both ends of the earth . . . Yonder for betraying the interests of religion; here for being its slave and missionary'. And he wondered whether, had he stopped at the Equator, it would have been admitted that he belonged 'to neither Antipodes of opinion'.

Less than a month after Duffy's arrival in Melbourne, a donkey-driver crossing Hampstead Heath came across a body a few yards from Jack Straw's Tavern. Beside it was a silver cream jug and a large bottle labelled 'Essential Oil of Bitter Almonds'. The body was identified as that of John Sadleir, former Lord of the Treasury, who had swindled the public by an amount estimated at one million pounds. Thousands of people had lost life-savings in the collapse of his complex financial empire. *The Times* described it as 'a gigantic fraud without parallel in England', and the *Banner of Ulster* wrote: 'His name will descend to posterity as that of one of the coolest, most consummate villains who ever lived'.

Despite the evidence at the inquest, many believed that the body was not Sadleir's, and that he had somehow contrived to enjoy the fruits of his villainy in some secure exile. Certainly there were more comfortable ways of committing suicide than swallowing poison on a winter's night on the open Heath. Sadleir's brother and confederate James, was expelled from the House of Commons, and fled the country. So did a third member of the 'Irish Brigade', the Commissioner for Income Tax — and embezzler — Edmund O'Flaherty. He fled to Denmark, where there was no extradition treaty, then to New York, where he established himself as a dashing man-about-town. The fourth of the infamous quartette, Solicitor-General William Keogh, was even more fortunate. He became a judge. Dickens used Sadleir as the model for Mr. Merdle, the villainous financier in *Little Dorrit*.

WILLIAM Haines, who headed Victoria's first administration under responsible government was a London-born doctor, educated at

Charterhouse and Cambridge, who had become a gentleman farmer in Victoria. He was known as 'Honest Haines'. Duffy described him as 'a character without stain, and the cordiality which springs from a generous nature'. Nor was Parliament lacking in talent. It included graduates of Oxford, Cambridge, Edinburgh and Trinity College, distinguished lawyers, scholars and journalists.

But Victoria's first parliaments were inevitably unstable. As the ablest historian of the period, Geoffrey Serle, writes:

> The ideological assumptions of conservatives, liberals and democrats were overlaid by a profusion of complicating issues: pastoral, banking, mercantile, agricultural, mining, manufacturing and other interests struggled for economic advantage ... Protestants feared an unaccustomedly large Catholic minority; Catholics themselves fell into camps ... Despite long-drawn out sessions, the legislative achievement was almost trivial ...

Not only was it difficult at any time for a government to hold a majority in the Legislative Assembly; 'the incubus' of the Upper House, the Legislative Council, made effective government impossible. If, as Serle believes, 'Duffy never fulfilled his great promise' in Victoria, his failure must be seen against a background of political instability and sectarian prejudice.

'Nothing tended to impede the career of Mr. Duffy in Australia so much as his previous connection with *The Nation ...*' wrote 'Orion' Horne in his *Australian Facts and Prospects* (1859). 'It alarmed the prejudices of the majority of English and Scotch, not to speak of the native landowners, squatters and old settlers. They regarded him for a time as an Irish ogre, who had come for their gold, and whose sons would eat all their potatoes'.

He had to contend not only with sectarianism, but with corrupt, parochial and ephemeral governments. Between 1855 and 1868, Victoria had ten Ministries, most of them ineffectual. 'They all found the struggle for existence too severe to let them meddle with anything that could be put off' says the banker and conservative historian, Henry Gyles Turner. But despite these handicaps, Duffy's achievements were not inconsiderable. And he cannot be blamed for the failure of his two major political aims. He worked strenuously to bring about Federation in Australia, underestimating the intensity of inter-colonial jealousies, and not realising that commercial, rather than national considerations, were the determining factor. And he worked strenuously to unlock the best land for small farmers, underestimating the power and chicanery of the big landgrabbers — the 'squatters' — who were able, by various stratagems, to frustrate his attempts. The New South Wales Secretary for Lands, John (later Sir John) Robertson, failed even more lamentably in a similar attempt.

Duffy's experience in the House of Commons often saved the new Parliament from procedural mistakes, but some of his colleagues resented him 'playing the schoolmaster', with Erskine May's standard work on parliamentary procedure as text-book, and he himself admits that he was 'sometimes too peremptory and brusque'.

Henry Gyles Turner, who disliked Duffy and his politics, wrote:

Many who freely admitted his intellectual qualities and high literary reputation were repulsed by the assumption in some of his speeches that his brief experience in the House of Commons gave him the right to be only sarcastically tolerant of the amateur legislators who had never seen a real Parliament.

When Parliament assembled on 6 January 1857, Duffy gave notice of a private Bill to abolish the property qualification for members of the Assembly. There was no reason why politicians should be required to have this qualification any more than judges, naval or military commanders, or diplomats, he argued. There was no such qualification required for politicians in the United States, in France, Belgium or Canada, or in almost any colony. (New South Wales and South Australia had no such qualification, and Britain was to abolish it in 1858). 'The question they had to determine, 'he declared', was whether Victoria, instead of standing at the head of the new countries for free institutions and popular progress, was to retain the shackles and restrictions which the others had thrown away in contempt'.

There was a feeble show of opposition from the Government, but the Bill was passed by a majority of seven votes in the Assembly, and, more surprisingly, by a large majority in the Council. The *Age* commented: 'Apropos of Mr. Duffy and Parliamentary business, it is rather remarkable that he has been the first to lead the Opposition to victory against the Government, and the first to get a Bill through all its stages'.

Early in 1857, Duffy had persuaded the Government to appoint a select committee to consider the best way of federating the four colonies, New South Wales, Tasmania, Victoria and South Australia. (Queensland was then part of New South Wales and Western Australia a Crown Colony). The committee of twelve men included H.C.E. Childers, Commissioner of Customs, and three future prime ministers; John O'Shanassy, James McCulloch, and Duffy. Under pressure from Duffy, they deliberated for some months, and produced a comprehensive report, drafted by him, which specified the reasons for Federation, and the best way of bringing it about. In the report, Duffy stressed the national importance of a federal union: 'Neighbouring States . . . inevitably became confederates or enemies', he wrote. But few shared his enthusiasm for Federation, or his belief in Australian nationalism. He was years ahead of his time in regarding Australia as a nation, not a mere conglomerate of selfish regional interests.

The *Age* rebuked him for his arrogance as a newcomer in putting himself at the head of a movement for Federation, and he was warned by the *Argus* that he was aiming too high. The most that the colonies needed, it said, was a much more limited form of union. Undiscouraged, Duffy persuaded the committee to recommend a conference of colonial delegates to consider federal union. But nothing came of the recommendation.

Nor was another committee, convened in December 1857, more successful. New South Wales refused to appoint a delegate to a conference. Like all the other colonies, it was jealous of booming Victoria, and resented Duffy's leadership of the Federal movement. And the Victorian Government was indifferent. Duffy had his committee reappointed in November 1858, but again it achieved nothing. A year later Duffy organized a third committee, but the differences between the colonies, especially over tariffs, had grown even greater, and Duffy for the time being, turned from the struggle for Federation to the struggle for land reform in Victoria.

THE Haines Ministry fell in March 1857 and O'Shanassy, the leader of the Opposition, formed an administration with Duffy as Commissioner for Public Works. The *Leader* began a series, 'Men of our Time', with a rapturous picture of him at work:

> In one of the secluded little offices of the Government . . . surrounded by maps, tenders and specifications, sits one of the most remarkable men of our colony. He is about medium height; his figure delicate and fragile as that of an ascetic; and his face gives you the impression of one worn by continual thought and anxiety. But it would be impossible to find a face or head more indicative of good nature and genuine intellect . . . He is discharging one of the most important functions of the Administration. I have introduced you to Charles Gavan Duffy, Commissioner of Public Works.
>
> As student, journalist, state prisoner, statesman, his career has been one of the most extraordinary in these modern times; but what renders it unique is, that, through all these dangers and changes, he has preserved his character undimmed by one solitary stain.

The land question was the main preoccupation of Victoria's first parliaments, in which the 'squattocracy' — the big land owners — had great power. The gold rush, which had brought more than one hundred thousand migrants to Victoria in eighteen months, had lost its momentum. Easily-won alluvial gold was becoming scarce. As migrants continued to pour into the colony and miners abandoned exhausted fields, the hunger for farming land became acute. When Duffy and Wilson Gray arrived in Melbourne there was a clamant cry to 'unlock the lands'. Vast areas of the most desirable land had been leased to squatters for sheep runs, on very easy terms which gave them the right to acquire outright the best portions of the run. Men were now demanding that the land 'locked up' in these huge pastoral leases be cut up into small farming blocks and made easily available to 'selectors'. Duffy and Wilson Gray vigorously championed the popular cause, Duffy in Parliament, and Wilson Gray in public agitation.

O'Shanassy's Ministry lasted less than seven weeks, and in April 1857, Haines again became Premier. One of his first acts was to introduce a Land Bill which sparked off a bitter political conflict. In many ways, the Bill favoured the squatters, and Duffy, despite his personal regard for Haines, attacked it furiously. 'I pledge my life on it that it will never be carried', he told the House. 'I believe, on my conscience, that it is a swindle'. And he angrily denounced the betrayal of the people: 'Nothing would be accepted as a settlement by the people which did not terminate, on whatever basis appeared equitable, but terminate once and forever, the claims of a handful of graziers to the whole territory of this country'.

If the land were not made accessible, he asked, what in ten years' time was to become of the mass of the present diggers? 'They have been too long trained in their school of independence to pass to any servile pursuit . . . shut out of the homesteads which Nature intended for them, they would in a few years be the most ungovernable population in the world'.

When Duffy was attacked in Parliament as an Irish Catholic and a rebel, he replied with passion and eloquence. 'The speech of the night was Duffy's,' said the *Leader*.

> Everybody describes it as one of the most successful intellectual efforts ever made in the Assembly. The touching plaintiveness with which he related the sorrows of Ireland — the manliness with which he vindicated his personal and political honour — and the proud disdain with which he overwhelmed his slanderers, will not soon be forgotten. His impression upon the house, no language could realise.

While Duffy led the parliamentary opposition to the bill, the spirit of Eureka was not dead. (It was less than three years since the miners at Ballarat had staged their little rebellion.) Organisations of mass protest sprang up throughout the colony. In Bendigo, the Attorney-General, Archibald Michie, was burned in effigy, and a future cabinet minister John McIntyre, offered to lead the miners in a march on Melbourne 'to prevent the robbery . . . of the patrimony of the people'. Delegates from all parts of the country met in Melbourne, forming a Land Convention with Wilson Gray as president. The Convention affirmed the right of the small farmer to select land without auction at a uniform price. Duffy later claimed that the original idea was his: 'Wilson Gray came to consult me on what ought to be done to control the dominant squatters. I reminded him of what we had done in Ireland on behalf of the tenantry with such effect'. Certainly, both hoped to see Victoria become a land of independent small holders.

The Convention met for three weeks and its discussions and demands were widely reported. The Government took alarm and began to amend the Bill. Ultimately, it satisfied no one, not even the squatters, and the Legislative Council rejected it in one sitting.

The defeat of what the *Leader* described as 'the so much detested' Bill was celebrated on Hawthorn hill (not far from Duffy's house) with bonfires, gunfire, music and dancing, and, amid hearty cheers, another effigy of Michie with a white hat and holding a document representing the Bill, was committed to the flames.

IN the confusing whirligig of Victorian politics, Haines was again replaced by O'Shanassy, and Duffy became President of the Board of Land and Works. In this role, he had the privilege of naming new townships. Determined to honour men who had served Victoria, he began with his 'old antagonist', William Stawell, the Irish lawyer who had been Attorney-General from 1851 to 1857. Stawell gracefully acknowledged the compliment and named the streets of the new settlement after members of his own family. When Duffy named a township on the River Murray 'Carlyle', Carlyle wrote that he 'almost wept a little' at some of the street names, 'Stuart Mill' street, 'Sterling' street, and especially, 'Jane' street. (John Sterling was a London man of letters, and friend of Carlyle, Tennyson and John Stuart Mill.)

Duffy introduced competitive exams for entry into the Land and Works Department at a time when there was no Public Service Act, and what a Royal Commission in 1859 described as 'the degrading system of patronage' prevailed, with no recognition of merit in making Government appointments. Patronage, of course, was an inheritance from the eighteenth century, when sinecures were handed out with cynical prodigality. (Wordsworth was given the job of distributing stamps in Westmoreland. Another poet, Thomas Moore, was appointed admiralty registrar at Bermuda. And the versifer and wit Theodore Hook became accountant-general in Mauritius!)

Duffy himself was not averse from bestowing favours. As Commissioner for Public Works, he appointed 'Orion' Horne a Commissioner for Water and Sewerage. For his father's sake, William Carleton's son was given a sinecure that allowed him plenty of time to write bad poetry, and Aspinall's widow was made a post-mistress. 'The applications for appointments were very numerous', Duffy recalled. 'Scarcely a ship came into Port Phillip Harbour that did not bring me letters of introduction from political associates in Ireland or personal associates in the House of Commons. This was to be expected . . .' Cardinal Newman commended a young man 'from our Birmingham congregation'. The eminent actor, William Macready, through Carlyle, sought Duffy's assistance on behalf of a wayward son, who, after what his father described as 'a brief career of folly and extravagance' in the East India Company's service, had been obliged to resign his commission. Duffy offered him a position in the Civil Service, but he preferred to try the stage. At Duffy's request, George Coppin, Melbourne's leading entrepreneur, obligingly cast him as Captain Absolute in *The Rivals*. 'Macready drew one great audience, but not a second', says Duffy. Despite Duffy's many efforts to rehabilitate him, 'he gradually descended the theatrical scale, and died prematurely'.

One applicant, an Irish schoolmaster named Timothy Joseph O'Kane, though armed with impressive letters of recommendation, 'utterly disgusted' Duffy. O'Kane had been involved in a scandal which rocked London society when he sued his wife for divorce, naming the seventy-nine-year-old prime minister, Viscount Palmerston, as correspondent. Mrs. O'Kane, described as 'a jolly, short, and stout Irishwoman, with fine black eyes and darkly pencilled eyebrows', had been a nursery governess in the family of Lady Palmerston's daughter. In the words of the indefatigable gossip, Sir William Hardman: 'The potent septuagenarian nobleman proved irresistible to the easy-virtued nursery governess. Hence a connection which resulted in various letters, sundry banknotes and equivalent copulation'.

O'Kane withdrew his action, having made 'an arrangement' with Palmerston through the intervention of influential friends, and sailed for Australia with his errant wife and children. When under severe cross-examination, he gave Duffy details of the 'arrangement' which included fares to Australia and £100 in cash, Duffy coldly rebuked him for selling his honour, showed him the door, and tossed his letters of introduction into the waste-paper basket.

Soon after taking office, Duffy almost died from a violent attack of dysentery. He was delirious for days, and his death was solemnly announced in Parliament. When he returned to his Department of Land and Works, he found 'with painful surprise', as he wrote to the *Argus*, that O'Shanassy intended to throw 'an immense mass of agricultural land on to the market'. He succeeded in having this proposal rejected by Cabinet, but the incident brought to a head a long festering disagreement with O'Shanassy over land policy, which culminated some months later, in his resignation from the Ministry. There were other differences.

The scholarly Alfred Deakin, Australia's second prime minister, summed them up acutely. O'Shanassy was 'the peasant in build, gait and habit' with 'a marked subservience to the Church':

> His jealousy of Duffy . . . was only less marked than Duffy's jealousy of him . . . Duffy was liberal by instinct and on reflection, and remained true to his colours to the last. O'Shanassy . . . went on to build up a considerable fortune and . . . became in all good faith . . . steadily more Conservative.

Serle makes a similar observation: 'It was not merely that O'Shanassy was boorish and Duffy an educated gentleman. O'Shanassy was essentially the Catholic, and Duffy the Irish spokesman'. O'Shanassy was a die-hard O'Connellite who had left Ireland years before the birth of the Young Ireland movement. When O'Shanassy insisted that education must be in the hands of the Church, Duffy pointed out that he himself had been educated in a Presbyterian school without violating any dogma of his faith. In the bitterness of the quarrel between the two men — the only Catholics in the Government — shameful allegations were made against both. One was that Duffy had been an informer in 1848!

In a letter to Thomas O'Hagan, Duffy told of his resignation '. . . but I may predict that some day I will return to office: and meantime the only sacrifice is that of income — I certainly have not lost character or influence'. (Ministers received £1,000 to £1,500 a year. Members were not paid until 1870). As for his future plans:

> I confidently hope to go home for a year in about three years, and then to return and be content with Australia for the remainder of my life. There are half a dozen friends in Ireland I long to see again, but the sky and soil here suit me far better. I grow my own peaches, figs, grapes and walnuts, in addition to all the home fruits, and have become a great horticulturist — dividing my time between politics and the pruning knife.

At the next General Election, in October 1859, the O'Shanassy Government was defeated, and William Nicholson, 'the father of the secret ballot', a bluff, honest, self-educated grocer became Premier. The main business of the new government was to settle the land question, and Duffy was again offered the Land portfolio, but refused it because Nicholson would not allow him to nominate two of his Liberal friends for office. Duffy became the leader of the Liberal Opposition, with a policy of 'a friendly neutrality' towards the new administration 'as long as its policy justified it'.

THE Nicholson Ministry, which lasted thirteen months, passed a Land Act that was a miserable failure. It was designed to provide cheap land for genuine selection, but after it had been savagely attacked in the Assembly and further mauled in the stronghold of the squatters, the Legislative Council, it was practically useless. It allowed the squatters or speculators to discover easy ways of frustrating the intention of the Act. The *Age* described the amended Act as 'a misshapen, emasculated thing — a sham which offers no facility to industrious men of small means to settle on the land'. The Council had made about 250 amendments. Within two months of it becoming law, squatters and speculators had acquired more great tracts of fertile land. The men of small means acquired none.

Nicholson resigned in despair and Duffy was offered the premiership. He formed what he later described as 'the first democratic Ministry'. 'I was determined that it should be one which would steer by the stars, and not have to watch the shifting winds and tides of the hour, a Government whose policy should not consist in evading difficulties but in encountering them'. Unfortunately he was not able to practice this astral navigation. He learned covertly that a cabal was planning to conspire against him. Confident that the country would support him he sought the Governor's assurance that 'in case of such an unfair combination', he would be granted a dissolution. When Sir Henry Barkly refused the assurance, Duffy resigned his embryonic premiership and Nicholson was temporarily recalled.

Barkly's refusal roused the advocates of land reform to fury. A mass meeting of nearly six thousand assembled in the Eastern Market to denounce the Governor's decision. Wilson Gray told the excited crowd that there were three things every man in the country should have; first a vote (which they had); second a rifle (which many had, as recruits for the volunteer movement); and third, a farm, which they must have and would have, even if the second item had to be used to acquire it. There were cheers for Duffy, for Garibaldi, and other popular leaders, and groans for Barkly.

Next evening another huge crowd of people, many wearing red ribbons, stormed Parliament House. A door was smashed, windows were broken, and there were threats to tear the stately building down, and drag the obnoxious members from their benches. At Nicholson's orders, a force of mounted and foot police, truncheons flailing, charged the crowd, which responded vigorously with showers of stones. A dozen or more police, and half a dozen citizens, were injured, some seriously. Members of Parliament were mobbed as they left the House, and sporadic fighting continued in nearby streets for some hours, till the Riot Act was read and the streets cleared. But the tension continued for days. Field guns were trained on Prince's Bridge to guard the approach to the near-by Victoria Barracks, more than a thousand special constables were sworn in, and a hastily passed Disorderly Meetings Act outlawed political assemblies between certain streets. Gray was accused of having used seditious language in addressing the crowd but no proceedings were taken against him. He left Victoria in 1862 and became a district court judge in New Zealand.

The Nicholson administration was defeated in November 1860, and Richard Heales, a coachbuilder who had been a day-labourer, an honest man and a genuine democrat, became premier with a precarious and often unsympathetic majority. Heales favoured free selection, and in the words of the distinguished politician, lawyer and writer, Sir John Quick, 'laid the foundation of liberal land legislation'. He was defeated 'by greedy schemers, notorious renegades, apostates and traitors' before much was achieved. His administration had lasted just less than a year.

When Henry Parkes went to the United Kingdom as an Emigration Commissioner, in 1861, Duffy gave him introductions to Cobden, John Stuart Mill and Carlyle. 'I don't think I understand Carlyle', a bewildered Parkes wrote to Duffy.

> I have seen him twice, and had a long conversation with him . . . Each time, or more accurately speaking, I listened to long characteristic utterances from him. . . He sat on the floor and smoked, and he laughed outright with a terrible kind of full-heartedness at his own grand sarcasms. But I confess I could almost as well explain the meaning of thunder and lightning as the meaning of what he said . . . it did me good to see how well you were remembered . . .

Carlyle in turn gave Duffy his impressions of Parkes: 'We find him a robust, effective, intelligent and sincere kind of man, extremely loyal to CGD; which is not one of his smallest merits here'. Parkes seemed to Carlyle to be

> thoroughly at home in the anarchic, democratic, universal-palaver element, and to swim about it, with a candid joy, like a fish in water. . . The worst news Parkes gave us was that you did not seem to be in good health. . . Alas, alas! could not the Victorian people be persuaded to send *you* as their 'Agent' hitherward? Anything that would bring you home, how welcome were it to us! Or would not your means, though modest, enable you to live *here* as well as at Melbourne? What a book you might write on that wild continent. . .

ONCE more O'Shanassy became premier, and Duffy, President of the Board of Land and Works. He and O'Shanassy had been reconciled, at least temporarily, through the intervention of Duffy's friend, Dr. Quinn, the Catholic Bishop of Brisbane. Duffy was now resolved to settle the vexed land question 'in the interest of the industrious classes'. Early in 1862, he introduced a comprehensive measure known as the Duffy Land Act.

A map which he had prepared showed that of the thirty-five million acres held by pastoralists at an average rental of less than two pence an acre, ten million were choice agricultural land. Among other provisions, he proposed that within three months of the passing of the Act, four million of these should be thrown open for selection, whether surveyed or unsurveyed.

Duffy was proud of his scheme and went to great pains to expound it. He published a detailed *Guide to the Land Law of Victoria* in which he not only clearly explained the terms of the Act, but also advised farmers on how to make the best use of their land. He listed some new industries he hoped to see introduced in Victoria; the cultivation of cotton, flax, mulberries, olives, sugar beet, sorghum, tea, and particularly Indian corn — 'the prime resource of the settler in the American prairie, furnishing him . . . with a delicious vegetable, household bread, dainty pudding, and wholesome spirits'.

The *Guide* had an enormous sale, in four separate editions, including a London reprint. Duffy's message to the world was that Victoria was now the working-man's paradise. From London came warm letters of congratulations. 'You seem to be really doing wonders', Childers wrote. And Lowe wrote: 'The only thing wanted to place Australia on its true footing is cheap and abundant land'. He wished Duffy 'very heartily success'.

But Duffy, like Nicholson, had underestimated the resourcefulness of the squatter. It soon became apparent that the Act was so loosely drafted that the squatter had no difficulty in evading it. One of the simplest ways which he had perfected under the Nicholson Act, was to employ a 'dummy' who took up land as a genuine selector and, for a modest fee, transferred it back to the squatter. 'Dummying' became a profitable profession. Children, and on one occasion, an unborn child, were used as 'dummies'. 'Servant girls and ticket-of-leave men, negroes and cripples, blind fiddlers and tambourine girls, all are pressed into service', reported the Melbourne *Herald*. 'Dummies, sharks, surveyors, squatters, land officers and others were all links in the corrupt chain forged by the Duffy Act', says Margaret Kiddle in her classic study of Victoria's Western District, *Men of Yesterday*.

Duffy's offer of a reward of £100 for the conviction of any person evading the provisions of his Act, or the penalty of imprisonment which the Act provided, had no effect. Nearly all of Victoria's best land fell into the hands of the squatters. Within two years, about two-thirds of the one million acres sold under the Duffy Act, had been acquired by no more than one hundred men, and settlers were forced into more remote and less hospitable parts of the colony.

Looking back on the debacle years later, Duffy wrote: 'Now when the whole facts are familiar we can fairly judge the causes of the failure'. In truth it arose wholly and solely from the manner in which the measure was drafted. According to him, the villain of the Act was W.E. Hearn, a Trinity College graduate, and Professor of History and Political Economy at Melbourne University who received 'the unusual fee' of £500 for drafting it. But as every clause in the Act was submitted in proof to Duffy and to his law officers, it would seem that the Professor was not wholly to blame. 'Duffy's . . . trouble was that he was an idealist who had spent only a few years in the colony. Hearn . . . was an even greater innocent', says Margaret Kiddle. 'On the other hand the squatters believed that almost every man had his price. . . They could never have evaded the law as they did if they had not been given the support . . . of many others in the colony. Thus the Act was delivered into the hands of the colonial realists'.

In June 1863 the third O'Shanassy Government was defeated on a proposal to reduce an assessment for livestock, and resigned. The *Age* had been attacking the O'Shanassy-Duffy combination ever since the defects of Duffy's Land Act had been revealed. Once a supporter of Duffy, it had become his bitter critic. And it disliked O'Shanassy even more intensely. When the O'Shanassy ministry fell, the *Age* exclaimed, 'Thank Heaven! The country may breathe freely. The reign of scoundrelism is over'.

Duffy's hopes for a federated Australia were revived when the Tasmanian House of Assembly resolved that the Government should immediately discuss federation with the other colonies. Seizing the opportunity, Duffy persuaded the Victorian Legislative Assembly to reappoint the Select Committee on federal union. After two meetings, it adopted a report he had drafted that dealt with the vexatious questions of tariffs, defence and immigration. The report urged the colonists to think of a strong and united Australia worthy of its destiny and playing an honourable part in world affairs. But the colonists were more concerned with parish-pump politics than with Australia's high destiny as mistress of the southern seas.

In March 1863, Duffy persuaded all the colonies except Queensland, which had recently become independent, to attend a tariff conference in Melbourne. He hoped that federal union would also be discussed. But again, tariff policy was the stumbling block and the conference achieved nothing. The *Age* said the lesson of its failure was 'Mind your own business and let that of others alone'.

With the fall of the O'Shanassy government, Duffy qualified for a pension of £1,000 a year, a handsome annuity in those days, equivalent to at least £20,000 today. One of his first acts as a man of means was to repay the money Arthur Geoghan had lent him when he left England. 'Such a thing as interest should never, even for an instant, be thought of between us', Geoghan wrote. 'It was merely an offer, frankly and heartily made, and kindly accepted, and to the latest hour of my life the recollection of it will be to me a source of mingled pride and satisfaction'.

Duffy was also able to buy four hundred acres of land at Sorrento, at the entrance to Port Phillip Bay, and to build a sea-side cottage on it. He was now free to abandon politics, and take up the literary career he dreamed of. But the call of politics was still irresistible.

The new administration under James (later Sir James) McCulloch took over, and Richard Heales became its first Minister for Lands. He tried to amend Duffy's Act to remove its weaknesses, and drafted a Bill that would have reserved ten million acres of Crown Lands for bona fide agricultural settlement. But the Bill was rejected by the Legislative Council. Again, the squatters triumphed.

OUT of office, Duffy decided to visit Europe for a couple of years. 'A physique which was not vigorous, and highly sensitive, was strained by the emotions my career naturally produced', he wrote. 'And ten years' constant labour entitled me to a holiday'. Parkes, when he heard of Duffy's plans, asked if he could return Duffy's kindness in giving him a letter of introduction in 1861. 'The only person worth knowing I think is the author of *Tom Brown's Schooldays*' [Thomas Hughes] he wrote; but he could provide introductions that would 'open the sealed doors of Birmingham's manufacturing wonders'. His letters continued:

I owe much to you, my friend — for strength in moments of weakness — for consolation in severest trouble — for new lights of thought amongst the barrenness of life . . . Adieu, my dear Duffy. May your life be long and prosperous, full of usefulness and honour.

Duffy left Melbourne on 18 January 1865, accompanied by his wife and eldest daughter, Susan, and arrived in London in April. Among the many warm letters of welcome he received was one from Jane Carlyle, with a pressing invitation to dinner: 'Name any day you like, only let it be soon... for I am impatient to see you'. Other old friends in London and Dublin offered him their houses and servants. 'I came home for a rest and recreation after assiduous labour', he wrote, 'and speedily found myself entangled in more engagements and undertakings than embarrassed me in Australia'. Duffy spent most of his Sundays with Carlyle, gossiping in the little sitting-room, or walking for hours in Hyde Park or Battersea Park.

At John Forster's, he had the great satisfaction of dining with Robert Browning, whom he regarded as 'the first poet of his age and century'. Browning, then fifty-three, was 'middle-sized, grey-bearded, with a small but well-shaped head'. After dinner they adjourned to a 'singularly agreeable smoking room, lined with encaustic tiles, and cooled with ferns and drooping plants'. They discussed Palmerston, who had recently died; the *Pall Mall Gazette*, which had recently been founded; Wordsworth, whom Carlyle considered the best talker in England; the generous nature of Walter Savage Landor; Dickens' ungenerous caricature of Leigh Hunt as Harold Skimpole; and Southey's humorous poems which Browning admired, but Duffy thought dull. He preferred Moore, Praed and Canning. Duffy had always been passionately interested in literature, and table-talk such as this was what he hungered for in Australia.

Duffy found many misunderstandings about Australia in the English press, and in Parliament. Among them was the belief that responsible Government had been a failure. To vindicate his adopted country, and its institutions, he gave a lecture in the Society of Arts on 'Popular Errors Concerning Australia'. He pointed out that Australia's institutions, its social customs, and its intellectual enjoyments were identical with England's and that its material interests were closely intermingled with those of the mother country. Within a dozen years, more than four hundred thousand people had left England to settle in Australia, among them members of the families of Wordsworth, Coleridge, Arnold of Rugby, Brougham, O'Connell, Jenner, Faraday, Babbage, Dickens, Gladstone, Macready, Baptist Noel and Frederick Lucas.

Whatever was good in Australia was ignored or grudgingly admitted by writers and speakers in England, Duffy said. Whatever was not good was distorted and exaggerated. Instead of regarding the 'great social expedition' of the colonists with interest and sympathy, Australia was habitually represented as little better than the semi-barbarous and chaotic republics of South America. And he concluded:

'The Colony of Victoria, in which I reside, has never cost the mother country a guinea, has never done or wished her anything but good, has exhibited her sympathy in a practical way on many trying occasions, and has poured upwards of a hundred millions sterling into the coffers of her trade . . .

In the discussion which followed, a former New South Wales politician Mr. Marsh, dissented vigorously. Property was not secure in Victoria, he said. Stock, horses and cows were being constantly stolen. There was a bad police system, caused by political jobbery, and he had the best authority for stating that members of the Victorian Parliament were in the habit of receiving bribes ranging from £100 to £7,000. Duffy asked Mr. Marsh to give a single authoritative case, but Mr. Marsh did not oblige. Sir John Gray was loudly cheered when he said he had heard of cows and horses being stolen in England, and of garotting in the City of London. No one had attributed this to the evils of Government or to the corruption of the representatives of the people. Duffy's speech was published as a pamphlet by two competing Melbourne booksellers, neither of whom bothered to ask for permission.

When Duffy defended the integrity of Victorian politics, was he aware of the widespread corruption in the Victorian Survey Department? 'Government corruption began at high levels and continued all down the line . . .' says Michael Cannon in his authoritative *Life in the Country*. 'Many squatters subscribed to a secret fund used to bribe politicians whose influence enabled certain lands to be sold or withheld from selection'. The fund was controlled by a Melbourne stock and station agent, Hugh Glass, assisted by two members of Parliament, J.S. Butters and Peter Snodgrass. The Minister for Railways, C.E. Jones, during the hearing of some libel actions, admitted receiving a £600 bribe, and said that other members of the government had also been bribed. After a parliamentary inquiry in 1867, Jones and Butters were expelled from the House and later Glass was convicted of contempt and sentenced to goal.

A public dinner given to Duffy at London's St. James' Hall, 'revived in a curious and significant way the main incidents' of his life. John Dillon, a co-founder of *The Nation* sat beside him, and the guests included Sir John Gray, who had been tried with Duffy and O'Connell in 1845; D'Arcy McGee, who had been closely associated with Duffy during the trials and dangers of 1848, and now Minister for Agriculture in Canada; Sir Colman O'Loghlen, to whose legal skill Duffy largely owed his triumph in the trials; and all the survivors of the Independent Party of 1852.

In his speech, Duffy replied to criticism of Australian parliaments which Robert Lowe had recently made in opposing the Reform Bill. 'Mr. Duffy has more reason on his side than we like to admit', commented *The Times*, and Edward Wilson, who was in London, congratulated Duffy 'on taking up the cudgels against . . . the odious, slanderous propensities of John Bull'. Forster and the Tory M.P., Sir Emerson Tennent also congratulated him.

Duffy called on Lowe, who had sat with him in the House of Commons, and Lowe said that his hopes of a future for Australia were 'greatly mitigated'. He feared that when men educated in Europe ceased to go there and the governing men had to be taken from colonial classes, Australia would fall very low. It was hard to maintain a hope in popular progress and popular government. 'You tell me what great things you are doing now', he said smiling, 'but wait till the larrikin comes on the stage. There is a large native population in New South Wales and they will soon be the masters'.

DUFFY, of course, was anxious to revisit Ireland. Among the many greetings he received from his native land was one from Father Tom O'Shea, the Callan curate who had begun the land movement in 1850. 'My darling Duffy', he wrote 'Welcome, welcome to Ireland — would that I could say to *home* . . .'

When Duffy with his wife and daughter reached Dublin in June 1865, he found himself plunged into affairs as if he had been absent for only a week. There was the inevitable round of dinners, speeches, discussions. At one dinner, attended by many of Duffy's old friends, a notable absentee was D'Arcy McGee, though he was in Dublin for the International Exhibition. He was not invited to the dinner because of a speech he had recently made at his home town, Wexford. In this he had said of the Young Ireland fighters of 1848, 'Politically we were a pack of fools but we were honest in our folly and no man need blush at forty for the follies of one and twenty unless he still perseveres in them. . .' Duffy was affronted and wrote to McGee that he preferred the fool of twenty to the philosopher and statesman of forty.

At a public dinner, chaired by John Dillon, Duffy told his old friends that all that he asked for the Irish farmers had been attained for the Irish immigrant to Australia, a testimony, surely, that their claims in Ireland were not unjust or extravagant.

A General Election was at hand, and Dillon tried to persuade Duffy to nominate for a popular constituency. He thought that a genuine Irish party such as Duffy had projected in 1849 might be recreated. Duffy was tempted to accept, but he would have had to join a National Association of which his old *bete noir*, Cardinal Cullen, was the most active promoter. And he found the old Tenant League priests rootedly opposed to any co-operation with Cullen. There were other typically Irish dissensions, and Duffy wisely decided to return to Australia.

Dillon told Duffy of the growth of Fenianism, a movement born in New York about 1857, whose members were sworn to establish an Irish Republic by secret conspiracy or open warfare. The movement had been started by James Stephens, who had been with Smith O'Brien in the cabbage-patch rebellion of 1848, and many ex-Confederates were in its ranks. Dillon thought the conspirators were honest but incompetent men, and Duffy said Fenianism did not surprise him at all. It was the spontaneous and inevitable result 'of natural agencies'. In November 1865, Stephens made a sensational escape from Dublin's Richmond Prison and in February 1866, the British Parliament rushed through a bill suspending the Habeas Corpus Act in Ireland. It is curious that neither of these events is mentioned in Duffy's wordy reminiscences of the period.

Duffy was given a banquet at 'The Western Arms' in Monaghan, in the room where he had been farewelled a quarter of a century before. In his speech, he said that though much had changed since then, one thing had not:

When I was a dreaming schoolboy on the hills of Monaghan, I painted to myself the highest happiness that life could bring, the prospect of lending a helping hand to the dear old country. And now, when my hair is tinged with grey, when I have reached and passed the meridian of life, I would as cheerfully stake all that is regarded most precious in existence for the old cause and the old country.

He went on to compare conditions in Ulster, where there had been sectarian riots, with conditions in Australia. There the Catholics were in a minority to whom justice might have been denied, as it was denied in Belfast, but Protestants and Catholics had learned to live in harmony together. Between speeches, the proceedings were enlivened by Dolan's fine band, by Dr. Keegan, who sang 'Pat Molloy', by the Rev. Father Nugent, who sang 'Our Sainted Isle', by Daniel Phillips, who sang 'The Shamrocks of Old Ireland', and Master Maginnes, who recited Duffy's poem, 'The Voice of Labour'.

When London's fog and east wind became intolerable the Duffys turned their faces to Italy. For five months Duffy discovered the wonders of Rome with the eminent Irish Dominican orator, Father Tom Burke, as guide. He was pleased to find the works of Savonarola on the shelves of the Collegio Romano, and a portrait of Galileo in its observatory. He had a private audience with the Pope, Gregory XVI, but refused an invitation to meet the Queen of Naples, because he hoped never to see a Bourbon return to an Italian throne. In Genoa, on his way back to England, he stopped at the hotel where O'Connell died, but found that no one in it had ever heard of the Liberator. 'A people who have not a national existence cannot fix the attention of other nations', he reflected.

Duffy returned to London mainly to attend the debate on Lord John Russell's Reform Bill, on which the Government was defeated. Duffy had advised some of the Irish members to support the Bill because he believed that Gladstone, the Chancellor of the Exchequer, meant better towards Ireland than anyone else, except the Quaker M.P., John Bright.

Disraeli, the new Chancellor of the Exchequer invited Duffy to call, and they talked at length of Irish and Australian affairs. Of Ireland, Disraeli said it was his purpose to deal fairly and justly with the questions that agitated the country and as promptly as the enormous claims on Parliament would admit.

In Paris, on the way to Australia, Duffy tried to meet Count Montalembert, his ideal of a what a Catholic gentleman should be — 'genuinely pious, and a strict disciplinarian, but entirely free from bigotry or intolerance, the rooted enemy of despotism, and the friend of personal and public liberty everywhere'. But Montalembert was too ill to see him. In Paris, too, Duffy wrote a new preface for the thirty-ninth edition of his *Ballad Poetry of Ireland*, which in twenty years had sold 76,000 copies.

~Part 3~

Eleven

Victorian Premier and Australian Patriot

IN London Duffy had ardently defended Victoria's political institutions. When he returned to Melbourne after two years' absence, he found the Government, headed by the squatter James McCulloch, had acquired 'a dubious character', maintaining power 'largely by political corruption and setting at nought for selfish ends some of the main principles of the Constitution'. It had brought the country's affairs into 'dangerous confusion', and 'fatally lowered the character of Parliament'. And some of the measures Duffy had introduced — the system of competitive exams in the Land and Works Department, and the system of recording the services of officers with a view to their promotion — had been abandoned soon after his departure. Nor had the Government any intention of bringing out foreigners skilled in Southern European industries.

A few months later, the constituency of Dalhousie, in north-western Victoria, fell vacant, and Duffy was urged to contest it. Dalhousie was an immense territory ('as large as Yorkshire', he told Carlyle) and he had to travel great distances to address electors. At one meeting, he was repeatedly heckled by a man who shouted 'Ah, Irish rebel! Irish Papist!' There were angry cries of 'Turn him out' from Duffy's supporters, but Duffy calmed them by saying, 'What, boys, are you ashamed of an Irish rebel or Irish Papist? For shame! — the gentlemen describes me with great accuracy'. Duffy was duly elected.

DUFFY reveals little or nothing of himself in his published writings. His diary, which he kept for many years, has disappeared, and none of his family letters has survived. But he examines himself with clinical detachment in a remarkable scrap-book titled *Ars Vitae,* which was preserved by his youngest daughter, Louise. Much of it dates from 1867, but it is impossible to determine when he began to compile it. An inscription reads 'Recast and Revised December 1864'. The text is divided into sections headed: 'Aims in Life', 'Elements of Enjoyment', 'Dealing with Friends', Dealing with Opponents', Dealing with Neutrals', 'Faculties to Cultivate', 'Trust in God', and 'Training the Intellect', and takes the form of a dialogue between Duffy and himself. It begins:

My dear friend, I have known you intimately since we were boys together, and there is probably no person now living so familiar with your character and constitution. Let me make this knowledge useful to you by stating with perfect frankness my impressions of your present position and of the scheme of life which would harmonise best with your capacity and habits.

You are close upon fifty years of age, of a delicate and shattered constitution, and sprung of a family who have died early and of whom you are the *last*. It is perfectly plain therefore that *overwork* or *over-anxiety* in your case is suicide.

Duffy then recalls that during the Tenant Right movement, in the House of Commons during the intense heat, and on the ship coming to Australia, he was in a condition when speedy death did not seem improbable. Since then, he had been once on the brink of the grave, and in his ardour for any object in which he was interested, he constantly ran the risk of renewing this danger. He had done so, he believed, during the contests on the Land Question. 'Looking fairly' at his chances of life, he thought he might live fifteen or twenty years by avoiding 'undue anxiety or fatigue'. In a postscript, he tells himself:

You long for the excitement of the battle and the crown of victory. You find no compensating enjoyment, or next to none, in what pleases most men. You dislike general society; you detest a fashionable crowd or a popular one. When you dine out, you are usually weary of your evening, and sick after it next day. When you receive at a dinner party, the duties of host exhaust and depress you. . .

He catalogues many other characteristics. Shabby or unsuitable clothes depressed his spirit as certainly as indigestion. For years, he had longed for a garden, because he still had a boy's enjoyment of fruit. He had recovered his enjoyment of the theatre. Exercising on horseback stimulated him. Striking scenery and the seaside calmed and elevated his spirit, but he had never known 'except in glimpses and snatches, the fervour of religious enthusiasm or the unspeakable tranquillity of religious rest'. However, he copies into the scrap-book, passages from Thomas a Kempis' *Imitation of Christ*, which speak of seeking the will of God and the profit of one's neighbours as the way to internal liberty.

Duffy anatomises his public life dispassionately. He recalls that Michie, Melbourne's leading advocate, had told him that he was the best debater Michie had ever listened to, but was not a good speech maker. Duffy tells himself:

I have a radical unfitness to succeed with public meetings. In Parliament, I have sometimes attained a great success. At public dinners, also, and at councils and conferences, but never I think at popular meetings. I have had applause enough but I have never satisfied myself, and have generally come away disgusted. . . My voice is incurably bad, but many of the best speakers I have ever heard, employed a conversational tone in debate, as Macaulay, Disraeli, McGee, Bright and Davis. Gladstone is an exception, and so was O'Connell. . .

Duffy wishes to emulate men like Gladstone, Bright or Garibaldi — 'never a prosperous scoundrel like Louis Napoleon, or a successful trickster like Palmerston, or a gigantic sham like Victor Emmanuel'. One pleasure which had never failed him is reading. His brain is stimulated and his ambition fed by history and biography 'as generous wine feeds and stimulates the human body'. In the section 'Dealing with friends', Duffy writes:

> Deniehy with his remarkable talents and information would be a man of political importance, if a demonstrative self-conceit and petulance did not ruin all. My attacks on the policies of my opponents have nearly always been too fierce and offensive. . . Higinbotham said in the *Argus* that it was my demeanour in the House which made me so many enemies; which was substantially true, I fear. Remember O'Connell's patience with opposition in committee; Davis's open unruffled demeanour in argument; Dillon's placidity under contradiction and Pigot's unshakeable good humour.

'My real wants', he writes, 'are not many or costly':

To live tranquil days; to have a friend at hand whom I love;
to be employed upon work which I like; to have leisure for reading;
to be labouring for an end worth striving for;
to prepare for death

> These are blessings which are not refused to anyone who strives honestly for them, and they are not at the mercy of fortune.

In 'the vulgar sense of depending upon money', Duffy says he would not stake his peace of mind against a chance of a goldfield. Fortune, or rather a gracious providence, had given him enough for all reasonable wants. He finds that his present income ('taking it at £1500 a year') compares favourably with the salaries of ministers in Canada, New South Wales, and the other Australian colonies, and writes:

> You are fully justified therefore in resolving to devote yourself steadily and solely to the service of the colony, without any attempt to improve your fortune. You have been paid in advance for any time and toil you devote to the public. As regards your children, a good education and 'a good start' are better outfit for soul and body than a fortune made for them without having earned it.

Looking to the future, he plans to devote the next five years from 1868, to colonial work. He aims to 'accomplish in Parliament, without heat or hurry, the work which I have long desired to do there', before returning to Europe to write the books for which he had collected material. 'It is for writing, after all, that your faculties are fittest', he tells himself. Among the subjects he contemplates are the events of 1848, the rising of 1641 — which he was working on when Carlyle visited him in 1846 — a book about Australia, and perhaps a history of his own times. In addition, 'a novel, a play, and essays on life and books' had been 'floating' in his mind.

In a scrap-book apparently compiled about the same time as *Ars Vitae*, Duffy discusses the importance of effective oratory and analyses the technique of the public speaker. 'You may write books, you may make other men your agents, but publicly and ostensibly powerful you never will be till you have learned the art of oratory', he writes. 'The orotund voice is acquired by speaking from the back of the throat, with the throat expanded', he adds, and gives himself advice on improving his own speech.

IN November 1867, the Duke of Edinburgh, Queen Victoria's second son and Australia's first Royal visitor, arrived in Melbourne. 'The democratic community have of course fallen into a fever of loyalty', Duffy wrote to Carlyle. 'He seems an unaffected young man, who would rather be left alone to enjoy the pleasures which young princes cultivate than be pestered with addresses and demonstrations'. [The pleasures were said to include the hospitality of Sarah Fraser's fashionable Melbourne brothel. There is a legend that after the Duke's departure Mother Fraser asked permission to display the Royal Arms outside her premises.]

Duffy continued: 'To all powers, potentates, municipalities, Road Boards and Oddfellows who approach him with congratulations, he replies that "he will send an answer", which some secretary or chaplain, it is to be presumed, manufactures. There is a story that one considerate Mayor, instead of presenting an address, contented himself with expressing hope that H.R.H. had enjoyed his ride, and H.R.H. replied that "he would send an answer in the morning"!'

Melbourne spent the huge sum of £250,000 in welcoming the Duke. Among the street illuminations was one depicting the Battle of the Boyne. This led to a violent sectarian riot in which a boy was killed and two men seriously injured. Duffy did not report this to Carlyle, nor does he mention it in his memoirs.

At a harbourside picnic in Sydney, the Duke was wounded in the back by a pistol-shot from a half-witted Irishman named O'Farrell. In the hysteria that followed, Parkes as Colonial Secretary stirred up sectarian feeling by suggesting, with no justification, that O'Farrell was involved in a blood-curdling Fenian plot. When Duffy at a Melbourne function proposed at toast to 'the speedy recovery, health and happiness of Prince Alfred', he went on to say:

> I have never taken any part in the politics of Ireland since I made this country my home. I have never, for example, uttered one speech or written one line in respect to Fenianism since it came into existence, being quite certain that the only result of debating it here . . . would be to disturb and distract this community. One lesson, indeed, has been learned here . . . give Ireland the same Constitution, the same self-government, and the same control over her resources, which Victoria possesses, and there will not be a more loyal or contented people in the world.

Parkes' invention of the Fenian plot strained his relations with Duffy, and for two years their friendly correspondence ceased. But in December 1870, when Parkes had to resign his seat because of another bankruptcy, Duffy wrote to him sympathetically, deploring the interruption to his political career, 'though I, and all the race from which I am sprung, have good reason to complain bitterly of your conduct in office'.

His letter concluded:

> I see with pain and fear for the future of Australia, that public life is more and more engrossed by men without any fitness for such a position, and that the latest, and perhaps the last, experiment of creating a democratic dominion is to be made under disadvantages. My personal experience here makes me prefer men of brains, not only as allies, but as opponents. There is nothing so utterly disheartening as to contend with a fool . . .
> I never ride along the lonely sea-shore without thinking the world's prizes of less and less value.

Parkes replied that his personal regard for Duffy remained unaltered. He agreed with Duffy on 'the temper of the times and the portentous difficulties' that were rising up in the way of real progress . . .

> I fervently pray to God that a way may be found out for your 'race' to mix with mine as fellow citizens . . . Like you 'I prefer men of brains not only as allies, but as opponents', whether English or Irish, Protestant or Catholic. . .

MANY times Duffy had thought of starting a paper in Melbourne. Soon after his arrival, he had asked Parkes' advice on the cost of producing four thousand copies of a paper the size of the *Empire*, a paper 'aiming to be a *Spectator* with a soul in it, or a *Leader* with a creed and a purpose'. He deplored 'the naked lying of the Melbourne press', which exceeded anything in his 'tolerably wide experience of party warfare'. In April 1858, when Parkes was bankrupt and had lost the *Empire*, Duffy urged him to come to Melbourne.

> If you do, I venture to promise that the *Herald* or half of the *Age* would be purchased and put under your control and of course your proper place in Parliament and in a popular Government would follow as a matter of course. This is the capital of Australia, here the popular element is strong and triumphant, and this is your true field.

The economics of this ambitious proposal were not explained, and, not surprisingly, nothing came of it. Duffy next approached Frank Fowler, a versatile London journalist, and former parliamentary reporter, who had come to Australia for health reasons in the same year as Duffy. Fowler had spent three years doing literary work in Sydney. On the eve of his return to England in 1858, Duffy wrote to him,

> I had hoped I might count upon your assistance in a Quarterly Federal Review towards which I intended to invite the aid of the best intellects in Australia without reference to their politics or their locale. Something like the *Revue de Deux Mondes* in which every knight would fight under his own banner, and with his own battle-cry.

Four years later, Duffy invited Deniehy to come to Melbourne to edit a Catholic weekly, the *Victorian*. This announced itself in July 1862 as 'a new and original weekly newspaper of events, politics, science and literature', offering its readers 'all the Catholic intelligence of the Australian colonies, 'as well as news by European mails, and reports on the internal development of Victoria and on trade and commerce. 'The literary character of the new journal the conductors feel to be a consideration of paramount importance'. Who owned the paper, and what part Duffy played in the conduct of it, remains obscure.

The *Victorian* was the third attempt to establish a Catholic newspaper in Victoria. It promised to 'harmonise the views of the Irish population and to avoid any sectional partnership in the Catholic community'. But, despite much brilliant writing by Deniehy, it did not succeed. In April 1863, the Bishop of Melbourne, James Alipius Goold, declared that it had 'ceased to be the exponent of the Catholic opinion' in Victoria. Exactly a year later, it ceased publication, and Deniehy, a drunken wreck, ill and penniless, returned to New South Wales, to drop dead in a country town two years later. One wonders why Duffy was not as compassionate to him as he had been to that other unhappy genius, Mangan.

Undiscouraged by the failure of the *Victorian*, Duffy in February 1868 launched another Catholic paper, the *Advocate*, which has survived to the present day. He wrote the prospectus, and the first editorial in which he addressed the Irish Catholics in the Community 'as a body' with certain special and paramount interests '. . . religious education, the unlocking of agricultural and pastoral land, and increased facilities for bringing out suitable emigrants'. The editorial concluded: 'The interest of Irish Catholic electors is not to get men into Parliament of the same creed and nationality as themselves, but to place honest men there, who entertain views on public questions in accordance with the public interest'.

Early in 1869, Duffy learned that his dear friend Thomas O'Hagan had become a peer and Lord Chancellor. Congratulating him, Duffy wrote:

> I declare before Heaven you have no right to expect tranquillity till an Irish peasant can live in Ireland as prosperously, and an Irish gentleman of the Irish race, can feel himself as such at home there, as the peasants and gentlemen of other European countries in their native lands . . . When I first held office here there were next to no Catholic Irishmen in the public service, the magistracy or local force; and they were nearly as discontented as at home. I urged on my colleagues the policy of satisfying their just and reasonable demands, and it was done by Governments in which there were never more than two Catholics out of a Cabinet of ten. Done as a policy proclaimed and defended, not by stealth.

There had been sectarian riots in Belfast, and Duffy denounced the Orange provocation that had sparked them off, and 'the insolent and virtually penal law' that maintained the statue of William III in Dublin 'as a badge and symbol of conquest'. To conciliate Louis Napoleon, the battle of Waterloo was no longer celebrated. Was it necessary to insult Irish Catholics by celebrating the battle of the Boyne? The question is still valid.

DUFFY had neglected the federal movement during his fight for land reform, but in 1870, he induced the Victorian Legislative Assembly to appoint yet another select committee and later, a Royal Commission, to discuss federation. He chaired both. The most controversial matter raised at the Commission was defence. British troops had garrisoned Australia since its beginnings. Now the forces in Australia were being withdrawn, and at Duffy's suggestion, the Commission recommended that the colonies should have the right to remain neutral if England were at war. The colonies, Duffy wrote in his diary, 'were as liable to the hazards of war as the United Kingdom, but they could influence the commencement or continuation of war no more than they could control the movements of the solar system'. He argued that it was a maxim of international law that a sovereign State could not be involved in war without its consent, quoting the precedents of Hanover and the Ionian Isles, which, though ruled by England, had remained neutral when England was at war.

The neutrality proposal was widely criticised in Australia and England and Duffy wrote to a great number of politicians in both countries for their views on it. The majority opposed it as impracticable and dangerous.

Many historians believed that Duffy's unpopular neutrality proposals set back the cause of federation. His Report, like that of its predecessors, was soon gathering dust in a pigeon-hole, and Duffy at last gave up the struggle. Today, the Australian schoolchild learns that Parkes was 'the Father of Federation'.

It is extraordinary that Duffy in his detailed and often tiresome account of his Australian political career, never mentions any personal association with Peter Lalor, though Lalor had attended his welcoming banquet, and they sat together in Victoria's Parliament for many years. We do not know whether they knew one another in Ireland — Lalor migrated in 1852 — or what their relations were in Australia. Lalor's political position in the first Victorian Parliament was vague. He was elected unopposed at Ballarat, the scene of his little insurrection, but was soon accused of having deserted the people he had fought for. He voted for the plural property franchise, (which entitled you to vote in any constitutency in which you owned landed property worth £50) and absented himself from voting on the principle of manhood suffrage. He explained that he never was or ever intended to be 'an ultra-democrat', if the term 'democrat' meant 'Chartism, or Communism, or Republicanism'. But if 'democrat' meant 'opposition to a tyrannical press, a tyrannical people, or a tyrannical government, I have ever been, I am still, and I ever will remain a democrat'. Duffy, surely, would not have disagreed with these sentiments.

'YOUR soul ordinarily repressed only overflows in genial talk among congenial associates', Duffy told himself in his *Ars Vitae*. But he does not seem to have found many such associates in Melbourne. Wilson Gray, of course, remained a close friend until his departure for New Zealand, and the talented Margaret Callan had followed Duffy to Melbourne. Duffy had a warm regard for Dr. Charles Pearson, an eminent Oxford historian and educationist, who settled in Melbourne in 1873, but he showed little or no interest in the colony's embryonic intellectual life.

Duffy was not associated with Melbourne's Yorick Club which two Englishmen, Frederick Williams Haddon, editor of the *Argus,* and Marcus Clarke, a gifted, waspish writer, and a school friend of Gerard Manley Hopkins, founded in 1868. The Club became the centre of Melbourne's literary community. Though Duffy never joined it, he became acquainted with Clarke and in 1870, helped him get the job of secretary to the Trustees of the Public Library. That year, Clarke's classic novel of convict life in Tasmania, *His Natural Life,* was appearing serially in the *Australian Journal.* When he was preparing the huge work for book publication, Clarke asked Duffy if he could find time to criticise it. Duffy read the story carefully and found it 'singularly powerful and original', but marred by serious faults. He suggested a number of drastic amendments, which Clarke gratefully carried out.

'I confess that I feel a pang at your suggestions for vigorous cutting, but I am sure you are right. . .' Clarke wrote to Duffy. 'When I have altered the book according to your suggestions I think it will be readable. I shall then ask permission to dedicate it to the Hon. C. Gavan Duffy, as the only way in which I can express my thanks'. The revised book with the dedication was published in London in 1874, when Duffy was in England. (It is now generally titled *For the Term of His Natural Life.* Duffy had arranged for Mrs. Cashel Hoey to read the proofs, and Clarke wrote him that she was 'a brick'.

MᶜCULLOCHS' administration lasted for eight years, (1863—1871), with some modifications and two short interruptions; nearly as long a period as the seven previous governments had covered. When it fell in June 1871, on a proposed property tax of sixpence in the pound, Duffy became Premier and Chief Secretary, leading a ministry in which James Grant, a radical member of the first parliament was Minister for Lands, and Graham Berry, a suburban grocer, Treasurer and Minister for Trade and Customs. He was a protectionist and Duffy, a free-trader. But Duffy recognised the growing demand for protection and was prepared to compromise. The *Age,* temporarily burying its hostility to Duffy ('a fox in the midst of corn') welcomed his Cabinet as a ministry of action. 'No ministry should be refused a fair trial on merely personal grounds', it said.

Berry announced that this was the first truly radical Ministry. It contained no merchants, squatters, or bankers or a single Melbourne representative. 'I undertook the administration of public affairs with the confident determination that for once there should be a Government framing large and generous projects, and against whose exercise of patronage or encouragement of enterprises no man could utter a just reproach', Duffy wrote in 1898. And with that complacency in his writing, that not infrequently jars upon the reader, he added: 'A quarter of a century after the events of that day, I look back on them with the confident assurance that nothing was done which needs to be repented, or which I would not repeat if the occasion occurred'.

The London *Spectator,* a radical weekly edited by the distinguished theological scholar and essayist, Richard Holt Hutton, acclaimed Duffy's policy speech:

> If anyone wishes to know what the Empire loses by English inability to conciliate Irish affection, let him read the speech . . . we have not for years read a political manifesto so full of character and power. Mr. Duffy is an Irishman, a Catholic, and a rebel, a typical man of the class which we English say can neither govern nor be governed but he speaks like the man for whom the Tories are sighing, the born administrator, utterly free of flummery and buncombe, clear as to his ends, clearer still as to his means, ready to compromise anything except principle. . .

A few months after taking office, Duffy wrote to Carlyle:

> I have been employed in steering the ship of state and find it a toilsome and exhausting task . . . not to have a moment to read, not a moment to think, except upon the one problem, is a strange change of life for a man who has lived so long among books with only occasional incursions into politics, followed always by a retreat into my den.

But he was in better health than he had ever been, and he attributed this to Vichy water, which he urged the dyspeptic Carlyle to try. Carlyle described his chronic dyspepsia as 'the frightfullest fiend that lives in the Pit, or out of it; the accursed brutal nightmare that has ridden me continuously these fifty odd years'.

'Among the designs in which I have been baulked by the ignorance and prejudices of successors, the design of establishing new industries suitable to a southern soil and climate, was the most important, 'Duffy wrote in his autobiography. Determined to take it up again, he expounded this design at public meetings in a lecture titled 'What to Do'. Instead of concentrating on gold, wool and wheat, Victoria should develop other industries suitable to its climate. 'Whatever grows in France, Spain or Italy will grow here', Duffy said, 'and in most cases grow in soil worthless for wheat'. For example, the olive would flourish on deserted goldfields. Skilled European workers should be imported to teach Victorians how to produce olive oil, tobacco, dried fruits, flax and silk. And Victoria's penal settlements and reformatories could be turned into workshops and farms for these industries. The objection that prison factories would compete unfairly with free labour would not apply to new industries.

Turning from profit to pleasure, Duffy pleaded for a more gracious life in Melbourne, which he saw as a southern European city. There would be regular concerts in the Fitzroy Gardens, little open-air theatres in the Flagstaff Gardens, and facilities for pleasant drinking in both. Bourke street would be brilliantly lit at night, with twenty or thirty cafes, catering for various social groups. Melbourne streets would be shaded with umbrageous trees, and there would be window boxes in city buildings. And Duffy asked why there was no Mocha coffee in Melbourne, when mail steamers stopped each month at the next town to Mocha? Why was there no French bread? Had Australians tried to grow the mango? And why should they build unsuitable houses instead of copying suitable European designs?

An Australian gentleman builds an English mansion, and when he adds a verandah, he has attained his ideal of grace and convenience. An Italian gentleman, of less than half his income, when the hot winds blow, sits in a summer salon of exquisite proportions, lined and floored with slabs of cool marble, looking out upon gardens where hedges thirty feet high, like leafy walls, cast a perpetual shade, and the air is cooled by a flashing fountain or an artificial stream fed from a reservoir, and scented with the perfume of odorous plants. The boundaries of his fields are marked by trees laden with pleasant fruit, or by forest trees looped together by the swinging tendrils of the vine.

A less attractive suggestion was that the Fitzroy Gardens should become an Australian Pincian Hill, with an array of busts of great men adorning its leafy walls. Duffy asked the Agent-General to inquire from 'artistic people' in London which material less expensive than marble ought to be employed in busts exposed to the open air. Fortunately, the plan came to nothing. Today, Melbourne citizens can enjoy a stroll through the gardens without having to run the gauntlet of rows of assorted "celebrities".

Duffy also had a curious plan to improve Melbourne's Art Gallery. (He was Chairman of the Committee of Trustees.) 'The National Gallery gets on slowly. It is impossible to get an adequate grant for it', he wrote in his diary. 'One thousand pounds buys only one good picture: but I have been meditating other measures. Every gallery in Europe has duplicates, which could be spared, if we offered them, as we might, stuffed animals and birds in exchange'.

A week after his seventy-seventh birthday, in December 1871, Carlyle dictated a letter to Duffy, explaining that 'the process of engraving on lead' was beyond him because his right hand had become completely useless for writing. One thing he earnestly wished was that Australia should have ten times as much emigration. But he was pessimistic about this being achieved by popular governments: 'A government carried on by Parliamentary Palaver and Universal Suffrage, with penny newspapers presiding, must necessarily be a do-nothingism, and neglect not only the colonies, but every other interest . . . except that of getting majorities for itself, by hook or crook'.

Duffy was in office thirteen months, five of them with Parliament in recess. During his time in office he made a triumphal tour of the colony, buoyantly delivering eloquent addresses, and bravely digesting enormous banquets. Before long, the *Age* became more critical: 'He makes and breaks promises without being conscious of what he is doing', it said. He was editorially advised to stop 'unseemly boasting' and to try a mixture 'of dignity and humility', lest he 'cause a revulsion of public feeling now favourable to him'.

In the House, Duffy was faced with increasing hostility, mostly on religious grounds. Victoria's Irish population was increasing. The old cry of 'No Popery!' was heard again, and Duffy's openly proclaimed determination to give Catholics a fair share in responsible government stoked the fires of sectarianism. Despite this, he survived a vote of no-confidence in September 1871.

Launching his attack on the Government, Fellows had referred pointedly to Duffy's rebellious behaviour in Ireland. In a voice often quivering with emotion, Duffy told the House that the number of those who perished or fled from Ireland during the famine exceeded the entire population of the Australian colonies, and he ended a moving speech with an impassioned personal statement:

> I will soon have to account for my whole life, and I feel that it has been defaced by many sins and shortcomings; but there is one portion of it I must except from this censure. I can say without fear, without impiety, when I am called before the Judge of all men, I shall not fear to answer for my Irish career. I did what I believed best for Ireland, without any relation to its effects on myself. I am challenged to justify myself for having been an Irish rebel, under penalty of your fatal censure; and I am content to reply that the recollection that when my native country was in mortal peril I was among those who staked life for her deliverance, is a memory I would not exchange for anything that Parliaments or sovereigns can give or take away.

The speech had a remarkable effect on the House. According to Duffy, 'tears overflowed the eyes of hardened politicians'. What is certain is that the no-confidence motion was rejected by a triumphant majority, and a prominent member of the Opposition, Wilberforce Stephen, leader of the Equity Bar and a future Attorney-General, said that the result of the division had established Duffy as the leader of the House, and 'the most powerful Minister that this colony has seen since we have had Constitutional Government'.

Duffy faced another vote of no-confidence when parliament reassembled in May. Childers, who because of ill-health, had retired from the Admiralty, had succeeded Verdon as Victoria's Agent-General. He had written to Duffy offering his service, because of his 'sincere wish to do all in my power for the colony to which I owe so much'. Childers needed a secretary, and Duffy, perhaps indiscreetly but not improperly, recommended his friend Cashel Hoey for the job. Hoey, who had edited *The Nation* after Duffy's departure, was then a member of the English bar. The Opposition attacked the appointment. It attributed to Hoey articles that had appeared in *The Nation* before he became editor and declared he must be peremptorily removed from office. The Government was defeated on a no-confidence motion by five votes, and Hoey was sacked. Two of Duffy's supporters had stayed away from the division, and two others voted with the Opposition.

Duffy was convinced that an appeal to the people would return his party with a decisive majority. He claimed on constitutional grounds that he was entitled to a dissolution, but the Governor, Viscount Canterbury, refused to grant it, and a coalition of squatters, led by the wealthy Francis John Goodall, 'fierce Free Traders and devoted Protectionists', took over.

Duffy described Canterbury as 'an impoverished peer . . . whose business in the colonies was to increase his balance at the banker's'. He believed that Canterbury had acted in the interests of his son-in-law, a Victorian ship-owner and squatter, and he repeated with relish a story of how Canterbury, at a vice-regal lunch, had said patronisingly to a member of Parliament, 'I believe you were originally a tailor?' 'I was, your Excellency'. 'And pray, how are you employed at present?' 'I am employed at present taking your Excellency's measure'.

The controversy on Canterbury's refusal to grant a dissolution reached England, where it was debated on Imperial grounds. It was argued that he had violated the Constitution and thrown the principles of colonial government into confusion. The *Spectator* said it was the case of a Ministry which, by large and liberal measures, had attracted an unusual amount of European attention. Mr. Duffy had been defeated by a small majority and his request for a dissolution was absolutely unanswerable. He had not had a dissolution before, whereas his opponents had had five dissolutions. The Melbourne correspondent of *The Times* agreed that Duffy would have been returned, and commented:

> The Governor is bound to allow a Ministry to submit itself once within a term of years to the popular vote. This obligation Lord Canterbury disregarded, apparently for no reason at all except personal dislike. . . Partiality of this kind is as fatal to a constitutional governor as to a judge, and if not a reason for removal, is at least a final reason against continuing him in a similar appointment after his term of office has expired.

The correspondence between Duffy and Canterbury was moved for in the House of Commons. 'It is notable', Duffy wrote complacently, 'that he never after received any public employment'. In a letter deploring Duffy's defeat, John Forster described the affair as 'of unequalled shabbiness' and the Governor's behaviour as 'grossly unfair'.

ONCE more out of office, Duffy planned another trip to Europe. Before his departure, he received a surprising communication from Canterbury, saying that the Colonial Secretary, Lord Kimberley, had authorised him to offer Duffy a Companionship of the Most Distinguished Order of St. Michael and St. George. This is the lowest of the three Orders, and Duffy's Irish pride was affronted. 'I had much satisfaction in refusing the order, which I considered little better than an insult', he recalled.

A few days later, however, Canterbury inexplicably wrote again, to inform him that Kimberley had submitted his name to Her Majesty for the honour of a knighthood. 'It would have been a pleasure to decline this offer also', Duffy says, but in view of his disagreement with Canterbury, some of his colleagues thought a refusal would have been mis-understood. And they pointed out that he would have accepted a knighthood in Ireland if she, like Victoria, had a Parliament and Government of her own. Some of his former Irish colleagues did not approve, and to this day Duffy is denied adequate recognition in Ireland because of his knighthood. But he duly paid the sum of £115 demanded by the Imperial Government as the price of the regalia, and became the fifth Victorian knight since the establishment of responsible government.

Duffy explained to Carlyle: 'I accepted because it was the most conclusive evidence that I had performed the public duties I undertook with integrity, which in the case of an Irish rebel, of course, required some such evidence to become credible'.

'The honour was no doubt procured for him by his friend Childers, who was then a member of the British Cabinet, [he was not] and it was probably intended as a peace-offering to the Irish nation', commented Henry Gyles Turner.

The following year, O'Shanassy was knighted. Many nineteenth-century Victorian politicians believed that to accept a knighthood was to compromise their independence. Among those who refused to be honoured were Peter Lalor, J.G. Francis, James Service, Duncan Gillies, R. Murray Smith, and Alfred Deakin. Today's statesmen are not so fastidious.

In another letter to Carlyle, Duffy wrote:

I have made a modest independence, started my boys fairly in life, done as much work here as I was capable of doing, and I would not hire the remainder of my life at a hundred thousand pounds a year, to Australia or any other power, potentate, or dominion on either side of the Equator. Not that I mean to idle it away, but I have purchased by long years of labour the glorious privilege of independence, which, I take it, means the right to set one's own tasks.

ON 'a dazzling Spring day' in 1874, Duffy landed at Brindisi, this time alone. He had intended to take a long, idle holiday in the south of France before going on to London and Dublin. But his health was worrying him. He had lost his voice and decided to consult a London specialist.

Despite his voice trouble, London again meant a busy social round. In the first fortnight, he dined with, among others, Sir Charles Dilke, Lord Emly, Lord O'Hagan, and Lord Carnarvon. Dilke was then a rebellious member of the House of Commons, a republican who in 1872 had become notorious by moving for an enquiry into the cost of the monarchy, and Carnarvon had replaced Kimberley as Colonial Secretary.

Duffy was repeatedly a guest at Highclere Castle, near Newbury, one of Carnarvon's three country seats, and at his London house. Carnarvon's guests — statesmen, scholars, writers, historians, — were so distinguished that his house parties were compared with those of Cicero at Tusculum. Duffy could have wished for no more stimulating company. At one Highclere gathering, he met the historian James Anthony Froude, about to leave on a government mission to South Africa; the Dean of Westminster; the famous editor of *The Times*, John Thaddeus Delane; and the unconventional Mr. and Mrs. Auberon Herbert, who arrived sunburnt and dusty, in a pony carriage with a white Arab horse, and a dog.

Duffy and Carnarvon had long talks about Colonial and Imperial affairs. 'He was a Tory without a *soupçon* of the religious bigotry which I had so habitually seen associated with Toryism in Ireland and Australia'; wrote Duffy. 'He seemed to have arrived at the conclusion that the honour and interest of the Empire demanded some settlement of the Irish claims which would put an end to chronic disaffection'. Duffy later set out his views in a memorandum which he sent to Carnarvon.

Duffy also expounded his plans for Imperial Defence, and for strengthening Anglo-Australian relations, subjects in which Carnarvon was keenly interested. Carnarvon favoured the return of troops to the Australian colonies — the last had left in 1870 — but the War Office opposed this, and Cabinet decided that the Colonies must be left to raise their own forces, because Great Britain could recruit only enough men to meet her own demands.

'My "morbid vanity" for which the *Argus* will vouch, was abundantly gratified', Duffy wrote to his wife, after attending as guest of honour a whitebait dinner given by the Permanent Secretaries of the Colonies. (Whitebait and British politics had long enjoyed a curious association.) When he dined with the Archbishop of Westminster, Dr. Manning, a convert to Catholicism, 'in his strange, naked mansion', Manning cordially supported Ireland's efforts to undo the work of injustice and mis-government. As for England's Established Church, Manning regarded it as a bulwark against agnosticism which it would be a grievous error to remove.

Contact with men such as these sharpened Duffy's growing discontent with life in Victoria. 'I feel a strong distaste for the bitterness, the meanness and the pettiness of colonial politics', he wrote to Parkes in September 1874. 'And if all the offices in Australia were united in one, I would not consent to occupy it. . . I have thoroughly enjoyed returning among international men, and exhort you to do likewise. Life in London is as little like life in the colony as the tide of the Atlantic is like a waterhole in the Lachlan'.

Before crossing to France, Duffy visited the Royal Academy to choose pictures for the Melbourne Gallery. In Paris, he dined at the Palais d'Elysée. He thought the president, Marshal McMahon looked 'very Irish', not intrinsically different from an Irish soldier, or even a policeman. In Paris he saw much of John O'Leary, who had been released from imprisonment on condition that he lived abroad. Duffy described him as a Fenian of a class he had never seen before — 'moderate in opinion, generally just to his opponents, and entirely without passion except a devoted love of Ireland'. He had been a Confederate in 1848, and had become rather anti-clerical because of the priests' opposition to the Young Ireland movement.

Duffy's voice was still troubling him. The London specialist recommended a season at Aix-les-Bains, but a month's rest there did him little good, and he settled down for the winter on the Riviera, dividing his time between Cannes, Menton and Monte Carlo. 'I fear I am growing an old fogey', he wrote to his wife from a hotel in Cannes.

There is a family stopping here . . . consisting of the grandson and granddaughter of Lord Thurlow, Chancellor under George III. The lady asked me if I knew her grandfather. I replied that I did not, but that the fault was not mine, as he had placed an impediment in the way of our acquaintance, by dying before I was born.

At Menton and Monte Carlo, Duffy sat for a bust by the English sculptor Charles Summers, who had worked on the Australian goldfields, and in

Melbourne, before returning to Europe in 1867. Summers assured him that there was an abundance of sculptor's clay suitable for export in Moonee Ponds, a Melbourne suburb.

WHEN Duffy returned to London in the spring of 1875 he received a pressing invitation to attend the O'Connell centenary in Dublin. He was reluctant to accept, but yielded to the persuasions of the Lord Mayor of Dublin, Alderman McSwiney, who called on him in London, and of the Irish in Melbourne, who asked him to represent them.

In his formal acceptance of the invitation, Duffy wrote to McSwiney:

> It is great men who make a great nation, and it would be unwise as well as base and ungenerous for Ireland to be unmindful of the greatest man in will and intellect who sprang from the Celtic race for six generations and whose will and intellect were devoted exclusively to her service. . .

But in a letter to Lord O'Hagan, he expressed a less enthusiastic view of O'Connell. O'Hagan had composed an adulatory centenary oration on the Liberator, and Duffy wrote:

> The O'Connell you paint is as ideal a personage as the King Arthur of Tennyson. He was no more the generous, single-minded, unselfish hero of your prose idyll than he was the impostor ordinarily presented in *The Times* — but a strange compound of both. And unfortunately, the evil consequences of his moral deficiencies are still in full vigour.

For three days, Dublin celebrated the centenary exuberantly. There were religious ceremonies, banquets, picnics, fetes, athletic sports, a musical festival, a regatta, and a great procession. 'Speranza' reached for her lyre, and acclaimed the liberator in passionate Strophe, Antistrophe, and Epode:

He came in the storms of the years,
  When the world had grown weary of kings,
And Oppression and insults and fears
  Roused the bond slaves to bitterest things.

Dublin merchants did a brisk trade in souvenirs: green sashes, scarfs, neckties, handkerchiefs, badges, emblems, rosettes, and portraits. The *Irishman*, in a powerful leading article, appealed for 'strongest sobriety' during the celebrations. 'The public houses should be closed', it said, 'and if they are kept open the people should refuse to cross their thresholds'.

'Princes and ecclesiastics from Germany and France . . . arrived to grace the occasion, and the recognition of Ireland as an ancient, pious, and indestructible nation promised to be complete', Duffy wrote. 'But in all our annals before and since, the spirit of faction has played a fatal part'. The Centenary Committee was split into two fiercely opposed factions, one supporting Alderman McSwiney, the other, Isaac Butt. McSwiney and his followers wished to displace Butt from the leadership of the Home Rule League, which had replaced, with the aid of an ingenious euphemism, the movement for Repeal.

The conflict between the factions exploded at the Grand National Banquet, held in Dublin's Exhibition Palace, and attended by six hundred and fifty gentlemen, and an uncounted number of ladies demurely segregated in the galleries. The menu was not unworthy of the occasion:

Soups	— Clear turtle, turtle, English and Amontillado sherry.
Fish	— Salmon, turbot, sauce Hollandaise, and Lobster sauce. Hock.
Entrees	— Lamb cutlets and peas, sweetbreads and truffles, Ruinart pere, extra superior.
Releves	— Chicken Béchamel, haunch of Venison, haunch of mutton, sirloin of beef, sherry.
Second servings	— Ducklings, turkey poults.
Entremets	— Maraschino jelly, Italian creams, cream and water ices, brandy and curacao.
Dessert	— Claret, Château la rose.

After the feast came the toasts, beginning with 'The health of Queen Victoria'. By midnight, the Bishop of Nantes, the Polish Prince Radziwill, Count Wendt, a German parliamentarian, and many others had been duly honoured, but only half the toast list had been disposed of. Ignoring the cries of 'Order' and 'Chair', a number of guests then began to call for Isaac Butt. A general uproar followed. Above the confusion, the Lord Mayor proposed 'The Legislative Independence of Ireland, coupled with the name of Sir Charles Gavan Duffy'. The shouts for Butt were kept up with unabated vigour, mingled with counter cheers for Duffy, who had risen to respond. The Lord Mayor, standing up on his chair and waving his arms, entreated the guests to hear Duffy.

The *Irishman* reported, 'Sir Charles remained standing, and several times waved his hands for silence, but without effect. Those who cheered him had their voices drowned by the clamour of those who insisted on Mr. Butt speaking'. Butt rose, and by gesticulations, appealed for a hearing for Duffy, but the excitement increased. Nobody could be heard. Duffy sat down, the Lord Mayor abruptly left the chair and bade the meeting goodnight; and the Bishop of Nantes sprang on a chair and addressed a few impassioned words in French.

Resonant cries of 'Butt' and 'Duffy' continued. Father Lavelle jumped nimbly on the table. The gas was lowered and the ladies began to make their way speedily from the galleries. There was more animated discussion and violent pushing as people left their seats and crowded to the head table. 'Coat-tails began to be seriously endangered', reported the *Daily Express*. Then the principal gas lights were put out, and the guests fought their way to the cloak-rooms. 'What would have been a strength and honour to Ireland became a disgrace', Duffy lamented.

McSwiney invited him to a conference at the Mansion House to discuss the formation of a new Repeal Association on the old lines of 1843, with a national daily paper to support it, and asked him to stay in Dublin and direct these operations. When Duffy asked who was to finance such a costly undertaking, McSwiney told him after some hesitation, that Dr. Cullen, now a Cardinal, had promised a substantial share of the capital required. Duffy asked the Lord Mayor if he knew that his Eminence regarded Duffy as a man who ought to endure a long penance on bread and water before being permitted to serve the country again? McSwiney said that Cullen had entirely changed his opinion of Duffy's Irish policy. 'But alas!' Duffy replied, 'I have not changed my opinion of his'.

Duffy went on to say that he still thought the policy of excluding priests from politics to make way for bishops was execrable, and that he had always tried to rear a people able to judge for themselves, men and citizens, not grown children and obedient mutes.

IMMEDIATELY after Duffy's return to Melbourne, early in 1876, the constitutency of Gippsland, by far the largest in the colony, fell vacant and he was invited to contest it. He was suffering from bronchitis caught on the voyage out and could not take part in the election campaign. Despite this he was, in his own words, 'triumphantly chosen against a candidate whom the squatters as usual were pleased to send out against me'.

Within a few months, there was another dissolution, and Graham Berry became Premier. Duffy was re-elected, and unanimously elected Speaker. He had refused Berry's offer of any other office, not being prepared to accept a secondary position, he explained, after having occupied the first. But he was pleased to accept the distinction of Knight Commander of the Most Distinguished Order of St. Michael and St. George which the Queen, at the recommendation of Lord Carnarvon, was pleased to confer on him. 'I trust that it will be acceptable to you as it will be to all your friends amongst whom my recollections of much pleasant communication with you three years ago makes me hope that I may be included', wrote Carnarvon.

Duffy now had more leisure for reading and writing and in the Parliamentary recess, he began a long projected work — a history of his own time in Ireland, and a defence of the Young Irelanders. He told John O'Hagan of his plans:

> I propose to write the rise and fall of the National Movement, which otherwise will probably never be written and we, and our friends, will be for ever misunderstood. I might do some good in the House of Commons as you suggest, but surely I shall do more good in painting the sins by which our race has always fallen, and the virtues by which it has often risen again.
> I am weary of new countries and long for the green pastures where we wandered of old . . .

A few extracts from his diary about this time (quoted in his autobiography) show the diversity of his interests. For example, he asks the journalist and politician, Angus Mackay, why the Scotch so habitually hated the Irish who had never done them any harm?

> He said he believed they were disgusted with the superstition of the peasantry, and their servile submission to the priests. No wonder, I rejoined, Burns wished for his countrymen the gift to see themselves as others see them. Buckle declares that the most superstitious race in Europe are the

Scotch, and the most prostrate before their ministers.

Duffy's opinions encompass an original meditation on Australian life:

> The Australians will differ from their progenitors by a more decisive penchant for enjoyment. Marcus Clarke attributes it to the Irish element; but is it not rather more attributable to the sunshine? The Irish certainly resemble the continental rather than the insular races. Not merely the Latins, but the Teutons and the Slavs like to live their lives, whereas the English and the Americans generally live for some future generation — a practice better for the nation certainly, but is it better for the individual? Seeing we have but one life to live, it may be doubted.

Duffy shows penetration in a character analysis:

> I have been reading the *Remains* of Arthur Clough the representative man of the upright modern sceptic, who was not betrayed by passion or perversity, but perplexed by honest difficulties unwillingly entertained.

IN September 1878, Duffy's wife Susan died of tuberculosis, after a long illness. She had been his 'companion and counsellor' for more than thirty years, and borne him eleven children of whom three boys and three girls survived. 'I have lost the relish and enjoyment of life', Duffy wrote in his diary: 'Nothing interests me, my strength fails, and my appetite is gone. To arrange my affairs in the way most satisfactory for my children and to finish my book on the '48 are the only objects for which I feel it possible to work'.

He had become thoroughly disillusioned with politics. In letters to Parkes and others, he laments the 'naked selfishness of democracy'. Parliaments had become 'bear gardens', manhood suffrage, which he had championed, was producing an 'unexpected bad class of representatives'. He was 'a disappointed reformer'. As the session drew to a close, he announced that he would not be a member of the next Parliament. Years later, he wrote:

> I took farewell of a House in which I had served since its creation, to which I had given without stint toil of mind and body, and which had bestowed on me all the favours it could confer on a public man, I owed it much, and I should probably have finished my life on the scene which had occupied so large a section of it, but that I loathed the task of answering again and again the insensate inventions of religious bigotry . . . I determined . . . that I should never more become a member of any Legislature, or ever again mount a political platform.

Once more his thoughts turned to Europe. He was free to leave Victoria without surrendering his pension of £1,000 a year, and in 1880, he decided to settle in Nice, and to visit London occasionally. He chose a Mediterranean retreat because of his bronchial trouble.

A month before his departure, he wrote to Parkes:

> When I shall return I do not know . . . But I am resolved at any rate not to enter Parliament any more . . . It looks *so* petty and so rancorous, so dull and

driftless, that I lament so many years of my life in that wilderness. Where are the dreams of a noble, generous, free state in which the wise can rule, and the fool and the knave are absent?

When Duffy left Victoria, his four sons remained behind. None of them, inexplicably, is mentioned by name in his memoirs, though the eldest, John, was then a member of parliament, having won Duffy's old seat of Dalhousie, and another son, Frank, was a very successful barrister in Melbourne (see Appendix).

Duffy's departure from Melbourne was as inconspicuous as his arrival twenty-four years previously had been flamboyant. He was not among the many eminent Melbourne citizens who on 9 January 1880 held a public meeting to inaugurate a fund for the relief of distress in Ireland. The fund, in less than two months raised the substantial sum of £20,419.0s.1½d, but he does not seem to have contributed to it. Nor is there any record in the Melbourne press or his own memoirs, of him attending any farewell functions.

When Parliament was prorogued on 5 February, Duffy addressed it for the last time to announce his retirement. 'The long sittings, the late hours, the bad atmosphere . . . and the constant anxiety and responsibility imposed upon me by my office have so impaired my health that I do not feel able to encounter labours of the same kind again', he said. 'I intend to seek repose by a visit to Europe on private business'.

The Premier, Graham Berry, and a representative of the Opposition, Duncan Gillies, expressed their great appreciation of Duffy's services to the House, and Mr. W.J. O'Hea, 'as perhaps the only member . . . familiar with the House of Commons' said that 'not excepting even the ablest Speaker known to the House of Commons in recent times, Viscount Eversley' he was not aware of a Speaker who had exceeded Duffy in knowledge of the practice and law of Parliament.

Fifteen days later, Duffy embarked on the R.M.S. *Assam,* 1747 tons, bound for Brindisi with the fortnightly mails. The leading article in the current issue of the *Australasian Sketcher,* a Melbourne periodical, would surely have interested him. 'The subject of federation of the colonies, after having been on the shelf for some time, has of late been taken down, dusted and presented as a live topic of discussion', it said. Sir Henry Parkes in a review article contended that federation was now easy of attainment. As far as New South Wales, Victoria and South Australia were concerned, it could be reached within a year.

DUFFY arrived in London in the Spring of 1880, and immediately visited Carlyle. 'It was deeply touching to see the Titan who had never known langour or weakness, suffering from the dilapidation of old age', he wrote. 'His right hand was nearly useless and had to be supported by the left when he lifted it by a painful effort to his mouth. His talk was subdued in tone, but otherwise unaltered. "It takes a long time to die", he said, with his old smile, and a gleam of humour in his eye'.

Carlyle no longer walked, but invited Duffy to share his customary drive from three o'clock to five. They drove to Streatham, to Clapham

Common, and home by Battersea Park, Carlyle sipping brandy occasionally, and solacing himself with his pipe. The following year, he died. 'Time has brought to a close', wrote Duffy, 'not prematurely, but with many forewarnings, a friendship which nothing had disturbed, and which was one of the chief comforts of my life'.

In Nice Duffy was able to finish the book on which he had been working for years, drawing on his diary, and his vast collection of newspapers, documents and letters. Titled *Young Ireland, a Fragment of Irish History*, it told the story of the movement from its inception till 1845. *Young Ireland* was published in London towards the end of 1880, and soon after, in New York and Melbourne. Part of it appeared in a French translation. *The Times* reported that the whole of the first edition was sold on the day of publication. 'There has been nothing like this since Byron's *Corsair*,' wrote Dr. Murray from Maynooth. Duffy sent copies to a number of people, including Gladstone, Cardinal Newman and Lady Wilde.

In the letter accompanying Gladstone's copy, he wrote,

> One of my objects in writing it was the hope that it would induce *you* to reconsider the Irish question ... by sifting the evidence of men who have lived among the people and share their sentiments. I offer you my evidence for whatever it may be worth. At any rate, it is the truth as far as I am capable of understanding it.

Gladstone, who in April that year had again replaced Disraeli as Prime Minister, and was pledged to the pacification of Ireland, read three-quarters of the book in one day, and wrote pontifically to Duffy:

> I shall proceed with all the despatch I can make to profit by its perusal, mindful as I shall be all along that your career has supplied you with a peculiar experience which can hardly fail to have given you some very important advantages in dealing with the arduous subject of your choice ...

Cardinal Newman found the book 'very interesting and very instructive'.

> That we long have acted unjustly to Ireland is quite plain — the difficulty is how to make restitution — and what *is* a true restitution? Here it is that I feel my own ignorance — never having been a politician. I quite allow that Englishmen by themselves are not impartial judges in the matter. They are actuated by fear in all their decisions, though they may not know it. They consider that the greatness and capabilities of the Empire are at stake. But then supposing this apprehension proved true; if England was in misery, would Ireland be better off? Would not it be its own destruction, while it was ours? I have not come to any page yet of your book, which meets this objection ...

Lady Wilde praised the book's 'warm wit, passion and life ... Many times I could have stopped for tears. ... Some divine and undying impulse must remain out of all these glorious dreams, and to *you* and to your co-workers, whatever is good and noble in Irish national aspirations is due. Justin McCarthy spent a whole day reading the book and at parts, like Lady Wilde, felt his cheeks wet. 'I fear my old blood was heated for I spent a sleepless night after', he wrote.

From Sydney, Henry Parkes, who had bought the book before Duffy's presentation copy arrived, wrote:

> I heard a man not over friendly to you, Sir James Martin, say the other day, that your style excelled Macaulay. 'I detest his politics', said Sir James, 'but his book is delightful.' I am myself gratified that amid your literary labours and your other cares you could find time to think of me . . . Our friendship has been tried by circumstances which would have snapped less sterling links. . .

The Times acclaimed the remarkable literary quality of the book, its vivid and graphic style, and said that despite the 'genuine modesty' with which Duffy attributed the origin of the Young Ireland movement to Thomas Davis, he would always be regarded as its true founder . . . And the *Saturday Review* ended an adulatory notice with the curious observation that Duffy always wrote 'in the language and the spirit of a gentleman'.

From the other side of the world came similar acclaim. 'As a plea for Irish Home Rule, nothing more brilliant than the chapter titled "A Bird's-Eye View of Irish History" has ever been penned', said the Melbourne *Age*. And, more surprisingly, the *Australasian*, a weekly published by the *Argus* proprietary, serialised the book.

Young Ireland had been published at the price of a guinea, which greatly limited its circulation in Ireland. In 1883, Duffy sanctioned an 'Irish People's Edition', printed in Dublin, from which he waived his royalties. It was sold for two shillings. The same year, he published a sequel, which took the story up to 1849. In the preface, he wrote:

> A nation rarely changes its character, and in Ireland hitherto history has repeated itself with the fidelity of a stock piece at the theatre, where nothing is changed from generation to generation but the actors. The same mistakes in policy and conduct are committed over and over again . . .

This second volume, too, was very favourably reviewed. The *Spectator*, while not always agreeing with Duffy's political criticism, described the book as 'a very powerful, and for the most part, a very just, indictment against the Irish policy of Great Britain'. And the *Nation* wrote:

> It is not very often that a man retains up to the age of sixty-five years the faculties which in the prime of life enables him to thrill his readers, like wine; but it is scarcely an exaggeration to say that in these pages is to be found not merely the statesmanship which comes of experience, but the power of rousing the emotions which is usually associated with the glowing period of youth.

Despite some distortions of emphasis, these two works, based on a wealth of contemporary documents, and on Duffy's participation in the events he described, are invaluable source-books for a study of the times.

'In the shaping of the modern image of the eighteen-forties, it is difficult to overestimate the part played by Gavan Duffy's writings', writes a contemporary historian, Dr. Kevin B. Nowlan. He praises their restraint, and their 'easy, lucid style', and observes that Duffy at times understates his own part in repeal politics: 'Gavan Duffy never became an O'Connell or a Parnell in terms of political power and influence, but his personal contribution to the politics of the mid-nineteenth century remains a considerable one'.

The distortion which historians have most criticised is in Duffy's treatment of O'Connell. 'In Sir Charles Gavan Duffy's history. . .' Lecky wrote, 'O'Connell always appears as half-patriot, half-charlatan — a man of amazing abilities, sincerely devoted to his people and his creed, and in many respects in advance of his time, but untruthful, rapacious, unscrupulous, overbearing, very rarely acting through motives that were purely single-minded and disinterested'. And another contemporary historian, J.H. Whyte, writes: 'Recent research has not entirely upheld Duffy's view of events. The trend in modern writing . . . has been to favour O'Connell and to stress how much his critics owed to his achievements'. But many of Duffy's contemporaries, including John Mitchel, shared his estimate of The Liberator.

Duffy is also criticised for over-simplifying the part played by Dr. Cullen, Keogh and Sadleir in the failure of the Independent Opposition Movement. Nor do the files of *The Nation* support his claim that he and his Young Ireland colleagues had been dismayed by O'Connell's surrender at Clontarf. The files show, on the contrary, that they unanimously supported the decision.

IN Paris, on 16 November 1881, Duffy married for the third time. His wife was a beautiful red-haired girl in her twenties, Louise Hall, a niece of his second wife, Susan, and his own not very distant cousin. Her father, George Hall, was a banker and a sturdy Protestant who had spent some time in Australia.

Duffy had resolved never again to mount a political platform, but he could not detach himself from politics. During his stay in London in 1880, he had met the thirty-four-year-old Charles Stewart Parnell, who, in his short career, was to become the greatest leader Ireland had ever known. Like O'Connell he was known as 'the uncrowned King' of Ireland. Parnell was an enigmatic figure, a handsome, proud, reserved Protestant English aristocrat, with a passionate love of Ireland, where he was a large landowner, and a passionate hatred of the Union, which his great grandfather, Sir John Parnell, had bitterly opposed. Like all who knew Parnell, Duffy was profoundly impressed by him, whom he described at the time of their meeting, as 'a tall, stately looking young man of reserved manners, who spoke little, but the little was always to the purpose':

> He had not a gleam of the eloquence of Grattan, or the passion and humour of O'Connell, or any trace of the generous forbearance which Smith O'Brien aimed to efface himself. . . or of Butt's exact knowledge of Irish interests and annals, but he ruled with more unquestioned authority than any of them had done.

When Parnell questioned Duffy about his political intention, Duffy replied that he had come home to work for Ireland, though not in

Parliament. Outside of Parliament he should consider himself free to choose the course he thought best on public questions. Parnell had a high regard for Duffy, and publicly and privately acknowledged the importance of Duffy's role in creating the Independent Opposition in 1852.

During the five stormy years that followed, Duffy watched Parnell's career with interest, and they met occasionally when Duffy made his annual visit to London. 'Our conversation . . . generally consisted of my criticism of his policy or that of his supporters in Ireland, which he bore with consummate good humour', Duffy wrote. 'I thought they might have done more to suppress outrages and abate endless turbulence'. Ireland was still a most distressful country. The harvest of 1879 had been the worst since the Great Famine. In 1880, there were more than 2,000 evictions, many of them violently resisted, and 2,590 'agrarian crimes'. Poor peasants, driven to despair, attacked and sometimes murdered landlords and their agents, burnt dwellings and killed livestock. That year, Parnell was associated with Michael Davitt in forming the Irish National Land League. Davitt, the son of an evicted tenant, had been sentenced to fifteen years' penal servitude in 1871 for his part in an abortive Fenian attack on Chester castle, and released in 1878 on ticket-of-leave. The Land League was a sort of trade union of tenant farmers. It advised them to offer the rack-renting landlords a reduced rent. If he responded by trying to evict them, they were to impose a far-reaching ban on any attempt to deal with that landlord. This meant that he and his agent were completely ostracized, a process that became known as 'boycotting', because it was first applied to a Captain Boycott. It proved to be a very effective form, within the law, of passive resistance.

But 'agrarian outrages', a term which included sending threatening letters, continued, and on 24 January 1881, a Coercion Bill was introduced, giving the Irish Viceroy wide powers of arrest. After many stormily debated sessions the Bill was carried on 11 March, and speedily passed in the Lords.

Gladstone followed his Coercion Bill with a revolutionary Land Act which guaranteed tenants fair rent, fixity of tenure, and a free sale of tenancies at market values. It crushed landlordism and virtually conceded everything that Duffy's Land League and other tenant right movements had asked for. Duffy fervently supported the Act, declaring:

> If I were a bishop I would write a pastoral. If I were a priest, I would preach a discourse; if I were a journalist, I would make myself heard from the rostrum of the profession; if I could do no better, I would beat a drum on the highway in order to fix the attention of the Irish people on the splendid opportunity they possess of becoming prosperous and powerful.

Parnell was not satisfied with the legislation and denounced it and Gladstone so vigorously that in October he and other prominent Land Leaguers were arrested under the Coercion Act and imprisoned in Kilmainham Gaol. The Irish Leaders replied with an effective 'No Rent' manifesto, and the Government retaliated by suppressing the Land League. But these measures did not bring peace. 'The imprisonment of the responsible leaders of the national party had removed all check upon the fierce and dangerous forces which are always at work under the surface of Irish politics,' writes Justin McCarthy. 'The Chief Secretary . . . put into prison men, women, priests, according to his pleasure, and yet an ungrateful people refused to justify him by being pacified.'

Secret societies, which had dwindled while the Land League was in existence, became active again, and outrages multiplied daily, culminating in an event that shocked Ireland as much as England. Parnell and his colleagues were released from Kilmainham Gaol in May 1881 after the Government had agreed to extend the scope of the Act and Parnell had agreed to discourage agrarian violence. Four days later the newly appointed Chief Secretary, Lord Frederick Cavendish, and his companion, the Under Secretary, Mr. T.H. Burke, were hacked to death with surgical knives as they walked together in Phoenix Park. Though Parnell at once expressed his genuine horror and despair at the hideous crime, he was bitterly attacked in the English press, and resolved to retire from public life. He tendered his resignation to Gladstone, and suggested to his followers that Duffy might be induced to take his place in Parliament. However the request was never made to Duffy, who would certainly have refused it, as he twice refused invitations to stand for the Monaghan constituency. Gladstone would not accept Parnell's resignation, and Parnell remained leader of the Irish Party.

After the general elections of 1885, Parnell's party held the balance of power between Gladstone's Liberals and Salisbury's Conservatives. With Parnell's support, Gladstone took office. In April 1886, Gladstone presented his first Home Rule Bill, which provided for an Irish legislative body. Duffy acclaimed the Bill as 'one of the most courageous and disinterested experiments in human history,' but with ninety-three Liberals voting against it, the Government was brought down, and in the subsequent general election, the Liberal party was heavily defeated.

'I find here the life I have long dreamed of — a good climate, plenty of books, easy and habitual work, and domestic happiness,' Duffy wrote to Parkes from his Mediterranean villa in January 1884. And he recalled 'with horror' the long hours he had spent listening to dreary politicians in Melbourne. 'Life was surely given for some better purpose than this.'

He now devoted much of his time to writing. In 1882, he published as a book the chapter from *Young Ireland* titled *A Bird's Eye View of Ireland*. 'It has the force of a thunderclap', commented Lecky.

In 1886 appeared a history of the Tenant League movement, *The League of the North and South,* and the following year, Duffy contributed to *The Contemporary Review* an article, later reprinted as a pamphlet, titled *A Fair Constitution for Ireland*. He urged England to create an Irish Parliament and Government which it could trust, and to trust them accordingly. He described again the melancholy condition of Ireland:

Ireland presents a spectacle without parallel among Christian nations: its population — larger when any man amongst us was born than it is today — has dwindled year by year for more than thirty years; its ancient manufactures have disappeared; its foreign commerce, once considerable, is almost annihilated; the bulk of the population is pauperized and demoralized by a constant struggle for existence against unjust laws and pitiless authority. The produce of the island is carried away by absentees, and by fiscal exactions which have constantly increased while the wealth of the country diminished. The seed of the future — its young men and women — have been flying to foreign countries for longer than the existing generation can remember, because they have no career or pursuit at home.

And he set out in detail how an effective Irish Parliament could be created. It would be a bi-cameral institution of paid members, protecting minorities by a simple form of Proportional Representation, and with seats in the Senate — the nominated upper house — for ecclesiastics, university representatives, Supreme Court judges, and distinguished industrialists, manufacturers, lawyers, doctors and engineers.

Like Duffy's previous contributions to the Irish question, his 'Fair Constitution' was widely discussed and generally acclaimed. Parnell approved of its main provisions. Gladstone would not commit himself on all the proposals, though some of his colleagues gave them 'a frank and cordial acceptance'. Cardinal Manning thought it was the most adequate outline of a complex matter that he had seen, 'justly serious and practical'. Archbishop Walsh of Dublin thought Duffy's arguments 'admirable'. Justin McCarthy described the article as 'a splendid contribution to the great controversy,' and the distinguished jurist, James Bryce, invited Duffy to breakfast to discuss it.

In the middle of October 1884, Duffy was again Carnarvon's house guest at Highclere Castle. After they had discussed the Irish problem at length, Duffy undertook to write an article, showing that there was nothing in the hereditary principles or practice of the Conservative Party which prohibited it from favourably considering Ireland's claims.

Irish outrages continued. In January 1885, a portion of the White Tower was blown up, and part of the House of Commons, including the Speaker's Chair, was destroyed by dynamite. The following month, Duffy's article, at Carnarvon's instigation, appeared in the *National Review*, the monthly organ of the Conservative Party. It was a scholarly essay which reminded Tories that they got their historic name from their sympathy with oppressed Catholics whom the Whigs were persecuting. Duffy pointed out that William Pitt prompted by Burke, projected the complete emancipation of Catholics, and when Emancipation came at last in 1829, it was the Tories who carried it. The Tory party was the first to tackle the question of middle-class education in Ireland, and it was a Tory administration which laid the basis of colonial freedom in Canada and Australia. These 'prosperous and aspiring States' were now ruled as Ireland desired to be ruled.

The article excited great interest, and was widely discussed. *The Times* praised 'its moderate and conciliatory tone', and added: 'Sir Charles Gavan Duffy is too keen a politician and too sagacious an observer of public events not to see the favourable moment which is now presented for interposing as a mediator between parties which have hitherto been contending . . .'

A general election was approaching, and Duffy told Carnarvon that he had advised Parnell not to support the Tories unless they assured Ireland of a *quid pro quo.* He also urged Carnarvon to indicate his intention of trying to solve the Irish problem. Though sympathetic to Home Rule, Carnarvon replied cautiously that there were 'many difficulties on all sides', some aggravated by recent Fenian explosions. And foreign affairs were in a critical state. He wanted to avoid any premature step, he said, and not to promise more than he could fulfil.

In the election of 8 June, the Conservatives came to power with the support of the Irish members, and Carnarvon became Irish Viceroy. When Duffy, accompanied by his wife, went to Ireland to discuss Home Rule with him, they were at once invited to an official dinner at the Castle, and to a private talk at the Vice-Regal Lodge in Phoenix Park. But Duffy refused to go to the Castle. He had promised long ago 'never to enter its portals till it was occupied by a National Government, or a Government in sympathy with the aims of the people'. In their private talk, Carnarvon repeatedly said: 'I cannot answer for my colleagues. I can answer for no one but myself. But I will submit to them whatever information I can collect, and report to you frankly what they determine.'

From the Shelbourne Hotel, Dublin, in July 1885, Duffy addressed an open letter to Carnarvon, which was published in London. It was titled *The Price of Peace in Ireland,* and summed up the arguments he had pressed on Carnarvon personally. Half a century ago, he pointed out, the great colonies were more disturbed and discontented than Ireland in 1880:

> Lower Canada was organising insurrection under Catholic gentlemen of French descent and Upper Canada was in arms under a Scotch Presbyterian. Australia was then only a great pastoral settlement, but bitter discontent and angry menaces were heard in all its centres of population, provoked by the shameful practice of discharging the criminals of England like a deluge of filth on that young country.
> But Sir Robert Peel set the example of granting to the Colonies the control of their own affairs, and now Melbourne or Montreal was more exuberantly loyal to the Empire than London or Edinburgh.

He quoted a recent example of Australian loyalty. When news of General Gordon's death at Khartoum reached Australia, the acting-premier of New South Wales, William Bede Dalley, immediately organised a New South Wales contingent to assist the British forces in the Sudan. Moreover Dalley was a devout Roman Catholic of Irish descent. 'What has made Irish Catholics loyal on the banks of the Parramatta and the Yarra would make them contented and loyal on the banks of the Liffey or the Shannon,' Duffy wrote. And he concluded:

> For myself, as one Catholic Celt, I would say that the men I most honour in our history, and the friends I have most loved in life, belonged in a large proportion to a race and creed which are not mine. Swift and Molyneux, Flood and Grattan, were not only Protestants, but the sons of English officials serving in Dublin courts and bureaux. Curran, Tone, and Father Mathew were the descendants of Cromwellian settlers. The father of the best Irishman I have ever known, or ever hope to know, who has been the idol of two generations of students and thinkers, was a Welshman, wearing the

uniform of an English regiment. The price of peace in Ireland was simple and specific. To proffer reforms and revisions of the existing system in lieu of National Government was insensate. If a sane man had been put into a lunatic asylum and the administration of his estate given to strangers, it would be idle to offer him ameliorations of his condition as a remedy. What he wants is to get out.

Duffy wanted Carnarvon to meet Parnell, and when Carnarvon came to London to attend Lady Chesterfield's funeral, Duffy arranged for Justin McCarthy to act as an intermediary. The meeting took place in August in an empty house belonging to Carnarvon's sister who was out of town. The blinds were drawn and the carpets rolled up. It was a curious setting for an important conference. Carnarvon began by saying that he sought information only, and warned Parnell that as the Queen's representative he would not discuss separation. Parnell agreed, and spoke of the need to protect property and land rights in Ireland.

From Nice in December 1885, Duffy wrote to Gladstone with another suggestion on the Irish problem.

> There is only one way, it seems to me, to obtain the necessary light, to prepare opinion for a great change, and to bring the leading men of hostile parties to some approximation of agreement. That way is a Select Committee authorised to take evidence and report the result to Parliament. . . A final settlement of this quarrel between the two nations is possible if the pride of a sensitive race be not offended by a half measure. You see only the militant Irish in the House of Commons. You will deal with quite a different class by giving them their own country to govern and raise up from the dust.

After the death of her husband in 1876, Lady Wilde ('Speranza') was living in London in miserable poverty. Year after year, she applied for a Civil List pension, but it was not till 1890 that she was awarded £70 a year. Duffy from time to time sent her money, and visited her. 'I am deeply touched by the true-hearted kindness and sympathy and appreciation as regards my past and present,' she wrote to him in November 1888, thanking him for his 'generous gift' and for 'the noble and beautiful words that made the gracious gift more gracious still.' Sir William Wilde had owned several properties, but all were heavily mortgaged. 'Mine is indeed a sad case,' she wrote. 'My income of £200 a year entirely gone, while my eldest son . . . has nothing but his salary from the *Daily Telegraph* and on that it is difficult to keep himself, and the house and myself.' She did not say whether she received any help from her younger son, Oscar, then editing the *Women's World*.

Duffy's third wife, Louise died in February 1889, following the birth of her fourth child. With her, going he wrote to Parkes, he had lost nearly all the flavour of life. 'I work and wait neither unwilling to remain or to go when the summons comes.'

Duffy's three daughters by his second wife, Susan, Harriet and Geraldine came from Australia to look after him. Susan, aged forty, who had kept house in Melbourne while her mother was bringing up the younger children, again took charge of the household, and acted as his secretary. His sight was bad and he could not read or write without assistance. Harriet, aged twenty-nine, looked after her father's health. All three were devoted to their young step-brothers and sisters.

Twelve

The Closing Years

DESPITE the infirmities of age, Duffy's many-sided activities continued. He was a tireless diner-out in London, which he still visited annually. In Nice, he worked five hours a day at writing, and maintained a correspondence with many writers, politicians and churchmen. Among them were Lecky, Forster, and Sir Horace Plunkett, the Protestant agriculturist who had founded an Irish farmers' co-operative; W.J. Linton, the poet and wood engraver; and Bryce, then a cabinet minister, who consulted him on the workings of the bi-cameral system in Australia, 'for your opinion is to me of the utmost weight'.

Duffy sent the Fenian Michael Davitt ten pounds to buy seeds and plants for the distressed districts in Ireland, but Davitt reported that few peasants had applied for them. They were so used to getting relief that they were unwilling to make an effort at self-help. Davitt blamed the priests for this 'deplorable apathy'. They did not exercise their influence or set an example.

Nor had Duffy forgotten Australia's problems. In February 1890 he wrote in the *Contemporary Review* on 'The Road to Australian Federation', and sharply criticised Parkes, who had belatedly assumed leadership of the Federal movement. Parkes, he wrote, though a man of great ability, had rendered himself impossible as a mediator between the colonies. No man had done more to sow the local jealousies which it was the main business of an umpire to appease.

Duffy gave two examples. Victoria had been using the water of the River Murray, which divided it from New South Wales, for irrigation, 'to make immense tracts covered with a worthless scrub blossom like the orchards of Devonshire'. But Parkes, instead of blessing 'this beneficent work', had declared that New South Wales owned the water and was entitled to forbid Victoria's use of it. 'Fancy Surrey forbidding London to quench her thirst from the waters of *her* private river, and you will understand the feeling excited on the southern side of the Murray', Duffy wrote.

Equally divisive was Parkes' proposal that his colony should change its unsuitable name. Duffy agreed that "New South Wales" was a ridiculous name for a country larger than the British Isles.

The need of a change had been debated for thirty years, and it was one very proper to be made, for no Australian, we may be assured, ever consented to

Charles Gavan Duffy

call himself a New-South-Welshman. There was a good stock of suitable names available, but Sir Henry pushed them aside, and gravely proposed to his Parliament to change the name of the colony from New South Wales to Australia. The old penal settlement of Botany Bay, and the prosperous colony of which it is the capital, were to be *Australia,* and the colonies planted by the free enterprise of free men were to be content with the names bestowed upon them from London in the colonial middle ages. A jocose legislator at Melbourne suggested that if the object was to distinguish their territory from Victoria, they might call it Convictoria.

'Parkes' proposal, said Duffy, 'was an insult, and it rendered him for the time being, and probably for all time, an impossible founder of an Australian dominion'. There was no 'solid hope' of Australian Federation, Duffy argued, till its accomplishment was made an Imperial question. He believed that Imperial Federation would follow. But Westminster treated the question with 'ignorant and perilous insensibility'. Duffy was sure the prosperous Australian colonies were ready and willing to unite forever with England on terms of fair partnership and association.

> And they are no insignificant handful of men, these Australian colonists; they are more numerous than the people of England were when they won Magna Carta, or the people of the United States were when the stars and stripes were first raised to the sky: resolute, impatient, independent men, not unworthy to follow such examples on adequate occasion. But what cordial hand is stretched out to clasp theirs in affectionate embrace?

Duffy was convinced England should resolve that Australian Federation was of high importance to the interests of the Empire. It should appoint two Royal Commissioners, interested in Australian affairs, for example Lord Roseberry and Lord Carnarvon, to carry this resolution to Australia. These impartial Commissioners should visit all the colonies and listen to their objections. They should also represent the Crown at a conference at which delegates could thrash out the vexed questions of tariffs, national defences and a federal capital. This, he believed, was the road to Australian Federation, and ultimately, to Imperial Federation.

Despite his criticism of Parkes, Duffy wrote to him in October 1891: 'If you succeed in Federating the young nation, you will have good reason to be satisfied with your position, otherwise no labours seem to be more transient or resultless than those of a public man in a democratic community'.

And he voiced his own disillusion:

> In the Federal movement I not merely took the principal part, but practically did everything — every Parliamentary Report on the subject for twenty years was written by me, every Select Committee formed and managed and kept together by me, and all the correspondence with the other colonies conducted by me. The flowers gathered from so much seed make but a scanty bouquet.

PARNELL continued to support the Liberals in the hope that they would introduce a second Home Rule Bill. He was no longer the bogeyman of Westminster, and his reputation in England was rising, until a personal tragedy destroyed him. In December 1889, he was cited as co-respondent in a divorce action brought by a former Irish M.P., Captain William O'Shea. His wife, Kitty, and Parnell had been lovers for nine years. She had borne him three children, and they regarded themselves as man and wife. Parnell did not defend the suit, nor did he resign as leader of the Irish party.

Gladstone had a great regard for Parnell, almost certainly had known of his affair with Kitty O'Shea, and, as his diaries reveal, himself had a rather idiosyncratic sex-life. But to placate his noncomformist supporters, he threatened to abandon the Home Rule cause unless Parnell resigned. This split the Irish party. The majority supported by a viciously anti-Parnell Catholic hierarchy, voted to depose him. The feud between the two sections, which tragically weakened the Home Rule movement, continued long after Parnell died, a broken man, in October 1891.

Duffy was greatly affected by the upheaval. In public he proposed an end of all national feuds, but privately, he supported the anti-Parnellite faction. His attitude was perhaps based on both political and moral considerations. He had long resented Parnell's dictatorial manner, and as a pious Catholic, he had little sympathy with Kitty O'Shea, though he may not have gone as far as the parish priest in County Wicklow who told his flock: 'Parnellism is a simple love of adultery and all those who profess Parnellism profess to love and admire adultery'. But the names of Parnell and Kitty O'Shea were never mentioned in front of Duffy's children.

He continued to deplore the disunity of the Irish party and years later, when a Unity Conference was proposed, offered his services as a mediator, provided that his decision would be accepted as final. But the leading figures could not agree and the Conference never took place.

TOWARDS the end of the 1880s, a small group of Irishmen calling themselves the Southwark Irish Literary Club met weekly in South London, to discuss Irish literature. Members were encouraged to write on Irish themes and to read their compositions. Among those who addressed the Club were Duffy, William Butler Yeats, and Justin McCarthy. Yeats, the son of a Protestant Irish artist, had published his first book, a study of Irish lore and legends, in 1888.

In 1889, the Club died of apathy, but some of the more active members continued to meet informally, and this small group sought Duffy's help in forming an Irish Literary Society in central London. Duffy promised his support, and the group then approached Yeats, who proved a valuable recruit. The first meeting of the society took place at his house in Chiswick at Christmas, 1891. The following year when he returned to Ireland, he formed with Douglas Hyde, the founder of the Gaelic League, a similar society in Dublin. Yeats, in his *Autobiographies,* published in 1926, makes the extraordinary statement that he was arranging to publish a series of Irish books at one shilling each, when he heard 'an alarming rumour that old Sir Charles Gavan Duffy was coming from Australia to start an English publishing house . . .', and, he adds, 'I did not expect to agree with him but knew I must not seek a quarrel'. Yeats' memory, when he wrote this, was not very reliable. When Duffy came from Australia, Yeats was a boy of 15. And in 1890, when he was living in Chiswick, he wrote to Duffy asking for a loan of the Mangan letters which Duffy held, and gratefully acknowledged their receipt.

Duffy accepted the presidency of the London Society and gave it generous financial aid. The Society acquired rooms in Hart Street, Bloomsbury, and its membership grew rapidly. Among the foundation members were Lady Wilde, Oscar Wilde and his shiftless brother, Willie; the diminutive poet, Lionel Johnson and the distinguished war correspondent, William Howard Russell — a curious miscellany. (Lecturing to an American audience in 1884 on 'The Irish Poets of '48', Wilde said, 'Charles Gavan Duffy is one of my friends in London'. There is no supporting evidence.)

The society, which was non-political and non-sectarian, held 'Lectures, Concerts and Original Nights'. Duffy made long visits to London to participate in its work. 'Unfortunately, his sight has been very weak for some time, and his voice has almost deserted him', wrote D.J. Donoghue, one of the pioneers of the society, in July 1895. 'Yet he has delivered two brilliant addresses . . . full of wisdom, eloquence and humour'.

In the first of these, given in 1892, he preached the basic gospel of the Young Irelanders, 'Educate that you may be free'. While urging the Irish to acquire a knowledge of their own country and its traditions, he stressed the importance of education, 'not for ornament only, but for practical use'. He had seen young Irishmen arriving in Australia by every ship, wholly untrained for any profession or trade. Multitudes of them sank to be waiters, barbers and cabmen.

And he returned to two of his favourite themes — the contribution of the Protestant minority to Irish life, and the reluctance of the Irish to forget past differences:

> We regard all Irishmen who love their country, whatever their creed or pedigree, as equally near and dear to us. We rejoice in the splendid record of success in arms, arts, literature, and diplomacy which the Irish minority can exhibit . . . and we cannot look on the noble edifices which adorn the Irish capital, without thankfully remembering how much our country owes to the cultivated genius of the minority . . .

Parnell had died two years before, but the bitter feud between his supporters and his detractors continued. By the rules of the Society, Duffy was forbidden to mention it directly, although he said:

> It would be vain to deny that national quarrels are the most intractable of our troubles. The Celt is placable and generous in private transactions, but for public conflicts he has an unsleeping memory . . . surely no people ever were more emphatically exhorted by the circumstances in which they stand, to close their ranks and end their feuds. Our efforts here, will, I trust, indirectly promote that end.

For many years, Duffy had contemplated the publication of a new series of the 'Library of Ireland' of the 1840s. Yeats claimed to have conceived a similar idea independently, and in his later reminiscences, made little attempt to conceal his contempt for the outworn romanticism of Duffy and his followers 'who would have felt it inappropriate to publish an Irish book that had not harp and shamrock and green cover, so completely did their minds move amid Young Ireland images and metaphors . . .' Yet in 1890, he wrote to Duffy asking him to chair the inaugural meeting of the publishing committee, adding, 'the young men wish greatly that you would'.

But passions ran high when the publishing committee met, and the inevitable split took place. Yeats admitted that he 'was too full of the impatience of youth to be touched . . . by the spectacle of an old man coming back at the end of his life to take up again the patriotic work of his youth'. After many heated discussions, it was decided that the books should be printed in Dublin and published in London, and Duffy and Yeats formed an uneasy alliance to carry out the project. Instead of finding in Duffy 'an assistant upon equal terms', Yeats says he found 'a domineering obstinacy and an entire lack of any culture that I could recognise'. There was a long quarrel over the editorship of the series, which was resolved when Yeats' nominees, Douglas Hyde and T.W. Rolleston, were appointed assistant editors under Duffy. 'But', says John McGrath, a member of the publishing committee, 'it was a Pyrrhic victory for the young men. When it came to business, Duffy carried out his original idea, and selected and edited, for the most part, I believe, just as he pleased'. Yeats resented this, especially when Duffy insisted on publishing books which Yeats thought were out-of-date and irrelevant. One of these was Thomas Davis' unpublished *The Patriot Parliament of 1689*, which Yeats considered unreadable by the general public. 'We sold ten thousand copies before anyone found time to read it', he wrote with unconcealed malice. 'Unhappily, when they read it, they made up their minds to have nothing more to do with us and our books'.

But the book was generally praised by reviewers. *The Pall Mall Gazette* described Duffy's introduction as 'a brilliant and powerful indictment of the government of Ireland under the Stuarts', adding, 'It is impossible to mistake the accent of sincerity that runs through his pages, and very few have written history with such eloquence and force'.

Duffy's affection for Thomas Davis remained undiminished. One day when he began to talk about Davis, he burst into tears. Apologising for his weakness, he said that nobody could understand his feelings towards that most beautiful character. He paid a moving tribute to Davis in his *Thomas Davis: the Memoirs of an Irish Patriot*, published in 1890. More than anyone, Duffy was responsible for the revival of interest in Davis, now revered above all Irish patriots.

The twelve volumes published in the shilling series included Hyde's *The Story of Early Gaelic Literature*, Standish O'Grady's *The Bog of Stars*, lives of Swift and Goldsmith, and an anthology of ballads and songs written and published by the contributors to *The Nation* since 1845, titled *The New Spirit of The Nation*. It included four poems of Duffy's and was edited by Martin MacDermott who wrote in his introduction that while Duffy had written many great and vigorous poems, poetry was not his greatest gift:

It was not poetry he brought to the party so much as the power of initiation and organisation, without which, notwithstanding Davis' splendid talents, there never would have been a *Nation* newspaper, or an Young Ireland Party, any more than there would have been the old 'Library of Ireland', or the new . .

Yeats wrote that the new 'Library of Ireland' was killed after a couple of years 'by the books chosen by its editor-in-chief'. More charitably, John McGrath saw the new Library as 'a great effort for a man who had long passed his grand climacteric, and . . . a marvellous monument to his latter memory'. And he described the seventy-six-year-old Duffy: 'The mouth was large and mobile, the forehead expressive. But it was the nose of the veteran's face I best remember, a curious combination of the Roman and the Jewish type, with a deep furrow over each nostril.'

In 1892, Duffy published his *Conversations with Carlyle,* which had appeared serially in the *National Review.* 'The conversations', he explained, 'had been written down immediately after they took place'. The book was acclaimed for the intimate picture it presented of Carlyle. 'It is like another volume added to *Past and Present* and *Sartor Resartus,'* wrote Sir Walter Besant in the *Speaker.*

That summer, John Crone, the famous bibliophile and editor of the *Irish Bookman,* met Duffy at a garden party in Hampstead given by the artist Henry Holland. Crone 'gazed with absorbed admiration at one who seemed to have returned from another century, another world than ours'. As he grasped Duffy's hand he reflected that it was a hand that had been held by Davis, Mangan, Mitchel, Carleton, Smith O'Brien, Carlyle, Thackeray, and many of the survivors of '98.

GLADSTONE, who had resigned from the Liberal leadership after the disastrous defeat by the Lords of his Second Home-Bill in 1893, died in May 1898 at the age of eighty-nine. A memorial committee planned to erect statues of the grand old man in London, Edinburgh and Dublin, but the Dublin Corporation, preponderantly Parnellite, scornfully refused to make a site available. Duffy wrote to the *Westminster Gazette* indignantly protesting against this 'disgraceful and disgusting conduct', of 'a handful of Philistines'. After making the amplest allowances for what Parnell had done, he reminded them

> that if there had been no Gladstone, the Irish Church would still be established, the Irish Land System would still be unreformed, and the Irish franchise would still be a mockery of popular representation . . . and a Home Rule Bill . . . would not have passed the House of Commons.

Until the Corporation changed its mind, he concluded, Irish nationalists would be ashamed to look an English Home-Ruler in the face, or to meet a French or Italian sympathiser with Ireland. The Corporation did not change its mind, and Duffy was savagely attacked by the Parnellite organs in Dublin. One declared that if an attempt were made to erect a Gladstone statue anywhere in Dublin, the monument would require 'a substantial police protection'.

Duffy was now almost blind, but his daughters, and an oblate friend, Father John Fitzpatrick, wrote to his dictation and read to him, sometimes for four or five hours a day. His tastes were catholic. He enjoyed essays, poetry and fiction, particularly Scott, Thackeray, Conan Doyle and Edgar Poe, whom he defended against patronising critics. 'Poor Mangan', he said to a friend, 'was of the same rare school and was quite as caviare to the multitude'. It was more than half a century since Duffy had tried to succour the unhappy Irish poet.

His interest in world affairs was undiminished. 'Everybody here is debating the Dreyfus case', he wrote to H.M. Spielman. In January 1898, Captain Dreyfus, a young Jewish officer of the French army, had been convicted of betraying military secrets to Germany. Half France believed him guilty, the other half, including the eminent writer Emile Zola, who defended him passionately, believed he was the victim of a conspiracy, as was subsequently proved. The Catholic press in France waged a furious anti-semitic campaign but Duffy suspended judgment. 'I abhor secret trials and I cannot think a man like Zola would pledge himself so emphatically were the evidence not weighty', he wrote.

In 1899, noting the growth of Japan 'and the plunder of China by the great powers' he thought the consequence would some day be an invasion of Europe 'by the yellow races'.

DUFFY continued to work on his memoirs. His two-volume autobiography, taking his life up to his departure from Australia in 1880, was published in 1898, titled *My Life in Two Hemispheres*. This, his last book, is the least attractive, lacking the brilliance and coherence of his earlier writings. It is prolix and disorganised, and much of it, dealing in merciless detail with the tiresome permutations of Victorian politics, is heavily soporific to the present-day reader.

Duffy as usual distributed copies widely, and received an interesting comment from John Ingram who found the part dealing with Ireland 'a painful record' because of the view it presented of the character of the Irish:

> Intellectually they appear in it incapable of discerning character . . . and morally, very deficient in steadiness of purpose, and prone to discord and division. Critics from without have always attributed these failings to them, and it would seem not without good ground . . .

Though his health was failing, Duffy still had a great zest for life. He went for a walk each morning, returning to enjoy his midday meal, over which he would recall the old days, and the people he had loved. Davis, of course, and Dillon, Carleton and the Carlyles. He had many Irish visitors, among them Douglas Hyde, the poetess Dora Sigerson and the young John Dillon, who had been gaoled with Parnell in 1881, and who lived to see the burning of the Dublin Customs House by the IRA in 1921.

In the autumn of 1898, when Harry O'Brien was writing his *Life of Parnell*, (to which Duffy contributed a chapter explaining his negotiations with Carnarvon), he spent three weeks with Duffy. O'Brien found Duffy to be youthful in mind and manner, and 'the best raconteur he had ever met, with a keen sense of humour and a caustic wit'. Duffy had many local visitors, too, but his popularity with Nice's English community waned with the outbreak of the second South African War in 1899.

Like most Irishmen, and many people in other countries — including the Liberal politician Lloyd George in England, and the labour leaders, William Morris Hughes and William Holman in Australia — Duffy's sympathies were with the Boer farmers who were fighting the British Empire, and he did not hesitate to say so. Many of his friends shared his views. 'I am still hopeful that in spite of appearances the mad and wicked war with which we have been threatened will be prevented', Ingram wrote to him a few weeks before hostilities began. And two years later, when England had suffered serious reverses in the field, Bryce wrote, 'Things here in England are most depressing . . . the temper of the country and the way the press has misled it over the miserable war are what most grieves those who remember the England of Cobden and Mr. Gladstone'.

In February 1900, Duffy wrote to Mrs. C.H. Pearson, the widow of his old Melbourne friend, 'I am in sight of my eighty-fourth birthday and though I entertain some hopes of writing a book on the last twenty years of my life, I know how often such hopes prove fallacious. Charles Mangan, an Irish poet, describing such a condition sings:

Am I living now?
I was alive
Twenty golden years ago.

ON the first day of January 1901, the Commonwealth of Australia came into being. Unfortunately, there is no record of how the eighty-five-year-old Duffy received the news that the cause he had championed for so many years had at last triumphed. Federation was celebrated throughout Australia with gaudy ceremonial and great eruptions of oratory, but Duffy's role was not acknowledged. However it was fitting that his son, Charles Gavan Duffy had been secretary of the Federal Convention which led to Federation, and had helped to draft the Australian Constitution.

A month later, Duffy presented to the Royal Irish Academy, his vast collection of books, newspapers, and letters, which the Academy recorded, 'were rendered unique by the personal associations with them'.

Duffy died on 9 February 1903. His three daughters, Susan, Harriet and Geraldine were by his bedside. They heard the dying man talk of his childhood in Monaghan town, and whisper a verse of John O'Hagan's which began:

When comes the day all hearts to weigh
  If staunch they be or vile,
Shall we forget the sacred debt
  We owe our mother isle?

It was Duffy's wish that he be buried in his mother isle. A committee that included the Lord Mayor of Dublin, Cardinal Logue, and half the

Catholic hierarchy was formed to carry out his wish.

On the night of 26 February, in the midst of a great storm, the body of the last Young Irelander was brought to Dublin. It lay before the altar of the Pro-Cathedral where Archbishop Walsh offered a requiem, and on the following Sunday, followed by thousands of people, it was carried through the streets of Dublin, past the statues of Smith O'Brien, of Daniel O'Connell, of Sir John Gray and of Father Mathew. Duffy's body was laid to rest in Glasnevin cemetry under the shadow of the round tower that marks the tomb of the 'Liberator'. Duffy too, had tried to liberate his beloved Ireland — from the shackles of alien rule, of ignorance and of prejudice.

In the nineteen-twenties, when David Alec Wilson published his five-volume life of Carlyle, he alleged that Duffy even before 1849 had ceased to be a Christian and had kept up a pretence of belief for the sake of his children. When Susan protested, Wilson admitted that he had gone too far, and should have said only that Duffy had outgrown orthodoxy. He promised to amend his text in the next edition, but died before this was done. Duffy himself had declared: 'I was always a Catholic of the school of Newman and Montalembert, not at all of the school of Dr. Cullen. . .'

Appendix

Some of Gavan Duffy's Descendants

JOHN Gavan Duffy, Gavan Duffy's eldest son, the only surviving child of his first marriage, was born in Dublin in 1844, and educated at Stonyhurst, and Melbourne University, having followed the family to Victoria in 1859. He was a solicitor and politician, representing Dalhousie — his father's old electorate — in the Legislative Assembly, during 1874-86, and 1887-1904. He held office successively as President of the Board of Land and Works, Postmaster-General, in two Administrations, and Attorney-General. A devoted layman of the Catholic Church, he became Knight of the Papal Order of St. Gregory. He married one of Margaret Callan's daughters.

Sir Frank Gavan Duffy, eldest son of Duffy's second wife, was born in Dublin in 1852, and accompanied his parents to Australia in 1856. A few years later, he was sent to Stonyhurst. He returned to Australia in 1869, graduated at Melbourne University, was called to the Bar in 1874, appointed to the High Court in 1913, and became Chief Justice of Australia in 1931. He was a Privy Councillor and a Knight Commander of the Order of St. Michael and St. George. One of his sons, Charles Leonard Gavan Duffy, also a barrister, became a justice of the Victorian Supreme Court.

Charles Gavan Duffy, second son of Duffy's second wife, was born in Dublin in 1855, educated at St. Patrick's College, Melbourne, Stonyhurst, and Melbourne University. He was a barrister and held various public offices. He was secretary of the Federal Convention, one of the draftsmen of the Constitution, Clerk of the House of Representatives 1901—1917, and of the Senate, 1917—1920. He was a Commander of the Order of St. Michael and St. George.

Philip Gavan Duffy, third son of Duffy's second wife, a surveyor and civil engineer, was born and educated in Melbourne, worked on a railway survey in Siam, and joined the Railways and Public Works Department in Western Australia. He did the survey for the remarkable goldfields water supply, completed in 1903, by which water is supplied to arid inland areas of the State through 350 miles of pipeline.

George Gavan Duffy, eldest child of Gavan Duffy's third wife, was born in Nice, educated in France and at Stonyhurst, and practised as a solicitor in London. In 1916, he volunteered to act for Sir Roger Casement, on trial for high treason. He became a member of the Sinn Fein parliament, was one of the negotiators of the Anglo-Irish Treaty in 1921, and was Ireland's Minister for Foreign Affairs before becoming President of the Irish High Court. He married A.M. Sullivan's daughter, Margaret.

Bryan and Tom Gavan Duffy, second and third sons respectively, of Gavan Duffy's third wife, were both educated in France and at Stoneyhurst, and left home when young to become priests. Bryan joined the Society of Jesus and spent more than twenty years in South Africa as an Inspector of Religious Instruction, a writer and teacher. Tom joined the Paris Missionary Society and spent most of his religious life in India.

Louise Gavan Duffy, only daughter of Gavan Duffy's third wife, became an Irish language expert, taught in Padraic Pearse's progressive school, Scoil Ide, took part in the 1916 rising, and founded her own remarkable school, Scoil Bhride. She was made an Honorary Doctor of Laws of the National University of Ireland for her services to Irish education.

Select Bibliography

1. Manuscripts
Gavan Duffy Papers (National Library of Ireland)
Gavan Duffy Papers (Royal Irish Academy)
Gavan Duffy Papers (British Museum)
Gavan Duffy Papers (Latrobe Library, Melbourne)
Ars Vitae. (by courtesy of Dr. Leon O'Broin)
Parkes Papers (Mitchell Library, Sydney)
Lang Papers (Mitchell Library, Sydney)

2. Duffy's principal works
Duffy, Charles Gavan, *Young Ireland,* Part 1, (1880)
Duffy, Charles Gavan, *Young Ireland,* Part II, (1883)
Duffy, Charles Gavan, *The League of the North and South,* (1886)
Duffy, Charles Gavan, *Thomas Davis,* (1890)
Duffy, Charles Gavan, *Conversations with Carlyle,* (1892)
Duffy, Charles Gavan, *My Life in Two Hemispheres,* (2 vols, 1898)

continued

3. Other works

Abels, Jules. *The Parnell Tragedy*, (1966)
Ashley, Evelyn, & Bulwer, Lytton. *Life of Lord Palmerston*, (5 vols) (1870-76)
Aspinall, Clara, *Three Years in Melbourne*, (1862)
Carlyle, Thomas, *Reminiscences of My Irish Journey*, (1881)
Daunt, W.J. O'N, *Eighty-five years of Irish History* (1886)
de Vere White, T. *The Road to Excess*, (1945)
Edwards, R.D. (ed. with T. Desmond Williams) *The Great Famine*, (1956)
Griffith, Arthur (ed.) *Meagher of the Sword*, (1916)
Gwynn, Denis, *Young Ireland and 1848* (1949)
Hone, Joseph, *W.B. Yeats*, (1943)
Horne, R.H., *Australian Facts and Prospects*, (1859)
Kelly, William, *Life in Victoria*, (2 vols) (1859)
Lecky, W.E.H., *Leaders of Public Opinion in Ireland*, (1861)
Lucas, E. *The Life of Frederic Lucas*, (2 vols) (1886)
McGee, T. D'Arcy, *Memoir of Charles Gavan Duffy*, (1849)
McManus, M.J. (ed.) *Thomas Davis and Young Ireland*, (1945)
Mitchel, John, *Jail Journal*, (1854)
Norman, Edward, *A History of Modern Ireland*, (1971)
Nowlan, Kevin B., *Charles Gavan Duffy and the Repeal Movement*, (1963)
O'Brien, R. Barry, *The Life of Parnell*, (1899)
O'Broin, Leon, *Charles Gavan Duffy*, (1967)
Serle, Geoffrey, *The Golden Age*, (1963)
Stawell, Mary, *My Recollections*, (1911)
Sullivan, T.D., *Recollections of Irish Politics*, (1905)
Tierney, Michael, *Daniel O'Connell*, (1949)
Turner, Henry Gyles, *A History of the Colony of Victoria*, (2 vols) (1904)
Tynan, Kathleen, *Memories*, (1924)
Whyte, J.H., *The Independent Irish Party 1850-9*, (1958)
Wilson, David, *Thomas Carlyle*, (6 vols.) (1923-34)
Woodham-Smith C., *The Great Hunger*, (1962)
Yeats, W.B., *Autobiographies*, (1926)

Index